INVISIBLE INK

Invisible Ink

A Memoir

Guy Stern

WAYNE STATE UNIVERSITY PRESS

DETROIT

ISBN: 978-0-8143-4759-1 (jacketed cloth)
ISBN: 978-0-8143-4760-7 (ebook)

Library of Congress Cataloging Number: 2019957276

Wayne State University Press
Leonard N. Simons Building
4809 Woodward Avenue
Detroit, Michigan 48201–1309

Visit us online at wsupress.wayne.edu

The excerpt on page 162 is from Hilde Domin, Vorsichtshalber.
In: *Sämtliche Gedichte.* © S. Fischer Verlag GmbH, Frankfurt am Main 2009.
By courtesy of S. Fischer Verlag GmbH, Frankfurt am Main.

To my wife, Susanna Piontek,
beloved companion in life,
sage advisor, and fellow writer

CONTENTS

INVISIBLE INK

Invisible Ink

AFTER I FINISHED THE irrevocably last sentence of this autobiography, I started searching for an appropriate title. Three different ones seemed to be worth exploring. One of these described a series of events that recurred throughout my life and invariably changed its course. Few of these events could have been foreseen. I called them "chance encounters" and for a while I thought my book would bear that title.

Here are some of the events that made the label so compelling to describe the roller-coaster ride of my life. Chance encounters abound, with strangers emerging at various turning points. At fifteen years of age, my life was saved because of a brief meeting with a kind United States consular official. My family perished because of a half-hour encounter with a hapless, hidebound local attorney in St. Louis, who thwarted their rescue. After World War II, my postwar plans were sent helter-skelter. A rare meeting with one of my superior officers, a senior editor of the *New York Times*, sent me scurrying off to New York. One short telephone call led to my discovery of the whereabouts of a long-lost cousin.

I found my present wife because she had been pressured at the last minute into attending a public lecture of mine. I unearthed a hitherto unknown branch of my wife's family by taking a wrong turn during a nocturnal walk in a small Swiss town near Locarno. Finally, while writing this autobiography, some of my wartime experiences came rushing back to me because of a chance encounter with a British gentleman, a one-time resident of Bristol. That led me back in minute detail to those all-engrossing weeks, when we had been planning the most gigantic invasion of enemy-held territory in human history. Contrary to Einstein's observation, God (or fate) may play dice after all.

Another idea was to call these recollections "Of Life, Loss, Love, and Literature," for its euphonious alliteration and beyond. Love was lavished upon me by many people who walked alongside me during my long and variegated life. For all too brief a time, it was primarily given to me by my family. My losses can be summarized by the word Holocaust and the untimely deaths of my son, Mark, and my wife, Judy. As to literature, my immersion in books started in my childhood and accompanied me all throughout my career as a professor of literature and is still clinging to me even beyond retirement. Language has been my life's passion and my life preserver. The ability to use persuasive language was my intermittent ally at dangerous moments throughout my life. For example, as a dean in the 1960s, I squelched an escalating students' riot via an impassioned appeal to reason. Earlier, in 1937, I stood before an American consular official, pleading for a visa to the sheltering shores of the United States. Fifteen years old at the time, I stammered forth the right answers to his questions in acceptable English, received the appropriate US stamp and seal on my papers, and was thereby spared the fate of my parents, grandmother, brother, and sister—all victims of the Nazi Holocaust.

Throughout everything that has happened to me, language has been my mainstay and muse, my labor and leisure, lodestar and love. New words have always fascinated me; as a kid I soaked them up like a sponge and sometimes shattered the composure of the adults by my mature vocabulary. Owners of cigar stores in Hildesheim (where I grew up), whom we kids pestered for collectible pictures for our albums, ranging from postcard-like views of German cities to models of automobiles, usually shooed my playmates and fellow collectors unceremoniously out of their stores. But often they gave me a hearing, I suspect because my precocious eloquence entertained them, and some of the coveted cards of automobiles, animals, national flags, and city sites landed in my collection.

Two sources fed my insatiable appetite for delectable tidbits of language. There was my wildly indiscriminate reading, ranging from spurious Wild West stories to watered-down German classics. But even more important and enduring were the conversations with my mother. My German, then and now, comes from my mother—or rather my mother's tongue. She was a luminous woman who had an unerring instinct for just the right word. She was, amid our far-flung family, the occasional lyric poet. For my Bar Mitzvah she put together a multipage album of poems, in which she gently spoofed the foibles of twenty-one Bar Mitzvah dinner guests. Nor did she spare me: "Zigarrentabak schmeckt auch aus der Pfeife" ("You can savor cigar leaves smoked from a pipe"). I had dismembered one of my father's cigars, intended for customers, and had ignited the leaves in a clay pipe from a toy set.

My own attempt at humor was more boisterous. It came about because of my one and only and quite shameful encounter with foreigners. Come to think of it, we Hildesheimers were a bit provincial and xenophobic. One day when I was fourteen, I encountered two young French ladies, smartly dressed, with their faces stylishly made up. They were crossing the square in front of the Cathedral of Saint Andrew. A sizable group of youngsters and adults was following them like the satellites to the orbiting planets. Not having seen ladies with make-up before, we outdid ourselves with witty, nay, absurd, remarks. I offered the ladies the use of my watercolor box. While recalling this bit of juvenile fatuity, my face turns redder than the rouge on the faces of those two poor French women. Only one year later, I and my fellow Jews became the targets of verbal insults. But my penchant for language on that occasion was served. One of the French women responded with an expression I had not heard in my beginning French class in high school. "Ta gueule," she said to me. As I fled the plaza commemorating the saintly Andrew, it dawned on me that I was told to shut up in no uncertain terms. I was taken aback, of course, but then felt triumphant that I had acquired an expression that would have been banished from our French class.

When I reached the age of fourteen, my parents took me along to adult plays performed at our local theater. I can still reconstruct isolated scenes, for example, from a drama called *Uncle Braesig*. I remember mostly the protagonist's intermittent pratfalls, when least expected, and his inane, funny expletive, hurled repeatedly at a friend. "Why, just keep your nose in your face!" I didn't understand why this remark made the audience convulse with laughter. But there may have been something in the context or the acting that was suggestive beyond the comprehension of this fourteen-year-old.

No doubt my visits to the Hildesheim Theater were an early stepping-stone to my life's work as a professor of literature. My parents, had they been allowed to live, would have been elated by my choice of career and their catalytic role in it. That saddens me, of course, but that regret is as nothing compared to my torment when I imagine how they, lovers of the German language, probably heard it in its most debased form in the moments before their deaths at the hands of their murderers. A sentence coined by my late colleague Robert Kahn of Rice University says all that succinctly: "I hate the language that I love."

I can only speculate about how my parents or my brother, Werner, or my sister, Eleonore, were "liquidated," to use Nazi parlance. Werner probably also heard the beloved and accursed language at the time of his death. It was the ultimate death knell of his youthful illusions. When I said goodbye to the twelve-year-old, I wasn't aware of all his talents. But about ten years ago as of this writing, I received a letter from a person not known to me, who identified himself as a retired physician from the Rhineland: "I was a classmate of your brother at the Josephinum High School in Hildesheim. Your brother, I must tell you, was rather awkward at sports. But whenever our German teacher wanted the perfect recitation of a poem, he called on Werner. He could make even bad poetry sparkle." I read that letter with despair, more than seventy years after I'd last seen my brother. It seemed that Werner had a distinct gift, so carefully nurtured in both of us by our parents, and it never came to fruition. I'm sometimes ashamed of my own privilege, that of being the sole survivor of my immediate family, and thus the only one to bear my parents' legacy.

Finally I settled on a title that now appears on the cover of this tome and probably needs the most elaborate explanation. If there is an overriding caesura in my life, it occurred as early as age eleven, in 1933, the year the Nazis came to power. When the bitter news came at the end of January, that a dictator and demagogue was going to lead our native land, my father, rarely given to formal speeches, addressed his small family. An almost incurable optimist, he was neither despairing nor pollyannish. "We will be facing hard times," he said. "During the next years it will be imperative we don't call attention to ourselves. Wer auffällt, fällt rein. (Anyone who sticks out will get stuck.) We must all resemble invisible ink. Stay hidden till we can emerge again and show ourselves as the individuals we are."

I followed his advice all through the years of Nazi rule, from 1933 till 1937—and beyond. Yes, even after I entered the United States, the land of the free. You see, once you have drawn a cloak of invisibility around yourself, it becomes tough to divest yourself of it. The process proceeds in stages. A few of the more notable stages have stuck in my mind. The first partial shedding of that cloak happened within one day of my arrival in the United States. On my way from New York to St. Louis, I was treated between train rides to a cursory tour of Chicago. It led to Maxwell Market, a sort of flea market whose majority was Jewish traders in their kaftans. Their free and easy ways, accompanied by good-natured but loud laughter, nay, guffaws, gave me my first inkling of "freedom for all." Then, at one point during my years in a St. Louis high school, my government teacher, "Doc" Bender—Jewish, observant, and sensitive—took me aside one day. "I'm glad you smile at my attempts at humor. But feel free to laugh aloud like the rest of the class." The lesson wasn't lost on me.

I changed slowly, but I knew that part of my emergence into an extroverted youngster was still pretense or playacting. But that became more genuine a week before my high school graduation in June 1939. I was prevented from going to our prom by having to be on duty that evening at the Chase Hotel as a hired busboy. The prom was also at the Chase Hotel, in one of the rooms right next to "my" Fiesta Grill. Well, I had the temerity, gall, chutzpah to walk in on the prom—busboy uniform and all—as conspicuous as though I had come in wearing the gym clothes of Soldan High School.

My years in the army and as a teacher did the rest. A sergeant, as well as a teacher of freshmen, had better be extroverted and assertive. And thus the last vestiges of the "invisible-ink" persona, my father felt the need to instill in me, fell by the wayside—or did they?

No, the last stage was writing this book. I am given to reticence, but writing one's autobiography leaves no room for reticence. Thus, it is fitting that it sails beneath my father's injunction to his family—and with the hope that future generations don't have to suffer the kind of tyranny that makes it necessary to be like invisible ink.

CHAPTER ONE

A Nearly Idyllic Beginning

B Y THE SCALES OF the beginning of the twentieth century, the distance that separated the hometowns of my parents—approximately 130 miles—was considered formidable, the routes between them cumbersome, and the towns themselves were nestled away in the rural environment. It surprises me, even today, when recognition registers on a face, whether in the United States or Germany, when I toss the name of Vlotho in Westphalia or Ulrichstein in Hessia into a conversation. The former, where my mother was born, spreads out along the Weser River. Only one bridge led across in those times and Ulrichstein could boast of the fact that it was circling the highest mountain top in Hessia, and therefore, it was a "boon to the human lung."

And yet, despite distance and inaccessibility, the two met, or else this chronicle would not have seen the light of day (nor me, for that matter). Nor could I report that at age fourteen, I swam across the Weser River, nor that I climbed the Vogelsberg, driven by my father's ambition for my physical development.

How then did they meet, my mother, Hedwig Silberberg, the daughter of a successful Vlotho merchant and my father, Julius Stern, the son of a small-town clothing storeowner? He was parented by his older brother, Hermann, after their father had died when Julius was only ten years old. He first attended classes at the village school, supplemented by Jewish learning in a dwelling dating back to 1849, right next to another building, called unceremoniously, then and now, "das Judenbad," the Jewish bathhouse.

Dad went to a somewhat larger city for two years of desultory high school instructions, but also learned the basics of his future profession by helping out in Uncle Hermann's store. He knew textiles! I would never have penetrated the arcane vocabulary of clothing materials such as Beiderwand, Paletot, and Schlüpfer (woolsey, great coat, and panties, respectively), if my father had not used them constantly.

Of course that was but a beginning. He needed mercantile experience. One of Uncle Hermann's visitors, a traveling salesman, knew of an opening for a textile journeyman at the Kaufhaus Rüdenberg in a quaint place named Vlotho. Dad liked the place, he told me, and his position as premier salesman. But that was not his only reason.

Hedwig was the fair-haired daughter of Israel and Rebekka Silberberg. They had longingly awaited the arrival of a daughter after the birth of three stalwart boys, born in reasonably rapid succession. Hedwig and Julius met, so to speak, over the counter. To untangle that cryptic remark: my mother-to-be was making a small purchase at Rüdenberg's. My father waited on her. They never told us children of their romance, while photos testify to a happy, handsome couple, much attuned to each other. They wouldn't have dreamed of sharing intimacies. It was a time when the stiff collar my father wore five or six days a week was not only a piece of apparel but also a symbol of a social ethic. But there is evidence of the portent of that meeting across that fateful counter. Within half a year, my father had the temerity to face a seemingly impregnable obstacle.

Its name was Israel Silberberg, my venerable grandfather. Grandpa was the incarnation of a German patriarch whose word was law in the period following World War I. With the ousting of the German emperor, his unquestioned authority had evolved to the heads of households. Power and prestige transferred to less visible but almost equally domineering successors. Since power abhors a vacuum, it now came to rest on the family patriarch. My grandfather, though by temperament a lesser tyrant than the emperor, was ready. Had he not banished Benno, his youngest son, to America, when the kid, in his adolescent rebelliousness, had sassed him? Now my father had to face him, ask for the hand of his daughter, the apple of his eye, whom he had sent, just a couple of years before, to a "Höhere Töchterschule." That was an upper-middle-class school, teaching ennobling classes such as art and literature in tandem with domestic subjects. As best as I recall, she was sent to such a modestly ambitious school in nearby Bielefeld. A book on girls' education, fitting her time frame, lends more substance to my vague memory. Undeterred, my father approached the patriarch. He prevailed. Two years later, in 1922, I made my entrance via Hildesheim's Catholic Hospital, presaging my later exposure to Catholicism, when I started my career as a college student at a Jesuit university.

Writing this prelude was easy. I could rely on the narratives of my parents, relatives, and friends. But thrown back on my own recollections, I quickly rediscovered a truism that the German poet Goethe proclaimed about three centuries ago. He called his retrospective "Fragments of a Great Confession." I also deplore the fragmenting nature of those recollections, admit that occasionally they resemble "confessions," which, of course, never are far removed from introspection. And as an immediate confession, the mortar holding the fragments together are suppositions, makeshifts, and inferences. From the very beginning my parents' lives were marked by untiring labor. Their hard work paid off—till the inflation struck. Years later my mother told me of its impact. "I stood by the door, already in my hat and coat, shopping bag in hand, waiting for your father to come home. He would race up the steps, press his day's earnings in my hand, and I was off to the market. In another hour, your father's earnings would have shriveled to nothing."

And yet through bad years and good years, my mother hid her worries and my father rarely gave vent to them. We three siblings, born in Hildesheim, never felt deprived of anything. My mother could transform a most simple meal into a gourmet's delight. She would put soup dishes filled with milk close to a window until it had turned into sour milk. She would put some fruit and a layer of sugar into it and the combination of sour and sweet made for an exotic evening meal. (So much for today's modern refrigeration, of which we had none!) Or she could accomplish culinary transformations by words alone. When my father returned at times with some of his staple of sandwiches uneaten, my mother came up with the fairy-tale name of "Hasenbrot" for it, meaning a sandwich wrested from hares. My brother and I would fight for such magical morsels. Love has a stupendous wingspread.

They clawed their way upward. One domestic acquisition tells the story of their minuscule climb. When buying their basic furniture for their Hildesheim apartment, they had splurged on a luxurious easy chair. Both loved it as their repose for holiday siestas—and so decided to take turns sinking into its inviting arms. But when Dad's business soared after the years of inflation, they threw economics to the winds and bought the twin of that chair and held a celebration when it arrived.

Of course in 1938, my family's entire property, like that of all German Jews, was confiscated by the Nazi government, and my family was shunted to a so-called Jew House. To Shakespeare we owe the poetic remark that "he who steals my purse" (or my armchairs for that matter), "steals trash." But can you adopt that flippancy, if so much sweat attaches to the acquisition of "mere" objects? I now can infer from our weekly routine how my parents struggled, how the upward climb was accomplished. Dad got up first, shortly before six, Mother a few minutes later. She placed the sandwiches packed the night before into the pockets of his overcoat, quickly ground some carefully measured-out coffee beans, and poured him a self-squeezed glass of orange juice. She had read of its benefits long before juices became commonplace in Germany. Then a cup of coffee to accompany his marmalade-laden piece of bread and Dad was off. He picked up two suitcases, one small and one large, containing samples of the fabrics-in-season he would present to his prospective customers. He also carried an assortment of duplicate samples, intended as presents for the small daughters of preferred customers. These "Puppenlappen," once artfully stitched, became elegant additions to the wardrobe of their dolls. They were heavy, those suitcases. Wanting to show my masculinity shortly before being dubbed a "man" at age thirteen by the rules of the Jewish religion, I found that I, despite all my calisthenics, had to draw on every muscle to carry one suitcase a few steps. Dad, a diminutive forty-year-old, mastered both suitcases down four flights of stairs, three blocks to the next streetcar stop, on to the railroad station to mount a train to Elze, Gronau, or Nordstemmen, towns that even today command little space on the map of the State of Lower Saxony. I accompanied him there once or twice during school holidays and had trouble keeping pace with him, especially when he raced from one farm to the next. I once suggested buying a car. "That would eat up all our profit," he answered. Fortunately, whatever one could say about the Weimar Republic, the trains ran on time!

He would return home between six and seven, except from places like Gronau with its numerous customers. Then he stayed overnight at a pension, a sort of bed and breakfast. Otherwise he returned slightly before dinner. Werner and I were relegated to the care of our sleep-in maid and our parents would share an evening meal, variations on a potpourri of soup, fish, potato, and vegetables. Needless to say, both were in need of restoratives, both physically and mentally. Mom had in the meanwhile managed the household, tamed two boys, supervised their homework, and handled the customers who had strayed into town rather than await Dad's periodic arrival at their homes.

We joined the two for dessert. Dad wanted to know how we had fared at school, not only if my grades in algebra were improving, but also whether I had stopped my daily fisticuffs with that nasty classmate, Heuer. He wasn't paying tuition, my father threatened me, for dishing out or receiving body blows or a black eye during recess between classes.

After worship services on Saturdays, Mom and Dad became the store's shipping clerks. They packed up the orders Dad had taken during the week; all three of us carried them downstairs to a "firm-owned" hand-drawn wagon and then Dad and I pulled it to an inn about a mile away. That's where a "Fuhrmann," a deliveryman, spent the weekend preparatory to his rounds of endless commuting between Hildesheim and the rural villages. His carriage was horse drawn; later, the horsepower of a truck took over. He apparently made an adequate living by underselling the post office. That was, of course, the reason why Dad used him.

On Sundays Dad took the family on outings. He followed a citywide custom and hence, our excursions were incessantly interrupted by encounters with neighbors or fellow members of the Jewish community. Werner and I were treated to grownup gossip, which we deciphered before going to sleep. But the main treat was the Sunday afternoon coffee hour at one of the outdoor cafés, at the end of a hefty and prolonged walk through the park. Dad ordered exotic cakes, let's say with strawberries and whipped cream, plus coffee and cocoa. By way of variation Mom would pack sandwiches for our Sunday supper; we'd take them to a restaurant close by, order drinks, and return hours way past our usual bedtime. I still find that routine endearing, when these days my wife and I sit down with friends at a Munich beer garden, devouring our packed lunches.

On Mondays the routine would begin anew. It did not differ greatly from those of my Jewish classmates, except where much greater wealth allowed a more ostentatious lifestyle.

One of my classmates, a girl belonging to an upper-class family, disparaged our lifestyle as "a daily feast of rice pudding." I knew better. It also contained some exotic fruits. My parents belonged to a theater-going group that had branches in virtually all German cities. When I had outgrown typical children's performances, such as *Little Peter's Trip to the Moon*, my parents purchased an extra ticket for their son, stage-struck even then. After watching Friedrich von Schiller's *William Tell*, I reread the drama several times, until I could declaim whole passages, much to the chagrin of my father, who deplored some of the dramatist's more grandiloquent lines. My parents also took me along to musical events. Ironically, from my perspective today they sported an open ear for Wagner and a closed one for Kurt Weill. A gala performance, chosen as a farewell gift to a Hildesheim star lured away by a Berlin stage, was Weill-Brecht's *Threepenny Opera*. I was pointedly not taken. To their minds these worst fears of questionable language and situations were realized. "How could that great actress have chosen that trash as her farewell performance?" they asked as they came into the door.

But my mother also did not ingest Wagner uncritically, although I surmise they did not know of his blatant anti-Semitism. Mom and Dad had taken me, at the tender age of six, along to my first introduction to grand opera. "We have read you the stories of Siegfried, now you can see something like it at an opera house in Hannover."

What can I say? It turned the kid on. During the train ride home, I exulted about Lohengrin's bravery, his dueling prowess as he "smashed" Friedrich von Telramund in a duel and his permanent squelching of Elsa's rosiness. "Well," said my mother, "that was certainly not a very chivalric way to leave Elsa, for no real good reason at all." That was the first time I began to perceive that there is a feministic way to look at literature.

One other occasion, my sixth birthday, competes in the vividness of my recollection with the fusty Wagnerian event on the Hannover Opera stage.

At age fourteen my voice changed, announcing my transition from childhood to adolescence. My love for music, however, stayed with me. And when Cantor Cysner announced that he would team up with Mrs. Moses, the wife of the community's vice president, and with Mr. Rubenstein, a gifted violinist and prestigious member of our community, to put on Haydn's *Toy Symphony*, I was literally the first in line for tryouts. I chose the toy horn as my instrument. (Of course none of us knew at that time that Haydn's alleged composition was not his at all but likely Mozart's father's, as later research showed.)

I looked forward to the tryout with some trepidation, unnecessary as it turned out, since the toy horn, like most of the toy instruments of this symphony, gave out only one tone. The tryout was correspondingly simple. "I will now play the beginning of the *Toy Symphony* and you will interrupt when I reach the seventh bar!" said Mrs. Moses. I frantically started beating the rhythm and passed the test. We performed in the auditorium of the Jewish Community House, opposite our synagogue, before a packed house. I heartily blew my trumpet and earned loud applause from the Stern family. My friends and I basked in our musical triumph until an older friend, damn him, dampened my satisfaction in that virtuoso performance. "So you think all those people came out to hear you play? Well, think again! Don't you know that Katie Moses, appearing in public, brings out every male, twenty to seventy?" I called my friend a cynic; I was then unacquainted with the term "bombshell" or its German equivalent.

Another signifier of my setting-in adolescence was a streak of rebelliousness, notably against religion. During one of my visits to the ancestral home of my grandparents, I began to read Moses Mendelssohn and his followers and discovered some of the many rationalistic refutations of the Bible that were common at that time. The views expressed in those texts dovetailed with my grandfather's low opinion of the miracles that suffuse the Old Testament. They simply couldn't have happened, he declared. The doubts cast by the book and him fell on fertile grounds. Nor did I hesitate to spread my budding heresy with my contemporaries. My apostasy soon came to the attention of the community's hoi polloi. The pillars of our faith were tottering! Our youth leader, Seppl Cysner, was enjoined to cure me of my deviant ideas. He corralled me after one of our Saturday meetings. As a good debater he declared my sources spurious. But I stood my ground. Beneath his disapproval at my obstinacy, I could sense a certain respect for a mind ready to go its own way. My heresy would continue to withstand the arguments of rabbis and priests that chanced upon my wayward route at various stages of my life.

CHAPTER TWO

The Nazis Come to Power

B UT ALL THOSE BOYISH contemplations were overshadowed by an event that augured the end of the world in which we had lived, and it would soon spell the end of my childhood and adolescence. On January 31, 1933 all classes of our high school abandoned their syllabi. Most of our teachers and most of my fellow students acted as though the Messiah had stepped into our midst, heralding an event that would restore the glory of the fatherland. Our teachers also announced that on the coming evening there would be a parade of all true patriots in every town of Germany to pro-claim that Adolf Hitler was now steering the fortunes of our nation. Every student—no excuse accepted—was to join the glorious demonstration. Did any of my classmates notice, as we Jewish students observed, that Dr. Hein-rich, our math teacher, had quietly entered his class and merely announced that the given assignment was being held over till the next meeting, and then left the room as if on tiptoes?

When I arrived home, my parents were in dead earnest. We boys were told that we were not to leave the apartment under any circumstances. Then the telephone rang. Mr. Buchterkirchen, one of my father's in-town customers, was on the line. His orgiastic voice was audible across the living room. "My wife and I are coming over to your place this evening! You have a better view of that incomparable torchlight parade!" There was no way to refuse this self-generated invitation. Against our inclination we all looked out our liv-ing room window and all of us became spectators of this march of national hubris. At the twilight of this intimidating display of rampant power, there appeared a motley group of youngsters, the high school boys—no girls—of Hildesheim. I even spotted some of my schoolmates. They did not march in lockstep. They would soon learn.

Only years later, as I reflected on that infamous evening, did it occur to me that I had witnessed the first step of the Nazis' embrace of an evolving iconography, the symbolism of fire and destruction. Flames and fires accompanied the Third Reich from its strident inception to its apocalyptic demise. An endless torchlight parade had turned night into surrealistic day in my hometown and all across Germany. On February 27 that year, the flames of the Reichstag fire also consumed the last vestiges of the Weimar Constitution; on May 10, 1933, the Nazis burned books; five years later, on November 9 and 10, 1938, they burned the synagogues. In 1939 they commenced bombing and scorching European cities; in 1942 the gas ovens of the death camps were lit; and in 1944 and 1945 whole German cities went up in fire and smoke, including the corpse of the chief arsonist of that world conflagration.

That January evening in 1933 ushered in the removal of Jews from German civil society, forcing them into "an outcast state," to quote Shakespeare. But this sundering of our roots came rather gradually. Playmates and best friends were instructed by their parents, and likely by teachers too, to ignore us. They began walking by without a greeting. We were kicked out of our sports clubs and youth organizations, banned from swimming pools, nature walks, and discussion groups. For me, the most galling separation was removal from my beloved gym club, Eintracht. That hurt.

Some years ago, in 1994, a teacher in Germany, Harald Roth, asked me to contribute to an anthology for German high school students meant to acquaint them with the pain inflicted on German-Jewish youngsters during the Nazi period. Thus my thoughts and feelings became part of a collection titled, "Es tat weh, nicht mehr dazu zu gehören" ("It hurt to no longer be part of it"), which became a standard German textbook. Here is my English translation of what I wrote:

The time was spring 1934. I am twelve years old. Hitler has been in power for about a year. Please, think now of a breakfast table on a sunny Sunday morning: my parents, my brother, and I are having another cup of coffee, and my little sister is lying in her crib. We are relaxed; you can still, if only briefly, shut out the bad news that you hear on the radio or read in the newspapers. Suddenly, there is a ring at the door. Who could be calling so early on a Sunday morning? The outside world is suddenly breaking in on us, sweeping in like a gust of wind and spreading fear in its wake. My father goes to the door. But the five men standing in front of our apartment are not the dreaded Secret Police. Dad recognizes them as the Board of the Sports Club Eintracht, or "Harmony" in English, to which I belong. They walk in and my mother offers them seats, but they remain standing. They look awkward in their Sunday best, and then finally a member of the delegation, Mr. Stövesandt, begins to talk in a halting voice. I know him quite well. He is the father of Gustav, a good friend of mine. We are both on a boys' soccer team, and when I got a birthday present, a table soccer set with small metal players, and was making up teams, Gustav came over to our house to give the toy its inauguration. (I beat Gustav by a score of 8–7)

Mr. Stövesandt dragged the words out of his mouth: "You know, we really like your Günther. He is quite a whiz on the gym horse. Well, he is not so good on the parallel bars. And your Günther wrote such wonderful and funny reports about those outings that Mr. Behrens organized. But, you see, we got orders from high up: Cancel the membership of all Jewish members in your club."

I couldn't believe it. I was a good athlete and, as best I knew, I was the only Jew in the entire club. Couldn't they make an exception? My father's voice cut into those immature thoughts. With a sort of finality, he said: "We understand your position." And then they left. But at the door Mr. Stövesandt turned around and said, "Günther, if you want to come to our stadium and use the track, it's okay with us." I never did.

Of course our classroom instruction changed as well. The Nazi term was it was being "gleichgeschaltet"; it had to "toe the Nazi line." Each region was dealt a Nazi as cultural minister, and heads rolled, down to the instructors of kindergartens. Our high school principal was transferred to the boondocks and a party stalwart was dutifully installed. But to our parents' surprise the changes he made were, with one notable exception, merely cosmetic. As a university administrator in later life, I found an obvious explanation for his restraint. His administrative and pedagogical skills were no match for those of his predecessor, who had built up an exemplary high school. The newcomer, who initially did not even bar Jewish parents from PTA meetings, simply took over a smoothly running institution and, with rhetorical embellishments, attributed all the school's virtues to his leadership.

The one exception was his selection of candidates for faculty vacancies. All of us snickered at the eventual replacement for elementary French instruction. On the instructor's first day in class, he gave a dictation. Not even our prize French student, a descendant of Huguenots, had the slightest idea what he was trying to convey with his garbled French. More troublesome was the new director's choice of a geography cum art teacher. During his first class, the teacher asked us for a definition of German folk art. Our class, used to trick questions, observed a cautionary silence. After castigating our stupidity, he gave us his own effusive definition. I only recall one plank of his tottering platform: "For all those reasons, no Jew can ever produce German folk art."

Soon other propagandistic insertions into our syllabi followed. Perhaps as a follow-up to the Nazi book burning, further orders came "from above" to falsify our history textbook. Toward the end of 1933, Mr. Schwerdtfeger, our history teacher, entered our classroom carrying several packages of handouts and, as we learned shortly thereafter, several single-edged razor blades. He started writing numbers on the board. "I am passing out razor blades. Take your textbooks and cut out all pages indicated on the blackboard. Careful though, that you leave enough space on the margins to paste in substitute pages." We did as told. All positive achievements by Jews, other "inferior races," and political "deviants" were excised and replaced by historical distortions and falsehoods.

And then something even more galling took place. Paraphrasing Shakespeare—"fear also makes cowards of us all"—we felt compelled to become the censors, or rather the book burners of parts of our own library. We had amassed a solid collection of sociopolitical books on the shelves of our Saturday afternoon meeting room under the tutelage of Cantor Seppl Cysner, who really wasn't much older than we. During Saturday morning services, a frightening rumor made the rounds. Several of our community leaders had been arrested and their homes searched. We youngsters aggregated in the vestibule of the synagogue. We were struck by fear. Would our fathers be next? What could the Gestapo bloodhounds find? Someone mentioned our own library in the community house across the street. By Nazi standards several books could be considered "demagogic" or "subversive." We rushed across the street, started sorting books, and ignited a bonfire in the stove of the assembly room. All that in utter silence. Then someone, loud of voice, stormed into the room. To our relief, it was our shammes, Mr. Kaminsky, the caretaker of our community house and synagogue. "What are you doing?" he screamed. "You built a fire on the Sabbath?" His accusing words carried the conviction of orthodoxy. One of us threw a saying of the *Pirkei Avot* (*Ethics of Our Fathers*), learned in this very hall, at him: "The saving of lives takes precedence over rules." Bookish, I quoted the chapter and verse by way of reference. Mr. Kaminsky withdrew; the bonfire continued. Georg Prager, one of the youngest of our group, threw up right after the last contraband book had been reduced to ashes. His outrage at our cautionary action rivaled mine. But my persona as an "invisible ink" person restrained me from giving vent to my indignation, even though I felt as if those flames were lapping at me.

When I returned to my high school class on the following Monday, I found a tiny respite in the usual antagonism from my classmates. There was one fellow student in our class with whom I had exchanged blows ever since we started high school. My father had admonished me several times to lay off. That wasn't easy; our classmates egged us on. But then, after us three Jewish fellows had been demeaned and chivvied, he could no longer be urged to start the attack. It was a small gesture, but when you are surrounded by hostility, a token of decency goes a long way.

On a perfect June day in 1933, defiled by yet another outdoor activity of the Hitler Youth that kept us at home, a new dawn seemed to descend or rather burst upon us. It was wielded by four torchbearers from Hannover, the largest city near our hometown. I still remember three of their names. These were the obvious leader, Herbert Sichel, introduced as Hesi, Peter Heller, and Eto, the German abbreviation for "Ententeich" or duck pond, bestowed upon the fellow after his comrades had tossed him into a lake because of his outrageous behavior.

On that Sunday morning, they rang our bell and proclaimed that they held a letter of endorsement by Mr. Rehfeld, the vice president of our Jewish community. Once let in, they assumed a sort of military courtesy stance vis-à-vis my parents, reinforced by their uniform of spotless white shirts and dark blue knee pants. "We represent the Hannover branch of a German-Jewish youth group," they began, with the emphasis clearly on the German. "We are here to help found a Hildesheim branch of the Schwarze Fähnlein [Black Pennant]. We want your Günther as one of the founding members," they concluded. I could not take my eyes off these athletic, vigorous prototypes. I idealized them. The one-word characterization "zackig," borrowed from a word in vogue at the time, meaning snappy or snazzy, intoxicated my brain. "We won't let a bunch of hoodlums deprive us of our Germanness," they declared. The four heroes spread out the ideals of the Schwarze Fähnlein.

It appealed to my parents. "Well," said my father, "if you were recommended by Mr. Rehfeld and Günther wants to join, that's fine with us!" And then he asked whether they had found a leader for the group. Yes, they had: Fritz Schürmann, the son of my father's former employer. That clinched it. "Günther will join!"

I grabbed my father's shoulders as a manly sign of gratitude. A few weeks later I sported the same uniform as Peter, Hesi, and Eto. For the half year that it lasted, the Schwarze Fähnlein became a near-surrogate for much that we had lost. Fritz took over, after gaining clearance from the organization's central headquarters. Before Hitler's ascent to power, he had belonged to a group called dj.1.11, an anti-Fascist but suspiciously superpatriotic youth outfit. Under his guidance, we launched ourselves on exaggeratedly long hikes, assembled in the evening around a sparse campfire, learned traditional youth group songs stimulated by the guitar playing of one of us recruits, listened to our leader reading German youth literature and loved every line of the text, though it was sometimes undeserving of our enthusiasm. On outings we drank lukewarm tea out of thermos bottles and returned home with a halfway restored sense of self-respect. Of course the latter was hammered out of a thin overlay of patina. Sure, we felt some pride when we could sing those pathfinder songs better than the non-Jewish members of our high school choral class, often to the obvious resentment of our Nazified fellow students. But there were also some fear-inducing moments.

On yet another beautiful summer Sunday morning, we hiked to one of Hildesheim's landmark outings with the rather off-putting name of Galgenberg (Gallow's Mountain), a moniker recalling its function as a place of execution during the Middle Ages. Our path was narrow; we were walking in single file. Suddenly a group of men approached from the opposite direction. They were, to be sure, not dressed in Nazi uniforms but rather in the less malign camouflage green of hunters. Yet as they filed past us, the leader of the group, turning to Fritz, saluted us with the newly fashionable greeting, despised and feared by us, of "Heil Hitler." How would Fritz respond? To respond in kind was unthinkable and strictly forbidden to Jews. Fritz answered, "Good morning." This greeting and reply repeated itself as each hunter passed us. By the time the last hunter had gone by, our mounting fears had seemed to become a reality. Their lead-off hiker had turned around and was walking back to Fritz. "I just realized who you are," he said. "We didn't mean to put you down." Now we breathed again. But the youngest in our group had befouled himself out of fear. Fritz proved himself, once more, as a leader. He helped him to clean up.

When, within the year, one of the never-ending decrees of the Nazi government did away with the Schwarze Fähnlein, we were not really surprised. Growing more politically savvy, we saw the perverted logic of the Nazis at work. How could they tolerate a German-Jewish group that proclaimed its rights not only to its Jewish heritage but to their German one as well?

Prepared for the demise of the Schwarze Fähnlein, another, less pronouncedly German youth group stood in the wings. I immediately joined the Bund deutsch-jüdischer Jugend (Association of German-Jewish Youth). Needless to say, in our short-sighted perspective, joining one of the Zionist groups was not considered an acceptable alternative. The BDJJ was not only less ideological but also far more easygoing and relaxed. An outward symbol of this greater "Gemütlichkeit" was the fact that it also admitted girls as members. Another symbol of the transition: We no longer gathered around campfires and yes, some Hebrew songs snuck into our German repertoire. I remember one song, "Leilot Choref (Nights of Winter)," which Seppl sang for us so expressively that we echoed it for months. Sometimes we even could indulge in such an illusion of complete repose, for example, when the Berlin-based president of our organization, Günther Friedländer, did us the honor of a presidential visit.

But matters got infinitely worse for my family and me. Germany's most vicious anti-Semitic weekly, *Der Stürmer* (*The Attacker*), had "uncovered" the nefarious plot that world Jewry was all set to assassinate Hitler. Some clown had placed the first page, with its glaring headline, on the school's bulletin board. During a recess the most fanatical of my fellow students descended on us, his Jewish classmates. He and his faithful followers carried us from the schoolyard to the bulletin board, presumably attributing that murderous conspiracy against their beloved Führer to the Jewish students of our school. We emerged beaten and bloodied.

The final proof of the vicious lawlessness of the Nazi Party was agonizingly demonstrated to my family while my mother and I were away on a short trip to her mother in Vlotho. Late one evening my father, as on many occasions before, walked to the postal mailbox across the street after completing some urgent correspondence. As he was depositing letters, he was accosted by a uniformed SS man, who brutally beat him. He made it home with the help of a policeman but could not resume his route the next day, so he served customers at home. Toward noon my mother and I returned from our trip. Mom entered the store first. "Julius," she cried at the top of her voice, drowning out the customers, "they have beaten you up!" The shock to me was visceral. I turned heels and ran to the bathroom.

German law and order had taken a perverted course, disintegrating before our eyes. The policeman, still trying to do his job, had identified the assailant with the help of a witness by the name of Höhnlein, and a warrant for assault and battery was filed. A week later, when Mr. Höhnlein visited us, he said, "Oh sure," he would testify. But he was in financial straits, and "couldn't my father help him out a bit?"

A few days later, a high-ranking functionary named Dr. Pilz, a dentist by profession, and two of his flunkies came to our apartment, flaunting their full SS uniforms. They had hardly entered the living room when Pilz started shouting at my mother in a voice that carried every word to Werner's and my bedroom. "You Jewish swine have brought charges against one of my men. You, Mrs. Stern," he added in sarcastic politeness, "will call the police and the state attorney and tell them to withdraw all charges. Here are the numbers."

Mom got on the phone, and she had the incredible courage to tell the answering voice that SS-Standartenführer Pilz was at our house and was urging her to withdraw legitimate charges for assault and battery. "He tore the phone out of my hands," she told us the next morning, "identified himself to the police, and said that he was speaking on my behalf to close the case." The policeman on duty merely told him that such a request could only be made in person.

"You dumb cow," he yelled at my mother, before he and his flunkies stormed out. In addition to his physical injuries, my father had an emotional breakdown that night. As soon as the SS hoodlums had left, Werner and I rushed to the living room. For the first time in our lives we saw our father, usually unperturbable, crying without any restraint. The case itself became moot. Adolf Hitler, by fiat, granted a countrywide amnesty to all who felt that niceties of the law no longer applied to them.

When I left Germany, my youth group was still in existence. In my new American life, I made friends and joined American-Jewish youth groups. But I thought back, not infrequently, to my Hildesheim alliances, both with nostalgia and melancholy. My German-Jewish friends, through a sense of comradeship and total acceptance during a time when the outside world began to shun us, had given me, had given us, a tiny restoration of our former feeling of belongingness. The ranks of us adolescents was shrinking. Some of my friends had already been able to escape the Nazi hell. The two Goldberg girls, one a year older, the other, one year younger than I, were sending us letters from Washington, DC. The two Blomendal boys with some ancestral roots in Holland had crossed the border to Germany's neighbor. Their upbeat news from abroad made it appear to us, staying behind, more like an adventure story than a flight into exile.

My parents knew that the time for action had come. They had long acquainted me with their plans to send me to St. Louis, where my aunt and uncle resided. It had come as no surprise to me, and when I turned fourteen, my mother mailed SOS letters to them. She had corresponded throughout the years with her brothers who were still living in her hometown of Vlotho. One of them was no longer alive. Her brother Felix had served his country in World War I and had been killed in action. Uncle Willie answered his sister's letters only sporadically; he had been severely injured in the gas

warfare that concluded World War I, one of the most senseless wars in Western European history. Uncle Benno had lived in St. Louis, Missouri, since his
fourteenth year. How he ended up there is easily told. My grandfather was
a Prussian patriarch. When the adolescent Benno started to sass him, the
son was promptly dispatched to my grandfather's brother living in St. Louis.
Misbehaving children at that time were exiled to the wild Midwest. Ladies
and gentlemen, some of you may well be the offspring of one of those rebels.
As chance would have it, Uncle Benno's punishment turned out to be one of
the springboards to my escape.

My mother asked if Benno and Ethel could take in her eldest child, meaning me. Could they furnish the necessary guarantee—called an affidavit—
that I would not become a public charge? They wrote back that they were
most willing but were in no position to give such an assurance by themselves.
Benno, after coming to St. Louis, had become a unionized baker and pastry
maker, but like so many employees during the tail end of the Great Depression, he had lost his job. Fortunately, his union furnished him with enough
substitute positions so he could provide for his family. In the meanwhile,
my parents also contacted the newly installed Jewish governing body in Germany. They also promised their best efforts on my behalf.

At about the same time, Dad took me out of high school and hired an
English tutor for me. It was a relief not to have to endure the daily taunts.
My parents were determined to send their oldest child, me, out of Germany
with the mission of rescuing the entire family. That was a tall order and I
nearly succeeded, but that word "nearly" denotes a tragedy. At the time, I
obviously had no premonition that my efforts would come to naught. On
the contrary I had the strong optimism of my adolescent years that I would
succeed. Werner continued at his Catholic high school, which he started in
Germany at age ten. Eleonore, not yet of school age, was receiving home instruction from Mom.

As for me, hiring a tutor introduced me to American ways even before
my immigration. The tutor's name was Mr. Tittel. He had emigrated from
Germany during the Great Depression, landed a teaching position at an or-
phanage in Brooklyn, and then returned five years later, in 1931, to his home
town of Hildesheim. Now he was eking out a living by teaching Americanese,
only slightly tinged with Brooklynese, to various Jews in Hildesheim. Many

foresaw that English, in this watershed year of 1936, might soon be their primary means of communication, if they found asylum in an English-speaking country. He was a slight, stooped, somewhat emaciated, graying man of sixty, easygoing and eccentric. He sometimes would start humming an American ditty in the midst of a desultory English conversation. He taught me more practical English in a few months than my "Gymnasium" English teacher, a ruffian, box-on-the-ears specialist who bore the apt nickname "Der Boxer," had got across to me in three years.

Mr. Tittel, in his circumlocutious ways, also peppered his lessons with reminiscences. He had become a baseball fan in America and rose to something close to epic lyricisms when he extolled the pinpoint pitching of Grover Alexander or the mighty swats of Babe Ruth. When I ultimately arrived in the United States, my arcane training nearly dislodged the eyeglasses of my Chicago welcoming committee, a Jewish volunteer social worker. I accepted a candy bar, a Baby Ruth, from her, with a question as to why its name deviated by one letter from Mr. Tittel's venerated baseball idol. America, only dimly perceived before Mr. Tittel's arrival, was taking on concrete forms, and immigrating there was moving from a dream to a distinct possibility. Some of the other members of our youth group, for example, two girls and one boy, also foresaw the possibility of an impending departure from Germany. We felt joy and despondency at the same time. My private English teacher imbued me with the conviction that the passing of the American frontier had not diminished its unbounded opportunity for exotic adventures, ranging from coast-to-coast trains to coed high schools.

Because my friends and I had seen so little of our own homeland, we decided to undertake a very courageous adventure. We planned a long trip to Germany's fabled Rhineland on bicycles, even though we knew full well that Nazis might attack us while we were en route. Since Jews were no longer permitted to spend the night in youth hostels, we contacted Jewish communities in cities intersecting our itinerary and asked for their overnight hospitality. The plan worked and we traveled one thousand kilometers over a four-week period, arriving back safely. I should include that one of the girls on the trip was my beloved, Gerda, but I should also add that we, in our innocence, didn't indulge in boy-girl relations throughout the trip.

Our anticipation of enjoying the Rhenish landscape wasn't fulfilled. Germany had turned into an armed camp. The most vivid memory I have is a harbor that was filled at every anchoring place by small, fast boats equipped with the latest weaponry, as best I could judge. After my return from that trip, my parents immediately called me aside and spread out a document before me: "Uncle Benno and Aunt Ethel have sent you an affidavit. We will now try to get a date with the American Consulate in Hamburg."

How had my uncle and aunt managed to get a notarized affidavit, given their straitened circumstances? My uncle, having been told that he had to show the financial resources to support me, had hit upon an ingenious device. He called upon all his union buddies, friends, and relations, urging them to deposit goodly sums of money in his bank account. His loyal supporters came through for him. At the end of two weeks, he asked the bank for a notarized statement, which portrayed him as a gentleman of fabulous wealth. A few days later, he returned every last penny of that borrowed money.

The next hurdle had to be jumped—and at a dizzying pace. Two months later we were notified that I had an appointment with the American Consul in Hamburg. My mother was now torn between gladness for me and the sadness of separation. My parents had already worked out a modus vivendi. I would get a ride from another Jewish family scheduled to appear one day earlier at the consulate and spend the night at student housing. My trip to America started with the excitement of the longest automobile ride of my life and loaded down with a good portion of anxiety.

Here a bit of background is in order. We all had heard of the fearsome encounters with American consulate officials. Why? On little publicized orders from the American State Department, honeycombed with anti-Semites or personnel simply hostile to foreigners, these obedient or prejudiced consuls would turn down prospective immigrants for the slightest flaws in their papers or on trumped-up pretexts.

In early October 1937, I stood, only slightly awed and for only fifteen brief minutes, before the man who, unbeknownst to me then, held my life in his hands. The name of the American Consul General was Malcolm C. Burke, a massive, impressive man of fifty. In German he asked me my name, date of birth, schooling, and, apparently to keep America free of cretins, the sum of forty-eight plus fifty-two. My unexceptional answers produced his stamp and signature to my "Jugendausweis." In a few minutes I had acquired the papers that thousands at that time vainly coveted.

Only many years later, when I was fully aware of the near-miracle of those fifteen minutes, did I puzzle out my good fortune. My uncle's affidavit, I had long realized, must have appeared all but worthless to a seasoned consular official like Burke. Uncle Benno was an unemployed baker with a family to support. He earned his living through the goodwill of his union, which sent him out on fill-in jobs. Burke must have seen through my uncle's subterfuge. I wondered why this document passed muster. The answer came, as seems almost inevitable with an academic, through the pages of a book. After the war, when I knew nearly the full horror of the Nazi years, in part through the unfolding discoveries of my US Army Intelligence Unit, I, like so many others, sought explanations for the unexplainable, including the indifference of the many potential countries of asylum. And so I leafed through the first edition of Arthur D. Morse's *Why Six Million Died* at the branch of our public library. And there it was. The book's index led me to the American consul in Hamburg, Malcolm C. Burke, who was eager to find loopholes that would allow the persecuted to escape to America. He had saved my life. What a difference from the consul in Stuttgart, a bigot who kept Jews out under any number of legalisms.

And that is, in broad outline, my story as I would have told it. About seven years ago I learned that an essential part of my deliverance from Nazi Germany was hidden from me till the ripe old age of ninety-one. Of course, in retrospect I had often asked myself: isn't the event of my deliverance an unlikely story? Recall that my rescue depended on all sorts of lucky turns. There was my uncle, an unemployed baker who had pulled the wool over the eyes of a seasoned consular official. Or why had the deputy consul in Hamburg pitched that ridiculous question, "How much is forty-eight plus fifty-two?"—something that a kid half my age could have answered? And why, during my immigration, did I encounter so many members of a committee I had never heard of before? Surely there were gaps in my story!

But I have rushed the calendar. The letter from the New York committee reached us promptly. A date had been set for my passage and I was to be at the pier on November 5, 1937, several hours before the ship's departure.

A week prior to my departure my parents gave a farewell party for me and my friends—not a single non-Jew among them in this fourth year of National Socialism. The party boosted my sense of adventure. Looking back now, this roseate expectancy is expunged by the reality that followed. When I said goodbye to my parents, my brother, and my sister, I thought we would soon be reunited, and that tempered the grief of departure. I saw none of my family again. I believed at one time I could also write of their death in the Warsaw ghetto. But then, during sporadic visits to Hildesheim, I heard from strangers shattering details of their last days at home. My long years of suppression closed in again. We must all cope as best we can.

My dad added his own instructions before my impending immigration. Throughout the Nazi years he had constantly hammered into the heads of my brother and me that need for remaining inconspicuous: "You have to be like invisible ink," he cautioned. "You will leave traces of your existence when, in better times, the invisible ink will become visible again, but in the meanwhile. . . ." His voice trailed off. He also reminded me that my passage was booked on a German Hapag Lloyd ship and therefore I would not leave German territory until I had disembarked on American soil. My father's admonition took root. For many years I carried its psychological burden with me. But my father's words also became the metamorphosis from which I fashioned my life: to use the power of words in creating a career filled with teaching, writing, and speaking to thousands over the years about my life and the wisdom one possibly can extract from it.

CHAPTER THREE

Coming to America

N O FOREBODINGS ACCOMPANIED ME on the Hapag Lloyd boat that carried us, a group of Jewish youngsters and a German Jewish social worker, from Bremerhaven to New York. In fact we were rather full of practical jokes and bad manners in general, the natural compensation of long unnatural restraint, years when we were told on a daily basis that we, as Jews, needed to be better than good and at any rate inconspicuous, as was invisible ink. My own ill-timed sortie into rebelliousness—one that still makes me cringe—is my sudden assumption of a blasé attitude as we steamed into New York Harbor. As all the other passengers rushed toward the railing to be greeted by the Statue of Liberty, I casually strolled toward her in a spirit of nil admirari.

Before disembarking we said goodbye to an American gentleman who had befriended us en route. His expansive manner and his munificence—he treated our entire group to an exotic drink called Coca-Cola—convinced us that he was one of those fabled American millionaires. Toward the end of our voyage he told us that he was a vacationing mailman who had hoarded his savings for a European trip. We didn't believe a word of it; our "millionaire" wanted to stay incognito, we conjectured. My appreciation of the porousness of America's social hierarchy—perhaps calcifying as I write this—did not crystallize until much later.

The two days in New York contributed little to my Americanization. I was met at the pier and shoved through Immigration by a representative of a Jewish committee and by a cousin of my mother's from Essen. My Green

Card was in apple-pie order and would, fifty years later, help illustrate an exile exhibit of the *Deutsche Bibliothek* in Frankfurt. No such notoriety accompanied my first day in New York. Aunt Klärchen took me in tow, speaking a hard-to-follow amalgam of German and English. "Wir fahren jetzt mit der Subway. Duck dich mal unter die Turnstile, dann brauchst du keinen Nickel zu bezahlen!" Keeping with her instructions I committed my first American misdemeanor by entering the platform without paying. My recollections of New York are a jumble of skyscrapers ("Look out, die Wolkenkratzer," Tante Klärchen would exclaim), subways, and a curious type of gastronomy ("Automatenrestaurant," said Klärchen), where you inserted money to obtain the item of your choice. The meals were indifferent. I learned early on in America that technology often outstrips substance. Tante Klärchen said "Mahlzeit, my boy," as our ways parted at the exit of Horn and Hardart.

The committee in New York decided that my English would allow me to solo on my train ride to St. Louis, the residence of Uncle Benno and Aunt Ethel. As we sped from the East to the Midwest my awe at the largeness of America's geography—and of its vocabulary—increased in tandem. As to the latter, a curious omission of Mr. Tittel and "The Boxer" surfaced. After I had completed my main course in the dining car, the steward, the first black person I had ever spoken to, asked me monosyllabically: "Pie?" I thought that was his way of saying "pay," so I pulled out my committee-donated meal coupon. He then repeated his terse question two more times, his decibel level rising. The supervisor, called to the table, solomonically told the steward, after being equally thwarted by my apparent obtuseness: "Bring him some apple pie!" From that moment onward that word stuck to me like the gelatinous goo that held the pastry together. The experience came in handy. As a writer of textbooks I have always insisted on illustrations, even where pictures can't tie memory to the taste buds.

Yet another side of America, undreamt of by Mr. Tittel, unfolded before me in Chicago, where the aforementioned sophisticated committee-woman provided a city tour in her car during a three-hour layover. She concluded the tour with a stroll through the Maxwell Street Flea Market. Both sellers and buyers, at least at that time, were largely Jewish; some of them even wore yarmulkas. As I watched them in their unselfconscious transactions and relaxed by-plays, years of inhibitions, the need to crawl into myself, slowly, if yet incompletely, peeled off. I began to realize that in my new country I need not resemble invisible ink or that, conversely, I now had to rebel against my enforced inconspicuousness. Others, like those coreligionists milling around Maxwell Street Market, had already done that for me.

A bevy of relatives, familiar from diverse family albums, welcomed me at Union Station in St. Louis. Uncle Benno, working a night shift, was not among them. I met him at midnight, an undersized, squat person, floored but not counted out by the Depression. What sustained him were flights into popularized mysticism; even that first night he tried to make me a convert to Rosicrucianism. He lived a hard life and didn't apologize for the cramped flat, so different from his parents', my grandparents', spacious Westphalian house. Nor did he dwell on the fact that I had to share my bed with another refugee boy, boarded there, at some profit to my aunt and uncle, by the ubiquitous Jewish committee. Nonetheless my dreams of adventurous America didn't collapse those first days. Rather they now played themselves out on a reduced scale. Infinity, today's current chaos theory tells us, can be encountered in small spaces, if the measurements aren't applied to the cosmos but to atomic particles.

My exploration of America via cross-country trains began on my trip to St. Louis. It was not repeated until five years later courtesy of the US Army and then shrank to treks across St. Louis and environs. I had discovered America's subsidiary, cost-free mode of transportation called hitchhiking. I discovered South St. Louis with its "Dutch" (i.e., German) neighborhood, bordered by Italian Hill. I went swimming in Crevecoeur Lake, which I almost failed to identify to the kind lady who picked me up because I pronounced it the French way rather than in her Midwestern drawl as "Creavecar" Lake. I often thumbed my way to the downtown section of St. Louis with its sheltering library (and the nearby White Castle, ten cents for an egg sandwich and a glass of chocolate milk), and to Forest Park with its art museum and Jefferson Memorial where a replica of Lindbergh's *Spirit of St. Louis* was housed.

Together with my new family I would walk on Jewish holidays to a small prayer house a few blocks away. Few of us in our neighborhood could afford the substantial membership dues for the ornate temple of Rabbi Isserman or Rabbi Gordon, both of them riveting orators. Our makeshift synagogue was bare. It was presided over by Mr. Ansky, a volunteer cantor. But despite the soon-familiar faces the holiday celebrations weren't the same for me. I missed my hometown synagogue, even more the familiar ritual, the different pronunciation of the Hebrew vowels, and the annually intoned liturgical music. What I had imagined to be the easiest transition from one Jewish service to another turned out to be the most formidable obstacle course, in fact one never entirely mastered. Catholic exiles have told me that they found a spiritual anchor, wherever they went, in the "blessed sameness" of the then prevailing Latin ritual. I never sang the Hebrew melodies common in America with the same overtones of happy childhood memories that I had gathered in the Oriental-style synagogue of Hildesheim. But that was a minor religious adjustment problem, which faded into utter insignificance after the traumatizing news of November 9, 1938. A newsboy, hawking the St. Louis *Star-Times*, to which we subscribed, was shouting, "Synagogues burning in Germany! Read all about it!" Sometimes I hear his voice, the shouts raised to screams, at the most unexpected times and places: at services, before becoming fully awake, and certainly when I am in Hildesheim. And then I relive each time the feeling of loss and my maledictions against the perpetrators.

Occasionally I would walk with my aunt—her treat—to the Plymouth Movie House. Tuesday night was Ladies' Night at the Plymouth. That meant reduced admissions, coupons ultimately redeemable for "free dishes," and a steady diet of B-movies. Their saccharine quality didn't matter to me: the features with such faded matinée idols as Rudy Vallee constituted lessons in English and very basic Americana. What I had missed by not growing up in America I picked up at the Plymouth or in other curious ways. From a film about a love triangle with an utterly predictable happy end I learned the folk tune "Who's Coming around the Mulberry Bush," sung by one of the swains about his rival. I became as distortedly knowledgeable about America's West as a native-born, red-blooded American kid by walking to a sweltering outdoor cinema at the Wellston Shopping Center, where Gene Autry proclaimed, repeatedly and in song, that he was "a happy, roving cowboy." I learned English nursery rhymes, with which my American contemporaries had all grown up, by reading the Mother Goose murder mystery by best-selling detective-story writer S. S. Van Dine. In the evenings we adolescents gathered in someone's front yard, no less satisfying a gathering place than today's night clubs, drank weak lemonade, mildly and innocently flirted, and sang traditional American songs, such as "On Top of Old Smokey.'"

During those heat-baked St. Louis summer nights we confided to one another our own versions of the American dream. How ambitious we all were! Out of our neighborhood, confined to three to four blocks of St. Louis's predominantly Jewish West Side, emerged one of the city's most successful businessmen, a leading conductor and musicologist, a prominent physician, and Missouri's future lieutenant-governor, Kenneth Rothman. The dreams of my American contemporaries sustained and occasionally restored mine. That happened, for example, when my aunt and uncle, who were also my legal guardians, proposed taking me out of high school and enrolling me in a trade school. They had read somewhere that the path to later employment started with the learning of a trade. I fought the notion and won.

I knew instinctively that Soldan High School, where I had been enrolled within five days of my arrival in St. Louis, was ideal for me. Simply put, it was America at its best. James Hotchener later wrote *King of the Hill*, a novel about the school set during the Depression. In 1993 the novel, with the name of the institution and its administrators slightly changed, was made into an inspiring film. It tells about a boy's struggle, sometimes tragic, often wryly funny, to succeed despite a fragile family structure and against mounting debts. It is not quite my story; my life fortunately lacked that kind of drama and traumata. I was never completely broke. A distant, more affluent relative gave me an allowance of fifty cents every two weeks, when he didn't forget, and my aunt and uncle were never threatened with eviction. But the film did re-evoke Soldan for me as it then was. Students from fairly wealthy families rubbed shoulders with kids in threadbare clothes. And the teachers and principals, Mr. Stellwagen and Mr. Barr, were magnificent. They had set their sights on rivaling the best college prep schools, and on balance they succeeded. As an educator of some fifty-five-odd years myself, I am sure that, in chronicling those two years, I have not yielded to the temptation of idealizing the proverbial golden school days.

At Soldan I soaked up American history, political structures, culture, and literature. Ask me today about Andrew Jackson's Populism or the initial non-populist elections to the US Senate or the poems of Longfellow and I will still be able to regurgitate the teaching of Mrs. Mott, "Doc" Bender, and Mrs. Nagle.

The rules were as strict, or almost so, as those I knew from Hildesheim. No smoking within two blocks of the school building, no curse words (even mild ones) in class, no walking down the "up staircase," and absolutely no unexcused absences. But these rules were tempered, nay, sweetened, by personal attention and care. Sure, we also had a few villains hidden in our idyllic environment. Mr. Patrick, an English teacher, disliked foreigners, and the girl students avoided one of the math teachers, who doubled as the football coach and considered women unqualified for his discipline.

But in general the halls of Soldan echoed kindness. My first day at school betokened it. Mr. Stellwagen received me personally, told me that he had assigned me to the advisory (homeroom) of Mrs. Muller, the German teacher, handed me my program and asked whether I was interested in going for any extracurriculars. My quizzical look elicited further explanations and a menu of activities. "Swimming and the school newspaper," I responded. "Of course," he said, "I'll introduce you to the faculty advisors." And he didn't discourage me at all, despite the fact that my English, even to this day but then more pronouncedly, was tinged by an accent. "Our publications, the yearbook and the newspaper, are called *Scrip and Scrippage*," he said. "Do you know where those names come from?" A puzzled silence on my part. "Well," he explained, like a teacher would, "they come from Shakespeare's *As You Like It*: 'Let us make an honorable retreat, though not with bag and baggage, yet with scrip and scrippage.'" And then he took me to Mrs. Rasmussen, the advisor of *Scrippage*.

My first class was Mrs. Carmody's geometry class. "Ah, our new student from Germany! Well, we're having a test today. Why don't you show me what you can do? Just take a seat over there." I read the test and stumbled over a few terms. I walked up to her desk and asked: "What is an isosceles triangle?" She went to the board and drew one. "Ah," I said to myself, "Ein gleichschenkliges Dreieck." I got a "G" (for "good") on that test and still consider that a major triumph of my academic career.

Beyond shepherding me through my program, some of the teachers took a personal interest in me. Rose Kaufman, a Latin teacher, well connected in the Jewish community, got me my first job outside the occasional lunchroom work at school. I became a dishwasher at the Branscom Hotel, and a busboy at the Chase, the Jefferson Hotel, and the Bismarck Café. At the tail end of the Depression even those jobs were at a premium and Rose Kaufman interceded for me at the highest level with Mr. Kaplan, the owner of the Chase.

But my stint at the Bismarck Café became memorable for another reason as well. One of the owners had also found a job for his father, who did not want to be idle. His son had brought him to America from Bulgaria and he now eked out a wage and learned English at his old age. Well, he did not advance much. We, as fellow busboys, talked to him because he seemed to have some influence on his son. He reacted invariably in one of two ways to our conversations with him. He would say "Izza good," when he approved, "Izza no good," when he wanted to condemn. The other busboys and I tried to catch him in a situation where neither comment would be applicable. We did not succeed, but I never forgot this eccentric old man and his two responses can still be frequently heard within the walls of our house.

With these fledgling positions I was well launched on a "career" as room service waiter, then dining-room waiter with full union standing. My catapulting into that august standing came about through one of the most remarkable, if unheralded, exiles in St. Louis, Johnny Ittelson.

Ittelson had come to St. Louis after a brief mandatory waiting period in Cuba, had made successful careers, first as a liquor salesman—salesman of the year for the firewater producers of McKesson and Robbins—then as maître d' at the Jefferson Hotel in St. Louis, and in a further though unsuccessful venture, as the owner of his own European-styled establishment, the Continental, located at the entrance of the much-visited Forest Park.

His founding of the restaurant also brought about major progress in my career. I advanced from the lowly position of a busboy to the status of a waiter. (Actually my ironic remark is really ill-placed, because even such common jobs were at a premium during the tail end of the Depression.) Johnny had met me while he was a maître d' at the Jefferson and I a busboy. When he founded his restaurant he felt a sense of loyalty to the fellow exile and recruited me as a waiter at the Continental.

It is only in retrospect that I can fully appreciate the favors that Rose Kaufman and Johnny Ittelson did for me. Of course, my high school education at Soldan was invaluable, but of need, limited. By becoming for a while a member of America's working class, I gained perspectives, closed even to many Americans who were born in this country.

This added experience was threefold. I became a coworker of men and women who provided the muscles for America's well-being by their skills. There was Calvin, the dishwasher from Indiana, who threatened "to beat the sh—t out of me," and in fact, landed a punch because he felt that I had talked down to him when I just used my usual vocabulary. I soon learned to talk his jargon. Then there was the fellow waiter who only addressed me by the name he bestowed upon me, which was Abie, a reference to me being Jewish. Finally there was the only waitress in our group, the highly efficient Opal, with whom I partnered as a waiter and who promised to introduce me to certain adventures for which I was as yet unprepared.

The second new perspective supplemented what was lacking in my middle-class setting in Hildesheim. The Jewish community there was composed, for the most part, of established and well-provided professionals in industry and trade, the law, medicine, the arts, and music. There weren't any entrepreneurs who in many cases had to survive by their wits. But in St. Louis I became a close acquaintance of an intrepid, rare individual who exemplified such a person. That was Johnny. He ultimately succeeded in America because he could think beyond standard conventions and because he would often fail, but would never stay down. Somewhat by chance he assembled around him a group of immigrants with whom even most experts on Exile Studies never became acquainted. If I hadn't worked for Johnny, gotten to know him, his strengths and weaknesses—and learned to appreciate, perhaps to imitate his never-die spirit—I wouldn't have had that opportunity.

For a short while he also opened up to me one of the few centers, certainly in the Midwest, where nearly all the refugees from all walks of life in the city would gather and could be observed by a curious youngster. That came about because Johnny the Incredible had opened, yes opened, a restaurant. One observation of mine mirrors that group of exiles while not at their best. From the start Johnny had installed three pinball machines in a back room of the restaurant. Soon the players became tired of pitching their skills just against the machine itself. They started betting against one another for what would seem today ridiculously small change. The competition became as fierce as if the players had been in Monte Carlo or Las Vegas. In fact, Johnny had to intervene a few times when the rivalry threatened to become physical. However, upon one of those occasions, a participant had given the machine a forbidden push in order to correct the routing of the pinball and made a lame excuse for walking out with the loot he had taken from his opponents. This had led to a fisticuff. Because of Johnny's manifold managerial talents and their influence on me, I became much more pragmatic. Hence, I will draw a full portrait of him and our brief "association."

Johnny was at his best on the opening night of his restaurant. His planning had been meticulous. He had the financial backing from his cousin Henry and the décor of his restaurant left nothing to be desired. Tables and chairs called to mind the style of the Bauhaus. Beautiful light-brown napkins, folded in the form of crowns, matched the color of the table cloths. There was a music box that played tunes from operettas and burst forth, every hour on the hour, with the song "The Continental," borrowed from a Fred Astaire film. And Johnny's spirit hovered—yes, hovered—over the entire décor. He himself took charge of seating people and operating the cash register.

Johnny's planning paid off. I spotted members of the high society of St. Louis among the arrivals, hitherto known to me only from the society columns of our local newspapers. Even August Busch showed up with a large party. He was the famed proprietor of the gigantic brewery Anheuser-Busch. Johnny courted that party to a fare-thee-well, kissed the hands of the ladies— to their surprise and consternation—and put on a show reminiscent of Paris at its most glamorous period.

I returned from work dead tired. The tables in my station had been filled three or four times. The evening marked my less-than-smooth entry into my status as a waiter. But Mr. Busch rewarded my earnest efforts with a munificent tip.

Alas the triumph of opening night didn't extend to the weeks ahead. The good citizens of St. Louis had at first thronged to the new restaurant out of pure curiosity. Once that was satisfied, the aroma of the zesty spaghetti sauce, spreading from the citywide renowned Italian restaurant, Garavelli, located just across the street, made their mouth water much more than the hard-to-pronounce (and equally hard to digest) Cordon Bleu of our gourmet restaurant.

Instead of the leading citizens of St. Louis, the refugee circle moved in, but only for afternoon coffee and cake. There was a barber, more affluent than the rest of the refugees, who had had an exclusive clientele in Berlin and who became my favorite customer. He gave me one of the distinctive, if un-American, haircuts that I continued to sport in a period of my life when I still needed frequent trips to the barber. To indicate my rather sparse earnings the barber gave me a fifty-cent tip when he and his wife dined at the Continental, which I returned to him as a gratuity for practicing his original haircuts on me.

Despite a few such steady guests the income of the restaurant and with it the money from tips steadily declined. Johnny became moody. For example, he resented that I was not only a waiter on his staff but also a student at Saint Louis University because he realized that I wanted to become a member of The Establishment. "You're studying Spanish?" He was reverting back to his time in Cuba, when he added, "I, myself, could teach you that."

His first concrete measure to stave off the threatening decline of the restaurant was reducing staff. He started with us waiters. Admittedly we weren't prime specimens of our profession. When the positions for Johnny's experiment had been announced by the union, the demand for such employment was scarcely spectacular. Hence, among the hired waiters were some eccentric employees and a slightly senile retiree, who shuffled his way slowly through the dining hall. Then there was me, the fledgling waiter, and also a colleague, frequently less than sober and who in our dressing room sometimes told me, while in tears, what the demon alcohol had done to him in the past. I pitied him, but he found little understanding among guests whose orders he had hopelessly messed up for the second time. The union, used to the troubles they had had with him, finally endorsed his dismissal.

In order to be able to spread his charm even more palpably among our customers, Johnny had recourse for help from his parents. He turned the cash register over to his stepfather, a former Berliner architect and businessman, finally turned refugee. He stuck by the old German proverb: "He who doesn't watch his pennies will soon not have any dollars." And for that reason he watched every item on the bill with infinite care while waiting guests, in growing frustration, hit the counter with their knuckles. Johnny's mother, however, an aristocratic-looking lady, who had a piping voice and promptly had been given the nickname of "Chirpy" by her friends and old acquaintances, became a further addition to our motley staff as a sort of supervisor. Her measured steps took her from the kitchen to the dining room and back and she gave out well-meaning advice for cutting expenses. Our leading chef, a highly qualified master cook from the Philippines, turned red-faced as soon as he caught sight of her. In exquisite language she advised him that one simply shouldn't throw away the wrapping paper for butter. "It's excellent for greasing pots and pans."

One day the cook's patience was at an end. He tossed his apron on the floor, disappeared like a lightning bolt, and was discovered again after he had been hired by the competition across the street. His position was filled by the second in command, but that worthy was hardly capable of filling his former chef's shoes. This gradual breakdown of our infrastructure didn't escape the wide-open eyes of Johnny's wife, a chic but calculating woman from Berlin. She took action and confronted Johnny a few weeks later with an application for a divorce and soon after disappeared from our vision. Johnny, alternately depressed, enraged, and defiant, sought short-term substitutes with well-to-do customers who admired him as boundlessly as before. What was most on his mind was rescuing his restaurant. He wrote letters to the editors of important newspapers and used me as his ghost writer and editor.

Then one morning the telephone rang at my aunt and uncle's residence. Johnny asked me to come to the restaurant early because he had a colossal idea. Immediately after my first class I tore myself away from the Golden Age of Spanish Literature and ended up in the tough reality of an enterprise approaching bankruptcy. But Johnny's face was all smiles. "You will be the first one to hear of my rescue mission," he said. "We will imitate European customs and hold a costume party right in our own restaurant." Let me report that his costume ball attracted only the customary impoverished European refugees. My tips were below moderate. I had only one consolation: a young woman who had borrowed a rather daring waitress costume from her place of employment had come with the expectation of meeting a well-heeled American male at the costume party. We consoled each other and continued with that long after the last guest had departed. The restaurant lasted only about eight months.

I had to look elsewhere in order to practice my newfound skills. I ended up at the Rose Bowl, a bar and restaurant sought out by football fans. The combination of schoolwork and waiter's chores worked for me until high school graduation.

I soon lost sight of Johnny. Yet, I was destined to see him once again. World War II separated the two encounters. By 1957 I had become a professor at a good university and the German-Jewish American newspaper *Aufbau* had published a feature about me, giving out the name of my university and my department. Two weeks later I received an airmail letter. Wasn't I his former waiter at the Continental and didn't I frequently make trips to the Federal Republic of Germany, to which he had returned after retirement? Surely I could visit him sometime at his German home in Wiesbaden. In fact, in that very city I was to meet with a German writer for research purposes on my next trip scheduled shortly after hearing from Johnny. At first glance there was little left of the man of the world. He was walking on crutches, had aged badly, and was accompanied by an elderly live-in partner, who, as he whispered to me, was inclined for reasons of her own to do him kind services but hadn't turned romantic with him. But then I looked at him more closely. His light blue suit fit him as if it had been poured on, his shirt was immaculately white, his old cufflinks were glistening as in the days of old, and lo and behold, his car was a nearly new BMW. He had once more landed on his feet. He had become a special events director for the city government of an American city in the Midwest. Perhaps our luckless costume ball had served as a testing ground. So I asked myself whether this enterprising spirit, this man whom you couldn't keep down, this visionary of a miniature world: wasn't he also a loss for his home country? If the Berlin of the twenties had lived on without a dictatorship, Johnny Ittelson or Hans Ittelson would have livened up the most humdrum surrounding with his ever-present optimism and his irrepressible spirit.

I have jumped across the abyss of those eventful and sometimes horrible years between 1939 and 1957. In 1939 I was just on the verge of graduating from a wonderful high school. I have dealt above at some length with the intellectual rigor and prescribed discipline at Soldan, because I continue to believe that public education is the bulwark of a functioning democracy. My late wife Judith, a high school teacher of forty-odd years' experience, liked to quote Thomas Jefferson: "If a nation expects to be ignorant and free, it expects what never was and will never be." Today we stand in danger of selling public education to forces with profits rather than education as their goals and of confining the training of informed, broadly knowledgeable future citizens to those few who can afford the most prestigious private high schools. Is it really too late to return to the ethos and values of Soldan High School and other schools like it that enfolded me as a fresh-off-the-boat immigrant in those years of 1937–1939? After all, those years were beset by crises no less severe than those that purportedly necessitate the current dismantling of public education. I might add that I wrote the above paragraph in 1998.

The time for graduation and the prom was approaching. I turned to my benefactor, Mrs. Kaufman. She came to my rescue again. She found an anonymous donor who supplied a navy-blue jacket and white flannel trousers, an almost requisite outfit for the graduation ceremony and for the prom as well.

I consider one incident surrounding that graduation and prom as a barometer of my progressing Americanization. I couldn't go to the prom, because I had to bus dishes that night at the Chase Hotel. But the prom was also held at the Chase and during lag time in the dining room I had the temerity to stroll over to the adjoining ballroom, busboy uniform and all, and to greet my decked-out, jitterbugging classmates. But with that stroll, which I knew would draw everyone's attention, I had walked the long distance from the invisible-ink person to a healthily uninhibited American youngster.

If I had been able to attend, I would have escorted—as it was then called—a classmate with the improbable name of Idamae Schwartzberg. We had become friends soon after my arrival at Soldan, though we actually met at the YMHA/YWHA (Young Men's/Women's Hebrew Association), where I was working out to secure the not highly touted number three spot as breaststroker on the Soldan Swimming Team. Idamae contributed to my Americanization, beyond the usual "European boy meets American girl" stuff, in a most visible, audible, and certainly permanent way. She had little patience with my German name, Günther, which she termed a tongue-twister. She decided to retain the first two letters, and to add a "y." I became "Guy." The name stuck in high school and I retained it when I became a US citizen during basic training at Camp Berkley, Texas. People say it kind of fits me, especially in combination with my monosyllabic surname, which incidentally means "star" in German. Neither Idamae nor I had any money to speak of, so we would pack a picnic basket, stow our books for homework, and get to the St. Louis Forest Park outdoor opera at 3:30 p.m., right after classes, for one of the back row free seats that the city provided in conformance with the founding statutes. The time till curtain at 8:00 p.m. passed with homework, food, and tomfoolery. And then we were in the grip of performances of such musicals as Gershwin's *Of Thee I Sing* or Jerome Kern's *Showboat*. We lingered till the last curtain call and the dimming of the spots. I have rarely felt more intensely part of the American scene than at those times, when the two of us, humming the just-heard melodies, were walking home through a summery Forest Park—arm in arm, with a bit of necking thrown in, like virtually all the couples around us. My fondness for the American musical started then. And today, when I, as the vice president of the Kurt Weill Foundation, thrill to Weill's enrichment of the genre, I suspect that memories of those Forest Park summer nights, redolent of its flower beds and replete with simmering warmth and the joyousness of my first American love, are floating up to harmonize with the Weillian strains of, say, "Speak low, when you speak love."

During our incessant conversations Idamae and I not only advanced our romance but reinforced each other's interests. Idamae provided me with my first glances into the unknown world of Hollywood. Her artist elder brother worked for Disney Studios as an inker for the cartoon movies. His letters home were promptly communicated to me. On the other hand, I told Idamae of the occasions I attended performances at the Fox Theater in St. Louis. I was invited by friends from the YMHA to accompany them to this huge movie house. There is no way I could have afforded the ticket prices. It was only by the kind generosity and inclusion of my new friends that it was made possible. They reached out to the new immigrant in a way that would help him become an American boy more quickly. It was the era of Big Bands, famous choral groups such as the "Ink Spots," and solo appearances of performers. One moment of such a stage appearance has never left my memory. The comedian Oliver Hardy appeared without his trusty partner, Stan Laurel. At one point he had walked through the audience despite his sizable bulk and made spontaneous wisecracks about the people he passed. People roared with laughter.

My other afternoon outings, the quintessence of American leisure time activities, didn't interest Idamae, an energetic, attractive brunette with decided individualistic opinions. She was interested in theater, appeared in several high school productions, and wasn't enamored with baseball at all. But another neighborhood friend, Kurt Salomon, like me a recent arrival from Germany, had jointly foresworn our intense, even fanatical, attachment to German soccer in favor of baseball. We shared the incredibly useful intelligence that high school students could get so-called Knothole Passes, which entitled the bearer to free admission to the left-field bleachers of Sportsman's Park, home of both the St. Louis Browns and the Cardinals. There I became acquainted with the intricacies of the squeeze play, batting averages, and a more robust American language than the parlance absorbed in my English classes. I remember one diminutive student from another high school whose booming voice belied his small stature. He greeted each opposing left fielder, when he took up his position, with the choice sobriquet of "moldy rectum," this being a somewhat attenuated version of the actual quote. I also came to admire the powerful hitting of Joe "Ducky-Wucky" Medwick, of Johnny "The Big Cat" Mize, the fielding artistry of Terry Moore, and the spectacular pitching of the Browns' Buck "Bobo" Newsom. In fact once, while hitchhiking to Sportsman's Park from Soldan, I was picked up by the Browns' all-star pitcher himself. He detected my accent, asked me quite a few personal questions, and I gloried for years in my close, if only very brief, proximity to diamond greatness.

But another hitchhike acquaintance ended in an impasse that fills me even today with guilt and outrage. All this while I had vainly tried to find Jewish people in St. Louis wealthy enough to provide credible affidavits for my family left behind in Germany. One afternoon, on my way to work at the Jefferson Hotel downtown, a man picked me up in a car that implied affluence. I steered our conversation first to myself, then to the plight of my family. "What's involved in getting them over here?" he asked. "Someone with some means has to guarantee that they won't become a public charge," I told him, or words to that effect. "Well," he answered, "I could do that." I nearly hugged him even while he was speeding down Delmar Boulevard. But then he continued: "I'm not sure the government will accept my pledge." He offered no further explanation. "Are you willing to try it?" I asked. "Sure, absolutely, after all, life's a gamble!"

All the next week I hustled for an appointment with the lawyer whom the Jewish Committee had designated to do pro bono work for us refugees. The three of us met on a Friday afternoon in the fall of 1938. Mr. R., the lawyer, turned out to be a stickler for the niceties of the law and all but oblivious to the less-than-nice plight of Germany's Jews. He started fussing with papers and forms, asked my new acquaintance the usual routine questions, but came to an abrupt halt when my family's potential benefactor stated his occupation. "Gambler?" A pause. Then: "We needn't bother. The signer of an affidavit must be a stable citizen with an assured income." The terse verdict was uttered with supercilious superiority. I remonstrated, in less sophisticated terms, of course, that we could perhaps substitute a euphemism. A withering look: "Circumvent the law?" My newfound friend walked out of the lawyer's office, out of my life, and with him the last concrete chance of rescuing my family. I have never forgotten nor forgiven that afternoon in lawyer R.'s office. I am convinced that Malcolm C. Burke, even had he detected a subterfuge, would have validated my family's immigration papers. Until this day, beginning with that afternoon, I have retained a loathing for pettifogging, pigmy-sized, letter-of-the law officials, and a secret if selective admiration for America's free and generous spirits who, like that gambler or Azdak, the poor folks' judge in Brecht's Caucasian Chalk Circle, "broke the laws like bread to feed the people."

In 1939, during my senior year in high school, I became the feature editor of Scrippage and earned the nickname of "Scoop." Said appellation attached to me because I had obtained some interviews rarely found in high school news-papers. Within months I had interviewed the band leader Benny Goodman, which also contributed to my Americanization. He and his band were ap-pearing at the Fox Theater in midtown St. Louis. After watching the rousing performance—I had grown to be a jazz aficionado—I eluded a watchman to get backstage. I immediately ran into Jerry Jerome, a member of the band, and, with a bird in hand, developed my strategy. Had I asked Jerry directly and un-adornedly to lead me to the leader of the band, he might well have shown me the door. So I said, "I would like to interview you and later Mr. Goodman for my high school newspaper." "Sure, kid, go ahead!" And then he took me to the reigning idol of the jazz scene. "Bright kid here, wants to interview you," Jerry said. Benny Goodman spent half an hour with me. Even today I remember the lead sentence of my front-page feature: "Here he is, the King of Swing, whose clarinet and band delight jitterbugs across the land." Of the interview itself I remember one item of repartee. I told Mr. Goodman that I had become a jazz aficionado upon coming to America from Germany, where jazz had been outlawed by Hitler. He responded, "Well, that is just one additional folly of that madman!" For about a month I was a high school celebrity and my fellow students nearly forgot that I was a strange transplant in their midst.

Their brief admiration increased even more with my second interview with a prominent personality. I had devoured two news stories in the St. Louis *Star-Times*, the newspaper favored by my aunt and uncle. Two of my German cultural heroes were appearing in my new hometown, if under dif-ferent auspices. The Nobel Prize–winning author Thomas Mann, whose novel *The Buddenbrooks* I had read at my home in Hildesheim and long past my bedtime, was scheduled to speak at the St. Louis YMHA/YWHA lo-cated within two blocks of Soldan. Richard Tauber, the celebrated Viennese tenor—whose records of opera and operetta arias had frequently resonated through our apartment—had also found asylum in the United States and was appearing at Kiel Auditorium downtown.

Of course my allowance of fifty cents was laughably inadequate if measured against the price of admission to either event. Inspiration struck feature edi-tor Stern. I went to Mrs. Rasmussen, the advisor of our school paper, and she wrote a well-crafted letter requesting a free admission to the Thomas Mann lecture for the feature editor of *Scrippage*, Soldan's incomparable school newspaper.

I arrived at the Y in good time. But already a record crowd was beleaguering the stairway leading to the auditorium. I immediately noticed that all arrivals were closely checked by a Cerberus in the form of a ticket-taker. Several prospective attendees were unceremoniously shunted to the nearest exit. My chances appeared no better.

I decided on a stratagem. I handed him my trumped-up credentials and while he was reading, I vanished into a group of validated arrivals and triumphantly took a seat in the auditorium. Thomas Mann, reading from a manuscript, but ever so hampered by a curious pronunciation of the English language, held forth on "The Coming Victory of Democracy," a topic fully covered by the dailies. My moment of journalistic distinction came after the lecture and the question-and-answer period. He was assisted in the epilogue by his daughter Erika, who translated the questions into German and her father's answers into English.

As the crowd filtered out, Thomas Mann was led to a horseshoe-like semicircle of seats, near the exit of the auditorium. For whatever reason, Erika was temporarily not at his side. An eager group of reporters, led by an obtrusive correspondent of *Time* magazine, started the grilling. The *Time* representative couched his beginning question in the willful style of his magazine, to the bafflement of the famed author, who despairingly and vainly looked for his interpreter. When another journalist was similarly ignored by the eminent guest, I saw my opportunity. I threw in a question in German. As if he had been tossed a lifeline, he clung to several of my questions. My "colleagues" were fuming. In protest, I assumed, they capped their fountain pens. Then I spotted Erika Mann, hiding a wicked smile behind her hands, undoubtedly amused by the spectacle of these supercilious reporters scooped by a precocious high school student. Having composed herself, she joined Daddy and my fun was over.

In its issue of March 24, 1939, the school newspaper carried my report on the main event and my interview, together with a column by the "associate editor-in-chief," announcing to the world that "a *Scrippage* reporter scooped a *Time* magazine interviewer" and so forth.

For years I tried to retrieve that column and my report. My high school never responded and I thought it unlikely that the volumes of *Scrippage* could have survived anywhere else. But a colleague of mine, Professor Paula Hanssen at Webster University, St. Louis, was more persistent and more skilled. Soldan's news organ had been neatly shelved, all volumes of it, at the Missouri Historical Library.

I reread my report with a note of triumph, still reverberating into my advanced age. My first question to Thomas Mann concerned the past and was linked to something he had said during his lecture. "Mr. Mann, how is the socialization of which you spoke to come about, since you are aware that such attempts had failed in Weimar Germany?" His answer, given in German, was a prediction that the lower classes and particularly the "Negro" population, still resenting the hardships of the Great Depression, would become politically active and achieve those goals. A second question that I raised about education received an equally optimistic, if hitherto unfulfilled prediction. He felt that America was on the cusp of having universal college education. If I look at today's tuition, Thomas Mann's vision has moved backward rather than forward. It was an auspicious (and all but final) beginning of my journalistic career.

I graduated from Soldan in June 1939. My efforts to gain a scholarship for college succeeded, but ultimately led to naught. Westminster College in Fulton, Missouri, was ready to cover my tuition but could contribute nothing for my room and board and in fact told me that getting a job there, for example as a busboy, would be next to impossible. I had to find a different route to make the transition from high school to college.

So I did what my students of today are doing quite regularly: I decided to work for one year to have the funds for college. Carefully, I hoarded my busboy tips and salary. Finally when I was financially ready—well, more or less—I had a stroke of good luck.

I applied for a busboy job at a hotel within a half-block of one of the universities located in St. Louis and went for an interview with hope and trepidation. The interviewer for the position was Lukas Lanza, the head waiter of the Piccadilly Room of the Melbourne Hotel. I sold myself as a busboy of nearly superhuman capacities. I also interspersed an appeal to his apparent good nature. I mentioned that I was ready to continue my education at a university and that Saint Louis University would undoubtedly accept me because of my good high school grades and what I needed now was a job to pay my tuition. His kindness showed: "OK Günther, we'll try you out." My luck held. I proved to be proficient at my job as a busboy and Saint Louis University sent out a letter of acceptance in short order. With the help of a counselor I selected my program and found that the faculty was both outstanding and absolutely undeviating in their rigor. My prize example is our encounter with our logic teacher on a wintry day. Father Steven J. Reeve, who took delight in signing himself S. J. Reeve, S. J., had an uncanny ability to provoke his students into thinking. As a debate coach he would take on the affirmative team and deftly obliterate it, then turn around in mid-debate and dispose of the negative team with equal ease.

On a chilly February day we were scheduled to take our final exam. The central heating system had given up the ghost and we were sitting in our overcoats, hats, and gloves awaiting the arrival of Father Reeve. He came into the classroom clutching thirty or so blue books. Immediately one of the students, Nancy Bakewell, a prominent campus leader, rose from her seat. "Father Reeve, there is no heat in this building. You will have to postpone the final." He looked at her with an iciness that matched the room's temperature. "Miss Bakewell, you didn't come to Saint Louis University to get out of the inclement weather, did you now?" It is the first and only time that I, together with my fellow students, wrote the answers to an exam with my gloves securely in place. I might add that there's no way that Father Reeve could have prevailed in today's atmosphere even at a rigorously run university.

There was my history professor Father Bannon, who taught European history from an American perspective. For example, neither in Germany nor in my high school classes had I learned about the history of Ireland and the emigration of Irish citizens to America during the so-called Irish Potato Famine of 1845–1852. His graphic description and empathy kept us spellbound. But his empathy didn't stop with his (presumable) forefathers or with his present-day fellow Catholics. Before I left the university at the end of the semester for the US Army, I went to him to say goodbye. He kept me at his desk until the room had emptied, took me aside, and gave me his priestly blessings well-knowing that I was Jewish. I heard that several months later he joined the army as a chaplain. His kindness overwhelmed me.

And there was Father McNamee, the head librarian. He had set up a large desk at the entrance of the main reading room. One day Professor Sullivan, our English teacher, had given us a fairly complex assignment. I had the temerity to walk right up to Father McNamee's desk and ask him where I might find relevant material on the subject. He got up and urged me to follow him. Belying his seventy years plus, he climbed up a spiral staircase at top speed, then turned to a shelf and said: "You will probably find several books on the subject right here." I did, of course, and I found something else, a university administrator whose first priority was students.

As those intensely lived years progressed I learned to see America as it was, its wonders and its warts. But one additional person had simultaneously entered my life who showed me my adoptive land not only as it was but as it should be. Aunt Rae (short for Rebecca) Benson was no relative at all; she was the sister of Ethel, my aunt by marriage. While both sisters had been born in or near St. Louis, Rae had broken the mold of Ethel's homebody existence and humdrum lifestyle. Ethel had married an assimilated but still observant Jew, Rae an Anglo-Saxon Protestant. Ethel took no trips except into the close vicinity of the West Side and hence had little to report beyond neighborhood gossip; Rae, the wife of a railroad linesman supervisor, had gotten annual railroad courtesy tickets and showed pictures of fabled San Francisco, its stately hotels and Fisherman's Wharf with Joe DiMaggio's restaurant, a landmark of particular interest to me, since the Yankees always stayed at "my" Chase Hotel. Aunt Ethel played auction bridge; Aunt Rae went to lectures.

She took me along. When I first came to their house to play with her son Frankie, a few years younger than I, she sensed my unformulated hunger for a closer and deeper look at America's culture. She had joined the Ethical Culture Society. At least once a month I joined her at her invitation for a lecture by prominent speakers at the society's auditorium. It was there I heard Martha Gellhorn's impassioned plea for America's involvement in the face of Hitler's quest for global conquest. A magnetic personality, striking both by her eloquent, fiery delivery and her commanding beauty, she told of her experiences during the Spanish Civil War with her fellow correspondent and brief marital partner, Ernest Hemingway, and of the brutalities she witnessed during the German entrance into Prague. Aunt Rae and I walked up to her after the lecture and I asked her a few questions. Some fifty years later, during an interview I conducted with her for my article on Hemingway and the exiles during the Spanish Civil War, I reminded her of our first encounter. She indeed remembered her lecture in her hometown of St. Louis; but of course not the precocious youngster and his insistent questions.

Aunt Rae made me see the darker sides of American life and she offered correctives for them. She recommended that I read some of the muckrakers. I read Upton Sinclair's *The Brass Check*, an exposé of America's press and particularly its beholdenness to its advertisers. I was shocked at first by the boldness with which she discussed the book's title; Sinclair had taken it from the entry tokens bought upon entering a house of prostitution. So Aunt Rae also freed me, en passant, of a lingering prudishness. But she also pointed out how reportage can be twisted according to the wishes of large advertisers, an observation that even today has lost little of its relevance.

After Joe Louis's blitz victory over Max Schmeling in their second encounter, she ridiculed the myths of racial superiority and ethnic stereotypes. She pointed out America's discriminatory practices; in later years she took an active part in the integration of St. Louis's public swimming pools, effected only after some brutal beatings of some pioneering black youngsters. She looked at some of my high school textbooks and found them wanting. In David L. Murray's textbook she found his reference to the slaves as "samboes" incredibly offensive. She gave me an added perspective on my country of asylum. I began to see it more clearly without loving it less.

While Aunt Rae became my mentor, Aunt Ethel was my guide to the workaday life of America's lower-middle class. At dinner she would remind me of the difference between European and American table manners and, in general, prevent me from violating American do's and don'ts. Her benevolence wasn't perfunctory at all. She maintained a home for all of her family and sought to make our lives as comfortable and fulfilled as possible. Even with a five-year age difference, their son, Melvin, who lived with us for a while, and I often engaged in what can be termed "sibling rivalry." It was rooted in part by his resentment that he, who had never finished high school,

had to listen to my reports of my classroom achievements. By the same token, I felt that Ethel's motherly allegiance was lying with her son. Of course,
what Melvin had that I could only dream about was having his parents in his
life. If only my family could join me in my new world! There was really no
competition in that. He won hands down! When Uncle Benno and I spoke
together, frequently in German, we talked about his parental home. He asked
me for every tidbit of memory of my days in Vlotho. Although I was most
appreciative of his and Ethel's generosity, they were no loco parentis, except
for the emotional closeness of being biologically related. They also sheltered
me when I became despondent about being cut off from all the persons loved
in my homeland. They substituted their love and I shall never forget that. In
addition, they shared their vision of the American dream with me and under
their tutelage and despite the occasional demurrers of Aunt Rae, I became a
budding American patriot.

Yes, I was on the road to Americanization, a walk no one can ever complete, not only because America is different, as Carl Zuckmayer put it, but
also because it is so many things; it is protean and unpredictable. As for me,
Günther, I never became a completely American guy; I am, we all are a con-
glomerate of our experiences. But I am grateful to all those who pointed me
in that direction toward America, from Mr. Tittel to the Silberbergs to Aunt
Rae, and who gently chivvied me along. As those years of rapid acculturation
drew to a close, "I Heard America Singing," as Walt Whitman, the poet of its
democratic spirit, had exulted. It is my hope that the song will not grow faint
in the years to come.

CHAPTER FOUR

A Ritchie Boy in World War II

Preparing for War

URIOUSLY ENOUGH, THE FACT that I became a Ritchie Boy—the soldiers who were trained in military intelligence interrogation at Fort Ritchie, Maryland—in the US Army, I owe to the US Navy. How so? After Pearl Harbor and the US entry into the war, the walls of my university, Saint Louis University, were festooned with posters. One was from naval intelligence. If a young man had special skills, if he spoke the language or knew the culture of our enemies, he should by all means come down, the poster said, to the Naval Intelligence Recruiting Station. I did. "Do I detect an accent?" the recruiting ensign asked. "Are you a natural-born American?"

"No," I answered.

"Can't use you!" he said.

Naval Intelligence would soon change its policy, though too late to affect me, and go on to recruit one of the most inventive Jewish refugees to come to the United States, in the person of the colorful journalist, theater critic, and cultural historian Curt Riess. He brought some life into the staid and somnolent Washington establishment of Naval Intelligence. On his own initiative, he started to interrogate the first German prisoners of war to fall into American hands: the survivors of sunk submarines and surface vessels. He did not concentrate on the then standard military intelligence information but instead elicited gossip about Germany's naval officers, which ranged from sexual misbehavior to financial defalcations. Then he would broadcast these choice bits, along with some serious news, to German ships at sea. He heard subsequently from prisoners that these broadcasts created jealousies, suspicions, and several fist-fights among German naval personnel.

By a more circuitous road, I found myself enrolled in US Army Military Intelligence. Half a year later I was drafted. With dozens of other recruits from St. Louis, I was sent to the Induction Center at Fort Leavenworth, Kansas, and then after two weeks of idling there to Camp Barkley, Texas, the training center for medical administration. I was in good physical shape; a year of lifting heavy trays in restaurants had steeled me for carrying a full field pack during long hikes under the broiling Texas sun. The classroom instructions were moderately difficult, but they increased my respect for American teachers. The camp commandant had recruited women teachers from the local high schools and they taught us the fundamentals of the paperwork necessary for keeping medical records, a patient's case history, and other bureaucratic essentials. The teachers who faced us had done their (and also our) homework, as though it were their instructional forte. And they all came along to the most significant event during my stay in Texas.

I assiduously read the camp newspaper, and there, nearly hidden by announcements like the one that a group of Don Cossacks would be singing for us, was an item that would change my sense of identity. "Noncitizen personnel at camp are ordered to report to their respective headquarters for possible naturalization." I ran, not walked, to the command post, the newspaper in hand. "Request permission to talk to the First Sergeant," I said to the company clerk. That worthy came at a leisurely pace, complimented me on my close reading of the newspaper, and ordered our drill sergeant to join us. "Do you think Private Stern will make a good citizen?" he asked. Of course the sergeant didn't know me from among any of the other fitful recruits under his charge and mumbled something reasonably affirmative in response.

In 1942 I was asked to join a hundred or so other foreign-born GIs for a trip to the Northern District Court of Texas in nearby Abilene. In a mass ceremony, dignified and somehow awesome, we became US citizens. I, the outcast from Nazi Germany, had suddenly found a new national identity and simultaneously embraced a fervent new allegiance. I also officially made "Guy" my first name. Did anyone share this emotional event with me? I glanced at the gallery of the courtroom. Those women instructors who had guided me for the past months were watching, handkerchiefs in hand. When I came back to class, my admired teacher of Army Medical Reports broke military protocol and ordered me to stand up as a "freshman American." My new status didn't lighten that enormous field pack during those forced marches, but it surely helped me find my new identity as an American soldier. It seemed to me then that my perfectly fitting uniform also mirrored my inner attitude. My German citizenship seemed to be a thing of the past; after all, it had been taken away from me even when I was still living in my homeland.

After almost finishing basic training, I was called to company headquarters. "Orders are waiting for you! You are being transferred," said the first sergeant. "Where to, Sergeant?" I asked. "Can't tell you, confidential," he said in a Texas accent. In my time there, I'd also begun to acquire a bit of Texan authenticity. I packed my duffle bag and was off to a destination and destiny unknown.

The train traversed Texas. I found myself in the company of two other German-born GIs. Obviously during our conversation we tried to ferret out what the army had planned for us. Our hypotheses ranged from being discharged to being on the way to Officers' Candidate School. My guesses didn't include that last possibility. My classroom performance, I felt, had been pretty decent, but my skill at putting hospital corners on my bedding or carrying out similar mechanical tasks had often drawn severe criticism from the inspecting officers of our barracks.

Three hours into our travel, we opened our orders, as instructed. "Change trains in Baltimore for a local to Martinsburg, West Virginia. A jeep will be waiting." The mystery continued, though not for long. Toward evening our driver left us off at the gate of a Maryland army camp. Unlike our sandstorm-swept camp in Texas, it was studded by lush green lawns with a lake at the center—resembling a country club more than an average military base. A huge sign spanned the distance between the entrance gates. It said laconically, "Military Intelligence Training Center," less than an epiphany for us three. In the following weeks though, the mystery would yield to insight.

Camp Ritchie, named after a former Maryland governor, had been converted from a national guard post into the first subrosa intelligence training

ground in the history of the United States. (During World War I the secretary
of war had declined such an operation on the grounds that "reading other
people's mail is ungentlemanly.") But George Marshall, then the US chief of
staff and holding no such antiquated convictions, had given direct orders to
convert Camp Ritchie from a National Guard camp into a training camp for
future intelligence personnel.

When I first entered the barrack to which I was assigned, I felt I had joined
a successor organization to the League of Nations. Through the constant
babble of European and Asiatic tongues, we were encouraged to talk among
ourselves in the languages of our enemies. Ritchie slowly bared its secrets.
They were not to be shared beyond the grounds of the camp. Its new and temporary residents had been sent there because of those linguistic skills, cultural
backgrounds, and knowledge and, well, because of our presumed intelligence.
All that personal information was hole punched in a soldier's ID card upon
induction and spewed out again when the need for certain qualifications
emerged and the Ritchie selectees had passed the security checks of the FBI
or other government agencies.

Our physical training was as demanding as those marches through the un-
varying Texas landscape. At dusk a random team of three of us Ritchie Boys
was handed a map in an unfamiliar foreign language and a compass, before
being unceremoniously tossed out of a truck somewhere within a twenty-
five-mile radius of the camp. "Our assembly point is marked on your maps.
Be there by eleven or you will have a bit of a walk to get back to camp." That
meant if you didn't get oriented with the aid of the map and compass, you
might reach camp just in time for breakfast.

There were other challenges and hazards imposed on us trainees: an obstacle course, close combat instructions, a rifle range (I barely passed rifle
training with an M-1 on my third try), a forty-eight-hour continuous set of
problem-solving activities, such as putting a listening device on a telephone
wire. Those duties didn't excuse us from the usual BS of routine army duties.
But all those physical activities were topped by intellectual demands.

There were few aspects of up-to-date intelligence work that were not
covered in our classes between reveille and taps. We studied German and
Italian army organization and learned how to read aerial maps and to draw

contour maps (I am surprised I passed that course given my lack of ability at draftsmanship). Also we became skilled at sending and absorbing messages in Morse code, and recognizing the significance of a prisoner's attire and equipment. Those sartorial details ranged from the piping on a cap to the stripes, medals, and inscriptions on the prisoner's "blouses." We learned how to quickly extract vital information from documents composed in the legendary German bureaucratic style. We memorized whole passages from a newly published reference work, *German Order of Battle*. It had been composed by Ritchie Boys, posted to the Pentagon, and charged with assembling a roster of German armies and divisions likely to be our opponents during the invasion of the European continent. The book also spelled out the current strength of a unit and the names of its commanding officers.

The acquisition of those skills was just a beginning. We knew that sooner or later, we would interrogate German POWs. A lawyerly major told us the rules and techniques. "First off, you never touch a prisoner! That's a violation of the Geneva Conventions on Warfare," he began. "There are four basic techniques to extract information," he continued: "One: You overwhelm him with the info you already have, such as the name of his superior officers. Many prisoners will simply think, why needlessly defy the Americans when they know everything anyway? Two: If they are dying for food or a cigarette, eat something, or light up, and if they ask for a handout, say they can have it if they cooperate. Three: Play on their likes and inclinations. If your informant is a soccer fan, talk soccer to him till he forgets that you wear a different uniform. (One of my most successful interrogations during our advance through France used precisely that ploy. The prisoner's favorite team had frequently played against mine.) Four: Find out his anxieties and fears and make him think they will soon become a reality."

We were encouraged to practice interrogation on one another until, by way of surprise, a group of newcomers arrived at Ritchie. They were real German prisoners of war, taken during the African campaign—and they became our guinea pigs. They were briefed by high-ranking officers, in clandestine sessions, how to conduct themselves during scripted interrogations. If we, the trainees, asked the right questions and used the right techniques, they would answer. If we showed ourselves inept, they were told to clam up. Such interrogations conducted under the watchful eyes of our examiners were a standard part of our final examination.

All that learning, thrown at us in a little over a month, left us dizzy and fatigued. It was a course that rivaled anything I had to face in postwar life as a Ph.D. candidate at Columbia University. And yet we welcomed that challenge. This was our war, both as haters of the powers that had deprived us of our countries and by virtue of the fact that here we could help our new country through our past upbringing and education. Many of us would not become skilled warriors, but we felt confident that we could hold our own in a battle of the mind with our adversaries. A team spirit developed among us; we became possessed by a missionary zeal.

The time for finals arrived. We were tested, sometimes only cursorily, on every subject we had been exposed to. But when it came to interrogation, our performance was observed by some of the highest brass at Camp Ritchie. The first of my two tests was designed to really confuse me. The prisoner had been told to play an utter ignoramus, disguising his huge storehouse of information. I unmasked him by using a very sophisticated German vocabulary word, the understanding of which he failed to disguise.

And the ultimate test has occasionally recurred in my dreams. We were led to a huge meadow in the midst of the camp. For this occasion of mental torture, it was specially decorated with fifty items of enemy equipment, uniforms, weapons—you name it. Our torturers had carefully numbered them, one through fifty. Then my fellow examinees and I, spaced apart, were handed sheets of papers, speared on a clipboard with corresponding numbers. The instructions were terse. "Identify each object!" I don't think anybody scored fifty out of fifty; I certainly didn't.

After we thought that we had now passed each ordeal, we were told to assemble in the camp auditorium: "You will get your test results upon your return to camp. You are all going on maneuvers in Louisiana." In later years I have visited that state upon numerous occasions, toured the musical and culinary offerings of New Orleans and the lovely landscapes around the bayous. But that was not the setting that greeted us. We were clustered around Camp Claiborne and banished to the rural areas along the Sabine River and to swamps abutting such metropolises as Many and Natchitoches. We slept in pup tents, anchored in the mud, and were visited by an aggressive breed of pigs called razorbacks and by unfriendly tarantulas.

The pigs were our "extras" when we undertook a picaresque act of revenge on one of our comrades: Our ranking noncommissioned officer, Kurt Jasen, became the victim of our wish for egalitarianism—oh hell, let's call it by its right name—he was a victim of our jealousy. Kurt came from a very rich family, and when we arrived at those miserable camping grounds in Louisiana, he wired his parents for relief. They promptly sent a hammock, via special delivery, so that he didn't have to sleep in the mud and muck and among the tarantulas. He would undress at night, don a nightshirt, and stretch out comfortably, while the rest of us slept on the ground in our underwear. We thought of a scheme to break up his privileged nocturnal rest, enlisting the help of those pesky Arkansas razorbacks. The pigs constantly foraged for food; our mess sergeant had to cover garbage with rocks and even pour kerosene over all of it to prevent the garbage from being dug up again by the voracious porkers. While Kurt was on an assignment at headquarters one day, we dug a slit-trench underneath his hammock and filled it with garbage. Before his arrival we managed to keep the pigs away. Then we took cover in our tents when we heard Kurt return.

He had scarcely laid down in his hammock when his rest was interrupted by a hungry pig. He tried to scare it away by throwing his helmet at the beast, which availed him nothing. A single file of about a half-dozen pigs, led by an alpha boar, rushed toward the hammock, shaking it up. Out jumped our dear comrade, running ghost-like toward our tents shouting, "The pigs are after me!" For obvious reasons I never shared our secret with Kurt, not even during our long postwar years of friendship.

As for our work in Louisiana, it turned out to be a win-win situation. Each one of us was assigned to an interrogation team, part of either the red or the blue army. We had to interrogate the prisoners taken during the maneuvers. When we failed to get our "adversaries" to divulge any significant information, the line troops were praised for their security-mindedness. If we did break a prisoner, we were praised for our skill as interrogators. The maneuver in Louisiana led us Ritchie Boys back to our Jewish past and present. Until then the war had brought few such reminders. One day all Jewish soldiers were asked to report to Operational Headquarters. "I have some good news for you fellows," said a lieutenant colonel. "We have received orders that you have been excused from duty on the first day of Passover and you are authorized to take your vehicles and drive to Shreveport for services."

We were pleased by this sign of the fair-mindedness of our high-ranking officers, and the next day our team cleaned up with particular care. We drove for about two and a half hours to Shreveport, a town with a thriving Jewish community. Prior to leaving Ritchie, I had learned how to drive—that is, like the other neophytes, I was told to get into one of our jeeps, turn on the ignition, and try my luck. Now in the sparsely settled backwoods of Louisiana, I could solo without much danger of hitting a cow, a chicken, or a razorback. We arrived in good time for the public Passover observance, the service that takes place on the eve of the Passover holiday. When we filed out of the synagogue, the entire membership of the congregation had lined up on the steps. Whenever a soldier left the building, someone tapped him on the shoulder and invited him for the Seder service and dinner. For a few hours we became civilians. The highest-ranking officer who accompanied us was Lieutenant Victor Didinsky. We thoroughly disliked him because there wasn't one army regulation that he didn't enforce on those of lower rank. Consequently, we referred to him only by his unflattering initials. But for this occasion, he made one utterly unmilitary remark prior to the Seder: "Fellows, on this evening there are no ranks; we are just a gathering of Jews at this nice house to celebrate Passover." Our dislike melted.

For me, several things contributed to the uniqueness of this religious observance. It was the first time since my fifth year that I participated in a Passover service with complete strangers. Rather than my father as the amateur cantor, there was a younger gentleman with a distinct Southern American accent in his Hebrew recitation. And the house to which we had been invited was far more opulent than any I had ever been in before. It was a celebration of the Jewish holiday that I believe none of us ever forgot. The melodies we sang, even the pronunciation of Hebrew words, were different than I had experienced either in Europe or in St. Louis, but the tradition shone through and we soldiers enthusiastically participated.

After we returned to Camp Ritchie, the commander of each training company handed out certificates. I was promoted by several ranks, my document said, but by no means as high as some of my comrades in arms. Private Stern paid someone to sew the stripes of a staff sergeant on his uniform and was ready for war, he thought.

But first, in December of 1943, we found ourselves in Fort Hamilton, Brooklyn, for about a week. We were regaled with cultural events, among them a speech, or rather a put-down, by a nasty playwright, Lillian Hellman, who openly ridiculed questions by unsophisticated GIs. In my later years in academic leadership, I often thought back to her demeaning comments and told future teachers: "Never put down a student!"

No battle cruiser took us to England, but rather a banana boat borrowed from our Australian allies, named *The Rangitata*. The bowels of the ship had been readied for us; every inch of that fruit-and-vegetable boat was filled with hammocks for our nightly slumber. (Even our long underwear didn't keep out the chilling winter storms blowing across the Atlantic.) A dining hall was not in sight; we sat on stoops and emptied Australian tins for meals. Many of us drew night watch. German U-boats were plowing the Atlantic. Equipped with field glasses, it was our task to spot the tell-tale telescope of would-be U-boat attackers. My imagination was running away with me. Because of an apocalyptic vision of being thrown into the icy ocean, my watchfulness, even though focused upon a monotonous body of water, was as intense as though my life depended on it. Of course all our lives depended on it.

We made it to Birmingham and were housed at a makeshift army base called Pheasey Farms, already occupied by multiple British forces. There was no love lost between the two allies. When asked about their obvious reserve, our British co-inhabitants would spout their characterization of us: "You Yanks are overpaid, overfed, oversexed, and over here." Their kitchen person-nel found more imaginative ways to show their displeasure. At their request, enforced by the camp commandant, we Ritchie Boys were constantly put on KP (kitchen duty) and our allies as well as our antagonists pulled out, for assiduous cleaning, every quaint kitchen utensil, some of it probably dating back to the times of William the Conqueror.

Two weeks later we became part and parcel of an idyllic small town. Broad-way, England, seemed unchanged from the time of Shakespeare; one of his comedies, perhaps *The Merry Wives of Windsor,* could have been performed on the streets without additional sets. And we, intelligence personnel, as a security measure against spies, were billeted with the private citizenry of Broadway. We were invited to outings, social occasions, and dances in the evening. But during the daytime our training continued, enhanced by a guest lecture delivered by a seasoned British intelligence officer.

It became clear to me and to my fellow Ritchie Boys that Great Britain had become an armed camp. While Broadway had been spared aerial attacks, many of the towns we passed through were severely damaged. A high-ranking officer at headquarters felt that our line troops should learn some useful German phrases. So we journeyed to picturesque English towns like Honeywell and Evesham, all bristling with American troops. And soon their quarters would be resounding, choral fashion, with such practical commands as "Hände hoch oder ich schieße," asking Germans, none too politely, to raise their arms in the time-honored gesture of surrender.

The war came closer. Team 41, to which I was assigned, received orders in early 1944 to report for duty to Bristol, England. Unlike Broadway, Bristol, having been hit by German bombers, sported hundreds of captive balloons designed to hold off low-flying enemy aircraft. Again, as in Broadway, our quarters were scattered among security-cleared British families.

Each morning we mounted our jeeps at 6 a.m. We hastened to our destination, a British public school, according to the English designation. But to Americans, Clifton School in Bristol looked like a rather exclusive private school with a campus of manicured lawns that would have done credit to a small US liberal arts college. There were no students to be seen; Clifton School had been requisitioned by the US Army. But when we tried to enter the grounds, we were held back by formidable MP (military police) personnel. We suddenly had an inkling that we were going to report to an airtight security location. Also, letters from our "stateside" relatives had informed us that FBI agents had come around once again and had asked detailed questions about us. And we had been informed that we were given an additional security clearance, titled "BIGOT" for reasons best known by the army. That designation ranked even above top-secret. We soon found out why. Team 41 had been assigned, albeit in a minor capacity, to be part of the planning of one of the greatest military operations ever—the invasion of Europe.

The once (and future) campus bristled with brass. The commander was General Omar Bradley, followed by General Courtney S. Hodges. General Eisenhower frequently dropped in. If you wanted to enter the planning room assigned to us, you had to pass several checkpoints, and if you reentered the room after a break, the MP who had mustered you just a few minutes before acted as though he had never seen you in his life and suspected you of being a descendant of master spy Mata Hari of World War I.

Among our planning tasks was the selection of future sites of the POWs' enclosures beyond the initial ones on the beachheads. They had to be close but not too close to First Army Headquarters, the unit to which our team had been assigned. Camps had to be accessible to major highways for speedy evacuation of the prisoners and yet yield enough space for our bivouac area and that of ancillary units, such as MP guards. Our relatively minor task demonstrates the exquisitely detailed planning preceding the invasion.

Team 41, like everybody else, was often overwhelmed by thoughts of that impending invasion. Would everything go as planned? Yet we did not ignore the few chances for recreation, badly needed as a diversion from the reality awaiting us. We clustered around our Bristol host family. Their son, about fifteen years old, prided himself as an accomplished cricket bowler. He taught me how to twirl a cricket ball; in exchange, I showed him how a baseball pitcher executes a curve ball. We took mother and daughter along when we went to orchestra halls and theaters that were kept open in defiance of the German bombing attacks. Both women were delighted by the diversion. We once went on our own to a less classical performance on the initiative of our wheeler-dealer team member Paul. There we discovered, while the actresses divested themselves of their outer garments (and some otherwise invisible ones), that their delicate undies had given way to more robust textiles, a wartime exigency.

The high point of our theatrical experiences came shortly before D-Day. Trucks were made available to take any Bristol-based GI to Stratford-on-Avon. We theater aficionados returned at midnight from a riveting performance of *Much Ado about Nothing*. That first visit to Stratford is one that stays in my mind till today with every detail retained. I, of course, internally cheered the exoneration of the heroine, Hero; but as a lover of language, I was inordinately amused by the malapropisms of Constable Dogberry. I had been well prepared by my parents for the sophistication of this performance through our visits to the Hildesheim Theater.

Another leisure activity, more athletic in nature, sticks in my mind as well. At one point, I had the privilege of joining into competition with our British allies. Someone at USO Headquarters had hit on the less than innovative idea of turning the obvious rivalry between Brits and Yanks into a friendly sporting duel, through an international (hands-across-the-table) table tennis match between the two Allied forces stationed in Bristol. In my spare time I had played at the local USO; my nonexistent fame must have preceded me. I, a newly minted US citizen, was to help represent the Red, White, and Blue against its former colonial masters. I won my match; in fact, we resoundingly beat the Brits. Then they asked for an immediate return match—with darts and dartboard. In that competition we were blanked.

D-Day snuck in by surprise. As history now records, General Eisenhower made up his mind to launch the invasion on June 6, 1944, only after hearing the latest weather forecasts. Team 41 got its first orders; three of us were "to go in" the next day, on D+1. The other three team members, I among them, were on stand-by orders. To stand by meant being glued to the radio and trying to interpret every remark overheard at our listening post at Clifton School in Bristol. In the afternoon of D+3, I wanted to escape the tension. A large tent near our private headquarters had been converted into an army movie the-ater. I went in to see the hyped-up film *Shine on Harvest Moon*, starring Ann Sheridan, who pretended to launch into the title song within the first twenty minutes. More I do not know about that saga of romance under the lights of the harvest moon because, shortly, the very real lights in the tent went on. A voice came over the loudspeaker, "The following officers and enlisted men will immediately report to their quarters and be ready to join a convoy within a half-hour or less."

We were on the road to the seaport city of Southampton; I was driving one of our jeeps, the first time I did long-distance driving on the left side of the road, "not on the right side, as God had intended," one of us wisecracked. One street in Southampton had apparently been cleared of vehicles in antici-pation of our serpentine convoys. I parked. Ahead of me was a jeep driven by a dapper captain. He seemed to be the only US soldier not beset by anxiety.

He calmly took off his helmet, went into one of the houses, came out with his helmet full of steaming hot water, and started to shave. The proprietor of the house appeared, watched the intrepid captain for a moment, and provided a commentary for us onlookers: "I am sure this fine-looking gentleman never thought that one day he would be shaving in the streets of Southhampton!" The convoy started to move again. Vehicle by vehicle, we drove our jeeps onto a landing craft. The invasion had started for us.

CHAPTER FIVE

Going to War

S EVERAL OF US GIs, standing shoulder to shoulder, managed to hide our fears; none of us was free of them. As for me, not only did I share the anxieties of the soldiers all around me, I had a few special ones of my own, too. Naturally I painted a bleak picture of my future if the Germans were to capture me, a German-born Jew. Also, ever since boyhood, I was unreasonably squeamish. A cut finger chased me out of a room, and I refused to listen to records of songs or fairy tales with tragic episodes. How would I fare ashore with its predictable remnants of carnage?

The landing craft dumped us close to shore; our water-proofed jeep covered the remaining distance. I looked around. Yes, there were the expected vestiges of warfare. Corpses were lining the beaches. And surprise upon surprise: the me who shied away from a cut finger was utterly unfazed by the grosser sights. Even to this day I can't explain my childhood idiosyncrasy nor my recovery from it during the Invasion. One psychologist said that I must have had an unfortunate experience in childhood and that I banished it from my subconscious during the Invasion. But he failed to explain why it returned when I was a civilian again.

There was no time to absorb the French landscape. From somewhere in the distance, my teammate, Kurt Jasen, already two days on French soil, was hollering at me: "Get the hell over here, Stern! We've got too many f——ing prisoners."

Five minutes later I was confronting a tough-looking German noncom from an artillery unit. Abandoned crates had to do as interrogation chairs and tables. Like the makeshift furniture, I too must have looked improvisational. At any rate, my first prisoner responded to none of my questions. He'd obviously been thoroughly briefed on his rights. "I'm only obliged to reveal my name, rank, and serial number," he replied to one of my first questions. He repeatedly invoked the same agreement during subsequent questions. I felt utterly inadequate, stripped of all my Camp Ritchie skills. My subconscious hammered me with the words "failure" and "loser." Then a German shell came over; we both ducked. But I rapidly got up before him. Perhaps my opponent attributed that random act to a spirit of death defiance rather than my inexperience. He, of course, knew that artillery weapons were usually fired in successive spurts. I regained all my Ritchie resoluteness. My questions became more menacing. He answered, dammit and hallelujah, he answered—and in detail. I had won my first battle and felt that I towered over my prisoner, who in reality was a good bit taller than I.

Team 41 was together again. Two other IPW (Interrogators of Prisoners of War) teams joined us and pitched their tents at the same bivouac area. The next morning, our commanding officer, Captain Rust, who had learned German in Brownsville, Texas, gave out assignments. "Sergeant Stern, by all reports, you are supposed to be good at sorting out people. You'll be one of our screeners. Go pick out POWs who appear knowledgeable and who seem to be ready to spill the beans. We've gotta work fast!" His implied compliment assuaged my disappointment of being merely a screener rather than an interrogator. I followed orders and did my best during the first month in Normandy. Judging by the reports of the interrogators who had to question my selectees, I did pick some live POWs, though there were occasional complaints as well, pointing out that I had also hit on some real duds. My telltale mark was the readiness of the POWs to answer some revealing questions at greater length and their use of a more sophisticated German.

After about three months, the work became repetitive. Of course I knew better than to ask for a change of assignment. Chance encounters once more came to the fore. They took the form of three veterans of the Spanish Civil War, captured by the Germans and put to work for the Nazi cause. They were Spanish engineers who had fought for the Spanish Republic, escaped to France after Franco's victory, had been captured there after the German invasion of France, and were finally shipped to the Channel Islands to help fortify them against an Allied attempt to retake them.

Captain Rust briefed me: "They seem to know a lot about the fortifications of Jersey and Guernsey. They don't speak German or English, but then you are touted as our Spanish speaker. Go, interrogate them!" It was the easiest interrogation I ever had before or after. They were delighted with my college Spanish and only asked for large notepaper, pen, pencil, and eraser. I brought them food and drink as well. They were off sitting at a makeshift table and were drawing for hours. I occasionally watched; there was no gun emplacement nor underwater obstacle they left unrecorded. Finally, they turned several legal-size sheets over to me. Waving them in triumph, I rushed over to Captain Rust. He was awestruck. "Quite an interrogation, Sergeant Stern!" he commented in his slow Texas drawl. I did not disabuse him. His face became pensive. "I think I can make better use of you as an interrogator. I have something specific in mind. We are getting all these questionnaires from higher and lower headquarters. I'll show you."

Indeed, there was no shortage of them. Challenging questions were being showered on us: How did the Germans manage to repair bombed-out railroad tracks and rolling stock in record time? Were any infectious diseases rampant among the Germans that could, upon contact, also afflict us Americans? How did we estimate the morale of German line troops? What were our most and least effective propaganda leaflets? "I need a survey section," Rust concluded. "I will reassign some of our interrogators to report to you. And you'll be in charge, Sergeant Stern, of preparing reports in answer to those questionnaires."

I rushed back to my three Spaniards to share the captain's praise and asked them one final question: how had they managed to escape? But on that one they balked. One careless word and they would endanger the islanders who had obviously helped them. I sent them on their way, loaded with C-rations, to a camp for liberated allies. "If we are ordered to retake those islands," commented Captain Rust, "we are damn well ready, Stern."

I gloried in my new assignment. This was something I felt sure I could do. As a high school and college student, I had loved writing term papers, semester reports and reviews, pulling information together from multiple sources.

My new task was essentially no different, except I would now gather data not from printed sources of reference but from unwary or willing enemy soldiers. Oh, yes, we did it: over the following months my comrades and I would answer all those queries essential to the war effort. Railroad specialists told us that the Germans' rapid repairs rested on the manufacture of prefab tracks and other railroad parts. Medical personnel, from lowly medics to a one-star general, assured us that the German troops harbored no epidemic diseases. German line officers, with a bit of pressure, told us that the morale of German troops could undergo sudden shifts, depending on such vagaries as supplies, casualties in their ranks, and the availability of good leadership (that only they themselves were able to supply).

And the interrogated German "Landsers" (privates) admitted that they held on to a safe-passage leaflet signed by General Eisenhower. They displayed their typically German faith in printed assurances. However, they immediately discarded several of those flyers because they didn't understand them. We in the survey section suspected that these latter ones had been composed by some of the most rarified brains of academics serving now as composers of propaganda leaflets.

Three months into our war, the activities of the survey section spread out in new directions. The arrival of a replacement set off fireworks. Fred Howard, born in Silesia, raised in Berlin, known at birth as Fritz Ehrlich, arrived in our midst with a barracks bag full of ideas. Most of them, with a bit of toning down, were radically and erratically useful. On the day of his arrival I was writing a response to yet another questionnaire about the routing of German supplies, such as fuel, ammunition, and food, from the homefront to the front lines. The information was solid; what it lacked were graphics to make the complicated routes, interchanges, and rest stops more quickly comprehensible. As we broke for lunch, I asked Fred whether he could draw worth a damn. "Well, in civilian life I was a designer," he replied to my delight. With his illustrations added, I could reduce my expository remarks. The old bromide that a picture was worth a thousand words was validated. For example, when German equipment had to be transferred from one train station to another, the process was complex and hard to explain in words; Fred's detailed drawings made things crystal clear.

We soon found out that we complemented each other: Fred wildly creative, I more disciplined; Fred with an overabundance of chutzpah (gall), I a little bit better under control. Fred failed his driving test the first time because he didn't stay within the prescribed routine, but rather showed off with a spectacular maneuver, unappreciated by his driving examiner. With rare exceptions we could come up with outrageous ideas and actions while steering clear of reprimands. Later in this chapter, I will tell how Fred would abduct the famous movie star Marlene Dietrich from a USO performance to our prisoner of war enclosure about twenty-five miles away. For him the fact that we had no authority to either transport her in our jeep or bring her to an army enclosure, classified as restricted, only added to his zest for adventure.

We talked shop during meals. As the last arrival, Fred had drawn the most onerous task. He was to satisfy the constantly increasing requests by our air force for important targets. Captain Rust decided to initiate a second special section, labeled simply but accurately "Targets." Determined to lay waste to German supplies, the leaders of our flying boys wanted us to pinpoint exact locations. Their questionnaires were straightforward. "Supply us with the coordinates of the ball-bearing factory, the one near Schweinfurt! What are significant landmarks leading us to that target? Is the factory rail connected to the main railroad system?" Another: "We hit the Juncker works in February. Aerial photography does not show the extent of the damage. Can you find out?" Or another: "The optical factory in Remscheid has apparently relocated. The new coordinates, please!" And yet another: "A new plant opened in Wanne-Eickel. What's the product?"

Of course Fred, as well as anyone, had learned subtle interrogation methods at Ritchie. But how could you disguise a question dealing with the landmarks pointing to that Schweinfurt factory? The moment you asked even the dumbest, densest, or most deranged German soldier a question like that, he would know that we planned to bomb the hell out of that plant. And for good reason, he would clam up or invoke the Geneva Conventions, which obliged him only to reveal his name, rank, and serial number. The reasons for security-mindedness differed from one POW to the other, but all were compelling: A POW's parents or his sweetheart might be working at a potential target. Or he himself had been a peacetime employee there. From that vantage point, he might know that Germany, bleeding already from loss of equipment, would lose the war for want of vital war machinery. One POW had an even better reason: the factory we were inquiring about belonged to his father.

"How do you break such a prisoner?" Fred started to lament after a frustrating, futile interrogation. I recited the well-rehearsed Ritchie categories. Fred greeted each but the last one with an expletive borrowed from animal husbandry. "OK, fear," he repeated after me. "What scares those SOBs most, in your experience?"

"That's easy," I answered. "'Sieg oder Sibirien' [victory or Siberia]," as innumerable placards warned them. "They are scared shitless of the Russians. To be taken prisoner by the Soviets and to be sent to one of their prison camps, perhaps one located in Siberia—they think is a fate worse than death."

"OK," Fred perked up, "then let's import a Ruskie!" As usual I dampened Fred's off-the-wall suggestion.

"But how about one of us turning into one?" I ventured. In that heady, charged moment, Kommissar Krukow was conceived.

First thing the next morning, we went to see Captain Edgar Kann, the second-ranking officer of our unit. He was put in charge when Captain Rust was given a new assignment at G-2, First Army Headquarters. Younger than Rust and a storm-tossed refugee like us, he was a bit more adventurous than his predecessor. "Hell, why not try it?" he enthused.

Fred and I worked out the details. Kommissar Krukow's gestation took just one week. Going against typecasting, I was to become the irascible Russian. I had learned to fake a Russian accent in my native German pronunciation. My model? While I was at the home of my aunt and uncle in St. Louis, we all clustered around the radio each Sunday evening when Eddie Cantor's comedy show went on the air. One of the recurring minor roles was that of the "mad Russian." I could imitate his stereotypical impersonations of a demented Russian. I just needed a credible uniform. We went to some recently liberated Russian prisoners and traded our worn-out fatigues for parts of their uniforms. Then we asked our MPs who regularly searched our POWs to "confiscate" their trophies, whole assemblages of Russian medals, looted by the Germans from Russian captives. Kommissar Krukow was born and baptized with the name that would accompany him henceforth. It was the invention of Sergeant Johnny Kirsners, our Russian expert. (Only during my years as a language professor would I learn that wry Johnny had dubbed me with the Russian equivalent of "Kommissar Hook.")

A few stage props were still missing. Johnny devised a trilingual sign that identified my interrogation tent as belonging to a Russian liaison officer. Johnny also found a portrait of Comrade Stalin, which the ruler of the entire Soviet Union had dedicated to his friend, Kommissar Krukow. Johnny signed a fervent, nay fulsome dedication to the good Kommissar, to which Stalin might have pointed with pride for its rhetoric.

When the next air force questionnaire landed on Fred's desk, the interrogation-by-duo received its trial. When asked about his hometown industries, Fred's very first prisoner hid behind the Geneva Conventions. As we had rehearsed, Fred put on his most sorrowful mien. "I understand your position. But please understand mine. Last month we received orders from high up that we must turn uncooperative prisoners over to our Russian allies. I don't like it," he added in a voice resurrected from the grave, "but please come with me now."

Off he marched with his charge to the tent with the ominous inscription. He solemnly greeted me. "Here is a prisoner and the transfer papers." At that moment the mad Russian had an attack of apoplexy, and the following carefully rehearsed dialogue ensued.

Kommissar K: Sergeant, what kind of sorry specimen are you bringing me here!? That Nazi won't even survive the transport to the salt mines!

Fred: Kommissar, I must ask you to respect my uniform and don't shout at me or I will take this prisoner right back to my tent!

Kommissar: You can't do that! This tent is Russian soil!

Fred, having introduced the beast, me, wordlessly walked the prisoner back. Oozing sympathy for his captive, he confided to the prisoner that he could not square it with his conscience to leave him at the mercy of that unspeakable Russian. "I feel so sorry for you," muttered Fred, "you are still so young and from all I hear you are probably throwing your life away." Mental anguish already written all over his face, the prisoner now faced one more confrontation with my alter ego. I picked up my telephone before ranting at

Fred that he was provoking an international incident between allies by his sympathy for a German enemy. When my rage had reached a crescendo, I turned once more on the hapless prisoner.

"What have you done to that naïve American? You don't have to answer that! I'm having orders cut to send you to the so-called prison camp of the living dead in Siberia." It now looked as though Fred and I were going to come to blows. Fred grabbed the prisoner and led him back once more to the interrogation tent, as though rescuing him. Within minutes this particular prisoner was telling Fred all he knew about his hometown and its industries.

With older prisoners, Fred would deplore the likely possibility that the prisoner would never see his family again. The best he could do for him, Fred would say funereally, was to allow him to write a final letter before relinquishing him to the Russians. "The Russians," he would sorrowfully explain, "do not recognize the Red Cross even for such humanitarian services as sending a letter."

We didn't break everyone. Some of our captives may have reflected on the impossibility of transporting prisoners across half a continent to face the feared Russians. But mostly the stratagem worked. Our highly pleased air force command caused a unit citation to be authorized and sent our way. Our success silenced any thought about the roughness of our method. I shared those sentiments one time with a battle-hardened MP officer. I said, "You know, if someone believes he is actually writing his final farewell to the person he feels closest to, we are inflicting a trauma upon him." The MP lieutenant looked at me and answered with an unmistakable touch of sarcasm, "Sergeant Stern, haven't you learned the first lesson of warfare yet? War is hell!"

Literally hundreds of such battles of the mind followed, as we rushed through France, Belgium, and Germany, until we met the Russians at the Elbe River. In between came one major bloody holdup: a German counteroffensive in the Hürtgen Forest, which became known as the Battle of the Bulge. Everything might have ended for me during that battle, had our unit retreated through the Belgian town of Malmedy instead of through the city of Eupen. I would have been a victim of the massacre of American prisoners ordered by SS General Sepp Dietrich. Even closer to our nightmares, a lower-ranked Nazi officer had specifically ordered the killing of captured German

Jews. Two Ritchie Boys, for example, having been identified as "Jews from Berlin," were summarily shot by that officer. The news of that war crime went through our unit and prompted a promise to ourselves that we would from that moment on gather every bit of evidence against this officer if we captured him. We were totally successful. We even found the makeshift graves of our murdered comrades. I never forgot their names. Seventy years later I stood in front of those graves when I visited Normandy for the first time. I put my hand on both gravestones and then reached for my handkerchief.

During our retreat we were ordered to establish a temporary POW camp at the old fortress town of Huy. That short sojourn sticks in my memory because my routine duties were interrupted by two extraordinary events. One morning one of our screeners brought an average-looking prisoner to me. "This Austrian noncom said that he brought a valuable diary along." The prisoner, Sergeant Karl Laun, was sent to me after the screeners had discovered that this vaunted diary was written in German shorthand and that I was the only one of the Ritchie Boys at First Army Headquarters listed as "conversant with German shorthand." That was owing to the foresight of my parents. They had insisted that I take a relevant course in addition to the standard high school curriculum in Hildesheim.

The prisoner appeared in my tent; his diary turned out to be a gold mine of overheard classified information and, equally important, an informed assessment of morale among German soldiers. Sometimes it reported the rude awakening of a disillusioned Nazi or, less frequently, an account of a long-nurtured rebelliousness against German rulers. In both cases I felt that their "rude awakening" in late 1943 had come a bit too late. Laun and I transcribed the diary. The material generated twenty-three issues of our daily report. I supplied a title, "From the Bulge to the Rhine."

As we found out, it was widely read by various headquarters up and down the line. In fact, after the last installment had been distributed, one officer asked for more: "Didn't the talk of the German soldiers also center on sex?" My informant, Karl Laun, who became my good Austrian friend after the war, had nothing in his diary to offer. "Well," he said, "I can supply an erotic sequel with a bit of fiction thrown in." This addition in collaboration with me also became a resounding hit with our readers. Did we have a knack for purple prose? We were never tested again. But Laun's diary has a chance of immortality because a copy of it is now housed in the Truman Presidential Library.

As the author of this informative diary, Karl Laun became one of the earliest recruits for a rapidly growing roster of trustees. These were prisoners with particularly useful skills for our purposes and with a verifiably unblemished political past. They were given a multitude of tasks. For example, there was Private Korn with decided Communist leanings, who had been a concentration camp inmate for the better part of a year. He was invaluable in procuring information gathered at night when we slipped him into the holding cage and he emerged with intelligence collected from our "guests," especially those with a loose tongue. Then there was Konrad Modrach, who had talents as a forger and as a sleight-of-hand magician. He showed his ingenuity, prior to being drafted, by bribing a Gestapo official. Through generous gifts of jewelry, he was able to gain the status of a "quarter-Jew," instead of becoming an incarcerated "half-Jew," which is what he really was. His father was Jewish, his mother was not. "Quarter-Jews," often at the whim of the local party leader, had a chance of being spared deportation.

It was Karlie, as I called him in postwar years, who became our key helpmeet in my second extraordinary encounter during my duty as an interrogator: my direct confrontation (along with Fred Howard) with one of "Hitler's willing executioners," by the name of Dr. Gustav Wilhelm Schübbe. Of course, we were somewhat prepared or should have been, because even before we met this despicable and self-righteous ideologist, we saw and heard evidence of extirpation, even when it was not (yet) our assignment to uncover war crimes.

The unmasking of Dr. Schübbe was owing in equal parts to Fred's interrogation skills and to the improbable concentration of fortuitous circumstances during one day in the spring of 1945. The precise date was April 12, 1945, the day President Roosevelt died. Earlier that day Fred had interrogated an unreconstructed Nazi who boasted that he was the nephew of the leader of the SS, Heinrich Himmler. The SS was selected for its unquestioning loyalty to the Nazi Party and its instant readiness to murder Jews and other "undesirables." Our MPs, when searching Himmler's nephew, found a photo of his infamous uncle. They turned it over to Fred. He took out a pair of scissors, separating the photo from its background, put a string around Himmler's neck, and hung him up in effigy around his gooseneck lamp. He couldn't know how that picture would become a most important prop in the drama of that day.

Fred had already worked considerably past midnight and had exchanged his uniform for some civvies. Weary, he turned to the two trustees at his side, Korn and Laun, and ordered the last selected prisoner, the aforementioned Dr. Schübbe, to be brought in. Fred was multitasking. While interrogating, he listened to a German radio station. How was the enemy going to exploit the death of Roosevelt propagandistically? He didn't have to wait long. "The arch villain, the provoker of this war, is dead. Now our victory is in sight," proclaimed the radio.

Schübbe, apparently taking in both the photo of Himmler and the German propaganda broadcast, greeted Fred with a smile and casually remarked, "Na, ich sehe, wir sind unter uns." (Well, I see we are among ourselves.) Fred was about to explode. But Korn was out of his seat, reached over to Fred and handed him a slip with a one-word message, "Opium!"

Fred caught on at once. In a skeptical voice he said, "I sure as hell know who *we* are, but who, do tell, are *you*?"

Schübbe became formal. "Please, if you look at your files there, you will find my name and position. I'm in command of the euthanasia station at Kiev."

Now Fred didn't let go anymore. "I need more details. Tell me more!" He egged Schübbe on; the complete confession of a war criminal was in progress. Karl Laun was rapidly taking down every word in shorthand. And then disaster struck. Fred passed his informant a cup of coffee to keep him going. The strong brew seemed to cut through Schübbe's opium-induced delusion. The second disaster was that I, or rather Kommissar Krukow in full Soviet regalia, came in ready to tell Fred to call it a day. That sobered the doctor completely. He refused to say another word. A Russian officer was certainly not part of Schübbe's imaginary scenario.

The next day we used a traditional method of interrogation, asking the same questions over and over again, assisted by Laun's transcribed stenographic notes. And we succeeded. Herewith is some of the dialogue, when

Schübbe "justified" his heinous deeds. I believe it is an accurate reflection of an executioner's state of mind during his murder of handicapped civilian prisoners.

Fred: You surely are completely conscious of what your work meant for Germany, but you also certainly know that a large section of innocent people were annihilated through your institute in Kiev?

Schübbe: We were clear, in the circles of German physicians in Kiev, about the effects of this assignment, which we were carrying out under orders of the chargé d'affaires . . . I still maintain the point of view that just as one prunes a tree of bad, decayed branches during springtime, in just the same way, a certain hygienic watchfulness, alertness is necessary regarding the body politic. Pruning is essential. We also count sterilization as a means to that end.

Time magazine summarized our report in the May 7, 1945, issue under the heading "Out of the Pit":

> To US Army questioners a captured German doctor, Gustav Wilhelm Schübbe, casually admitted that the Nazi Annihilation Institute at Kiev had killed from 110,000 to 140,000 persons "unworthy to live" during the nine months he had worked there. Schübbe, a crippled drug addict who was head of the institute and scientifically detached from his motives, added coolly that he himself had killed twenty-one thousand people.

You may well ask what happened to the Doctor of Evil? My colleague and fellow researcher Stephen Goodell found that Schübbe was sent to the Dachau internment camp in September 1946. He was held there as a war crimes suspect and was interrogated twice by Ritchie Boys. It was determined that he was irrelevant to the trial proceedings of German physicians at the so-called Doctors' Trial, which began in December 1946. Hence, he was released from the Nuremberg Jail, and was returned to Dachau on May 1, 1947. Two months later he was discharged from Dachau and returned to the custody of his wife in Hamburg.

Fate or justice was to catch up with Schübbe. He was indeed an unreconstructed Nazi. His daughter reported that he would regurgitate the glories of the Third Reich and of the Nazi ideology at every meal. Apparently his son was traumatized by these recitals. The Hamburger *Abendblatt* of April 12 and 13, 1976, reported that after one such diatribe, the son took a shovel and killed both of his parents. The total extent of Schübbe's involvement in Nazi war crimes has never been cleared up, neither to Fred's nor to my satisfaction.

But we have certainty about the crime and punishment of still another trial of a German war criminal, whose crime had outraged us both as humanitarians and as soldiers. We at First Army Headquarters Interrogation Cage received a command from the Judge Advocates Office. They had found out that a US pilot, forced to bail out, had been summarily shot by a German infantry lieutenant. "If you find out his name and can take him prisoner, obtain further proof." Through members of his unit, we quickly identified him and found he was among a recently arrived batch of prisoners. He was, of course, in denial. At the suggestion of our Trustee Korn, we put the suspect in solitary with Korn. In the morning Korn came out of that meeting with every conceivable piece of incriminating evidence in place, and he told us the story. Upon entering the German lieutenant's makeshift quarters, he didn't so much as acknowledge the presence of the lieutenant. He started looking for a convenient hook and started to hang himself. The startled German officer asked him what on earth he was doing. Korn explained that he had committed several crimes upon American soldiers and that he feared the worst possible treatment, since apparently the Americans had the goods on him. "Better to make an end of it," Korn said to the lieutenant. The latter tried to dissuade him, but Korn faked proceeding with his suicide. Finally, the lieutenant blurted out that he himself was guilty of a war crime but that he would tough it out. He urged Korn to follow his example. In the course of their debate, he told Korn the details about the shooting of the American pilot. We turned that evidence over to the Judge Advocates Office and were reliably told that the German war criminal was tried and executed.

I should like to lift out one more successful interrogation, which in all likelihood hastened my being awarded a Bronze Star. Toward the end of the war, Hitler swooped up every man still capable of carrying a weapon or merely of marching, if haltingly, in formation. Hitler called it "Der Volkssturm" (The People's Attack), but in reality, they were a ragtag group of over- and underage men and boys, or others who were suffering from a disease that had prevented their having been drafted previously. An order came down from G-1. "We have no book on these Volkssturm members. What is their fighting capability?" I was charged with providing that information, and I sensed that routine interrogations, one-on-one, would yield no conclusive answers. So I started mass interrogations. After the newly arrived POWs had jumped off the trucks, I had them line up by units, down to regiment or ancillary battalion. By following my command they were already committing a breach of security. Then assisted by one of our trustees, a tough German noncom, I commanded them to raise their hands in response to my questions: "How many of you had training at the rifle range? How many of you were trained with a machine gun? How many of you had training with howitzers or mortars?"

Then came a crucial question, prompted by the G-1's query as to whether the German Army was ready for gas warfare. Hence, I asked, "How many of you carry gas masks? How many of you were issued protective clothing? How many of you passed through a gas chamber?" Without the slightest hesitation, the prisoners did as they were told and raised their hands, if the question applied to them. I had our trustee record the results. For example, only twenty POWs of the 129 members of the 62nd VG Division (Volkssturm) had received gas mask training. I sent in my first analysis to First Army Headquarters that evening and followed this stocktaking as soon as new truckloads of prisoners came in. An almost spontaneous order came back from headquarters. "Sgt. Stern is to report immediately to Warrant Officer Gold this afternoon for instructions." I was puzzled. When I reported to Gold, the paymaster of First Army, he said, "Sergeant Stern, I have orders to teach you statistics this afternoon," and he did, though handicapped by a slow learner in mathematics, to wit, me. I was now able to support the finding of my mass interrogations in terminology borrowed from statistical vocabulary.

I surmise that these statistical reports, later proven to be completely accurate, alleviated the minds of our High Command. A sentence in the citation accompanying the Bronze Star and signed by General Courtney H. Hodges seems to confirm this. It contained the following sentence: "[Stern's] detailed statistical analysis of enemy divisions facing First Army were of inestimable value to both higher and lower headquarters."

Of course, I am only one of many hundreds of Ritchie-trained interrogators who contributed to the war effort to the best of their abilities. A high-ranking army officer, who was charged with writing the history of military intelligence during World War II, asserted that sixty-seven percent of essential information was supplied by the Ritchie Boys. We ferreted out information about enemy positions, details on German research on atomic weapons, German plans, for example after we captured and interrogated General Schrimpf of the 5th German Parachute Division, and the ups and downs of German morale. Our unit at First Army alerted higher headquarters to the machinations of Einheit Stielau, with its scheme of penetrating our lines with English-speaking spies wearing GI uniforms. We also learned that Einheit Stielau had made tentative plans for an assassination attempt on General Eisenhower.

You might gather from all this that the Ritchie Boys were a group of obsessive workaholics and not much fun. Let me disabuse you of that notion by telling you of the time that Fred was able to persuade a world-renowned movie star to share a jeep ride with us to our prisoner-of-war enclosure. It happened at a time when our mood was at its bleakest. We had retreated, as a result of the German counterattack, during the winter of 1944 to 1945. One wintry morning a message came down from First Army Headquarters: Marlene Dietrich was bringing her USO show to a catering hall within twenty miles of our encampment.

We knew of her courage. Unlike us, she had not been driven out of Nazi Germany but, to the contrary, had been consistently importuned by ruling Nazis, especially Propaganda Minister Joseph Goebbels, to return to Germany and become the idol of German filmgoers. She didn't tell Goebbels, via vulgarisms of which she was quite capable, to "shove" his offer, but she came close. Instead of returning to German studios, she volunteered to entertain US troops.

My buddy Fred, always ahead of me as an initiator of adventurous enterprises, took the lead: "Let's get over there, Guy!" he bellowed when he heard about the show. Our commanding officer, Captain Ed Kann, did not object when we asked for the use of one of the jeeps. The show was taking place at a catering hall, part of a rural inn. It was already overcrowded when we arrived. No chairs, of course. We squeezed into a row past the middle and, like everyone else, sat down on our steel helmets. About fifteen minutes later Marlene Dietrich appeared on a podium only a few steps from her audience, astride

an upright piano manned by her regular accompanist. The glamorous star
of films and concert halls was dressed most unglamorously in the same olive
drabs we sported as a dress change from our fatigues. Yet the allure, no telling
how, was there undiminished. She stepped up to the microphone and said
something that established a bond, a sense of camaraderie between her and
the GIs, officers, and the men sitting in front of her. During our unforeseen
retreat, our water supply had been contaminated; virtually all of us were suffering from diarrhea, an affliction known in army parlance as "GIs." "Fellows,"
Marlene Dietrich said, "if I should suddenly disappear, even in the middle of
a song, you boys will know why."

She sang, mostly in English, the songs that would later fill her so-called
OSS albums, some Cole Porter songs and hits from her films. Deprived of
alcohol ever since the German breakthrough, we really identified with those
boys in the backroom in a ditty from "Destry Rides Again," titled "Let's Hear
What the Boys in the Backroom Will Have."

After her performance Fred again took the initiative. "Let's meet her," he
suggested. I discouraged him. "She'll be surrounded by all that brass we saw
during the show." Fred wasn't to be dissuaded. And he got her attention by
addressing her in German. "Mrs. Dietrich, I bring you greetings from my
mother in New York!" "Thank you," she said, "and who is your mother?"
"Paula Erickson," Fred shouted. The Hollywood legend walked over to us.
Paula Erickson, having come to the United States responsible for an adolescent son, had acquired the skills of a masseuse. Dietrich, when in New York,
had become one of her clients. She returned the greetings.

Fred was not satisfied with his temporary triumph: "Mrs. Dietrich, have
you ever seen a prisoner-of-war enclosure? No? Ours is only a short distance
away. Perhaps you would like to see it?" A few minutes later Marlene Dietrich
had informed her pianist that she was taking a little side trip.

We piled into the jeep, just the three of us, and drove through the fortress
town of Huy and up a winding road that led to the fortress. On the left-hand
side of this huge fortress, there were barbed-wire enclosures on both sides,
with a walkway in between. On the left side were the captured enlisted men,
and on the right side the captured German officers. Scarcely had she taken a
few steps, ascending the walkway, when the word spread like wildfire: "Mar-

lene Dietrich is here." The officers as well as the enlisted men rushed to the barbed-wire fence to get a look at her.

After a few moments, the enthusiastic outcries of the German prisoners reached the command post. The captain of our military police detachment, Captain Amacher, came storming out. "What the heck is going on?" (He used stronger language.) As he saw what was going on, he shouted at us, "Get her out of here! We will have a riot on our hands right here in the prisoner-of-war enclosure." So we drove her back to the inn, to the catering hall, where her accompanist was at the stray piano, waiting for her.

But on the way back, she told us a wonderful story. She had decided to stay in America and to embrace the cause of the Allies. She had been placed by the US Army into its entertainment branch known as the USO. Throughout World War II she entertained US troops, often not far from the front lines. In the spring of 1945 she had entered Stolberg, near Aachen, the first German city taken by US forces. The town was gutted and the people of Stolberg, mostly women, had little to eat. She had entered with apprehensions as to how she would be received by her former countrymen, because it was well known that she had changed allegiances. But she left with a sense of triumph. The first woman she encountered on the street immediately recognized her, and went from house to house to collect the ingredients for a cake. She told us she ranked that impromptu baked cake above the gourmet food she had enjoyed in Paris.

We left her off at the same inn and said goodbye. I didn't expect to ever see her again. But my luck with chance encounters prevailed. As an instructor at Columbia some dozen years later, I became a close friend of famous stage and screen actress Lotte Lenya, who was also the widow and foremost interpreter of the works of composer Kurt Weill. In the summer of 1956, Lenya asked me to escort her to one of her performances at the City College of New York. En route from her apartment in Tudor City, I learned that I would be seated next to Dietrich. She had no personal recollection of Staff Sergeant Stern, of course, but she remembered clearly, as we reminisced, many of the details of that memorable day in the vicinity of a provincial town in Belgium during that winter of our despair. After Dietrich and I had clapped for Lenya in unison and left for intermission, she said, "There is no audience with whom I have been more in tune than you boys in the US Army."

I have been an aficionado of Marlene Dietrich ever since and was thrilled years later when I was granted the opportunity to share the story of my encounter. I received a call from Dr. Heike Klapdor, a well-known scholar and old friend and, incidentally, a trustee of Deutsche Kinemathek, Berlin's famous film museum, which is home to the largest collection anywhere of Dietrich's films, costumes, and props. "Guy," she said excitedly, "we had a call from David Riva, the grandson of Marlene. He asked for the use of our archive for his project about her. And he also requested names of US soldiers who may have wartime recollections of her. We gave him your name."

The expected call from Los Angeles came several months later. "Could we interview you?" David was at work on a collection of essays and interviews with people who knew his grandmother. He had thus far been disappointed by prospective publishers, all wishing to sensationalize Marlene. I recommended his project to Wayne State University Press, which turned out to be more than appropriate. Unbeknownst to him and me, David's own father was an alumnus of Wayne State. Maria Riva was thrilled to have her late husband's university involved in the project. David later sent me a very flattering note, which gratified me as much as any academic accolade: "You have added the kind of magic to our story which she would have appreciated." My one-day wartime visit with Dietrich, similar to the experience shared by thousands of American soldiers whom she entertained and fascinated during World War II, had a surprising consequence. Our brief encounter found its way into her grandson's remarkable prize-winning documentary, *Marlene Dietrich: Her Own Song.*

Needless to say, not all of our entertaining and humorous encounters included glamorous movie stars. A rather different episode involved the most entrepreneurial member of Team 41, Sergeant Paul Rabinek. One of his unconventional initiatives almost got members of Team 41, including me, captured by the enemy. We were returning from an assignment at First Army Headquarters. Paul, who had deservedly earned for himself the nickname of "Shortcut Rabinek," was at the wheel. His penchant for finding shortcuts was working overtime. "I am taking a different route that will get us back much quicker," Paul tried to assure us. As he was speeding along, we suddenly heard voices, German voices.

Kurt Jasen, the ranking noncom, was getting agitated. "G–d damn, turn this frigging jeep around!" Paul, now upset himself, hastened to comply. But, alas, the jeep stalled. "What the hell is going on?" Jasen was heard to shout.

"Out of gas," muttered a subdued Shortcut Rabinek.

"Well, you got that canister in the back of the jeep," cursed Jasen. "Put it in that frigging tank."

Rabinek was down to a whisper. "It isn't filled with gasoline. I traded that in for Calvados." He was referring to a wartime variation of a French liquor distilled from apples, which he had acquired in a trade-off for gasoline from a French farmer and was selling to GI customers at an inflated retail price.

Jasen was having apoplexy. "Then pour that rot-gut in the tank!" he ordered. Shortcut Rabinek poured Calvados at lightning speed. Bless the Lord, a miracle happened. The jeep started again and we reached our quarters without further mishap, safe among our buddies rather than in a German POW camp. We blessed the efficacy of that Normandy firewater.

As a further indication of our wayward sense of humor, I could also share the nicknames we bestowed on German generals during our years in the field or my interrogation of Colonel von der Heyde. It was an interrogation by insults. Every one of my questions subtly implied a derogation of his leadership. He took the bait. Out of wounded pride he told me his entire military history.

The whole encounter with him in Huy started innocuously enough. "Stern," said Captain Kann to me, "we captured that whole outfit under Colonel von der Heyde without firing a shot. No point to interrogate any of them. But if you want to ask him a few standard questions, go for it!" I dutifully put on a set of captain's bars and led the colonel into an interrogation tent. Then I shot a question at him.

"Captain," von der Heyde snarled by way of a reply, "I have the right of being interrogated by someone of equal or higher rank."

I first marveled at, then resented his arrogance. "Fine with me," I answered. "We aren't really interested in you. Why, yours was the most incompetent maneuver I have witnessed during the entire war."

The colonel's face reddened. "Well, that was the pilot's mistake that we landed miles away from our target!"

"That's not what he says," I lied.

"I'll have him court-martialed!" Von der Heyde, now in full fury, bellowed out as an ineffective threat. He added, "I personally trained my entire unit back in Paderborn."

"Yes, but only for a very short time."

I thought von der Heyde would burst his collar button. "I used every moment we had to get my troops in shape. I knew my job!"

I maintained my barrage of insults, quoting a Hitler speech that a German soldier never surrendered, and ended my conversation by saying that I respected his right not to disclose any military information. He was mollified. Unaware that my sarcastic remarks had provoked him into a total disclosure of his latest operation, he answered, "I appreciate that, Captain." Years after the war I learned that von der Heyde had become a member of the law faculty of the University of Würzburg. I pitied his students.

And then there was the report we wrote for general amusement, all fiction, in which we claimed to have captured Hitler's latrine orderly. If only one humorless captain had not taken our ludicrous story seriously! I need to tell that story from the beginning. Although not the chief perpetrator, Captain Kann was the catalyst of a gigantic hoax. Soon after the Allies repelled the German counterattack during the Battle of the Bulge, Captain Kann called Sergeant Hecht (of New York City) and me to his command tent. He was grinning from ear to ear. "I want to show you something," he said. In his hand he held a copy of the daily Canadian intelligence report. The Canucks on our Northern flank, like us now freed from German encirclement, were expressing their relief in fun and games at our expense, having satirized the form and flavor of our reports. Picking as an easy target, they had begun by throwing a particularly envenomed dart at Sergeant X, our master of rich but not-so-beautiful prose.

The standard format for our report prescribed a short preamble, assessing the credibility and character of the informant, such as "the POW's statement is confirmed by other prisoners." In a bizarre non sequitur, Sergeant X had prefaced one of his reports: "POW is a tenor. That says everything." Combining X's idiosyncrasies with parody, the Canadians quipped: "POW is a bariturn [*sic*]. Does that say anything?"

"Fellows," Captain Kann followed up, "we could also use some comic relief." He handed us the Canadian funny paper on which he had scribbled, "Hecht and Stern, come up with something funny like this!"

In short, it was humor on command. We left the command tent, looking blankly and unsmilingly at each other. How were we to amuse the captain or, for that matter, the forty-odd headquarters who routinely received our intelligence reports, with something very funny? To put it mildly, this was no joke.

But inspiration was just twenty-five steps away, though a less likely muse would be hard to imagine. It took the form of one Obergefreiter (Corporal) Joachimstaler, dancing from one foot to the other in front of my tent, waiting to be interrogated. Everything about him was diminutive; he could have posed for George Baker's famous cartoon character "Sad Sack," the epitome of the put-upon US foot soldier. Joachimstaler had served as company clerk and sometimes important documents passed across the desks of such functionaries. But certainly not across his desk!

A few questions and I knew that Obergefreiter Joachimstaler, if asked, would be unable to tell his elbow from another part of his anatomy. But that part now explained his dance in front of my tent. He interrupted my final question with the desperate request, obsequiously advanced, as to whether he might "of course with all due respect and only briefly" please be excused "in order to answer nature's call."

My friend Hecht and I smiled at the bureaucratic quaintness of his question, so different from the parlance of soldiers in battle. But we hastily dismissed him. As Joachimstaler unbuckled his belt on his way to the straddle trench, to bring about his relief and to depart from our lives, an idea suddenly occurred to Hecht: "I've got it! We make out that Joachimstaler was Hitler's latrine orderly!"

Questions tumbled over and across each other. Where had he served Hitler in that important capacity? How and why did he find himself in the front lines, liable to be captured? Need we fear a rescue party to liberate this holder of such unvarnished secrets? And, most important of all, what secrets had we extracted from Hitler's "Privy Counselor" during an imaginary intense interrogation? I came up with the answer to that one: "He frequently observed that the Führer had a shriveled scrotum."

Fleshed out with some howlers by our friend Sergeant Fred Howard, our account was appended to our main report that same afternoon, albeit with the warning that "contents may already be compromised." Soon afterward, approving calls from headquarters up and down the line were flooding our field telephone. Lots of chortles, guffaws, and long-distance back-slapping. One item, an attached appendix, struck our readers as particularly comical. Pursuing once more our penchant for deflating Nazi pomposity and pretext, we had devised, with the help of our master forger Connie, a page ostensibly ripped from the latrine orderly's paybook. Upon that document the activities of honest Joachimstaler, the toiler in night soil, had been thoroughly sanitized, nay glorified. He now emerged as "Gefreiter Joachim Joachimstaler," sanitärer Unteroffizier und zuständiger Beaufsichtiger für Stoffwechselprobleme im Führer-Hauptquartier: or in plain English: "Sanitary noncom and duly qualified supervisor and observer of metabolic concerns in the headquarters of the Führer." Latrine orderly Joachimstaler, had he existed, would have been proud.

The applause showered on our report went to our heads. Vaingloriously, Hecht and I had visions of becoming gag writers for Eddie Cantor or Jack Benny, the leading comics of our generation, or of writing for the *New Yorker*. Our visions were of short duration. Shortly after midnight the field telephone in the command tent rang for me. I happened to have night duty. "Guy, this is Billy," the voice on the line said. Billy Galanis was a fellow student from Saint Louis University and was now, small world, a communication clerk at army headquarters. Whenever we got news from town or gown in St. Louis, we would get on the line, ignoring the prohibitions against private use of field telephones, and share news from home.

But this time Billy sounded ominous. "Guy, listen, that funny report of yours? Half an hour ago Captain A.—you know he is the liaison officer from OSS—returned from his leave in Paris, read your report, and now the fat is in the fire! That dumb ass believed that entire craziness! He just phoned his headquarters in Washington. Think of it. He wants an expert on Hitler from Washington to fly over and ask your 'latrine orderly' some more questions."

In a crisis like this you first try to protect your own backside. (Hecht and I were more blunt in advising each other of this.) We took a shovel, looked for an easily retraceable hiding place, and buried the Canadian report with Captain Kann's scribbled note. We feared that a wild goose chase across the Atlantic by a high-ranking officer as a result of our hoax would unleash a court-martial against its perpetrators, us. But we figured that the note by our CO, when disinterred, could serve as exculpatory evidence; it would show that we had invented the Joachimstaler tale on orders. And then, still seriously worried, we woke up Captain Kann. He appeared no less concerned. He himself got on the field telephone and woke up Lieutenant Colonel Specht, his immediate superior at army headquarters. "I'll take care of it," Specht tersely told Kann.

What happened next we learned in bits and pieces from Billy. Specht had run, not walked, to A.'s sleeping quarters, awakened him, and a few minutes later Billy had been told to place another call to Washington. "That fool A. has withdrawn his request for 'reinforcements by an expert,'" Billy reported triumphantly.

And so the humoresque of Obergefreiter Joachimstaler could, it would seem, be laid to rest. We had done our job and produced humor on request. But Gefreiter Joachimstaler, in spirit if not in body, re-entered my life decades later.

Please fast forward to the year 1990. The war is long behind us; the GI with chutzpah, Sergeant Stern, has long ago become a staid professor at Wayne State University and is writing a scholarly article on intelligence work during World War II. He has brought home a formidable stack of books on the subject. Just before supper his wife Judy comes home and sees said professor absolutely convulsed with laughter. "You usually don't find research so hilarious," she drily observes. The professor points to a book in front of him. It is by two British scholars, Ian Sayer and Douglas Botting, titled *America's Secret Army: The Untold Story of the Counter Intelligence Corps.*

The wife, all too frequently exposed to wartime stories, knows all about Joachimstaler. But now her husband reads to her the findings of the British colleagues, obviously gleaned from a copy of the "Joachimstaler Report" in the National Archives:

The news of the defection of Hitler's lavatory attendant was broadcast by Radio Luxembourg, now in Allied hands. When Hitler heard it, he was said to have fallen into one of his periodic depressions. As it was believed that Sergeant Johannisberg [*sic*] was in possession of information that could prove extremely embarrassing to the Führer, the order was given for the defector to be found and repatriated as soon as possible before he revealed all.

The man put in charge of this delicate task of retrieval was, inevitably, SS Colonel Skorzeny. In the presence of none less than Heinrich Himmler and General Sepp Dietrich, Skorzeny briefed the man he had placed in charge of this mission, Captain Franz Erich von Missenhofer, a resourceful young officer who spoke fluent English. Missenhofer's unenviable task was to cross into the American lines, enter the prison camp where the defected sanitary sergeant was held captive, and return with him back to the German lines.

The spurious report goes on for several pages more, all copied or extrapolated from our phantasmagoria. Corporal Joachimstaler, via his inspiring bowel movement, has thus gained immortality. Greatness had been thrust upon him.

It may seem that we were all of a sudden a particularly humorous group of soldiers, but it must be said that comic relief is a necessity in wartime, a means to cope with almost daily tragedy. It was only after the war that I came to this conclusion. In the meanwhile I was a witness, not a participant, even if a day later, in the liberation of Paris.

We had established our latest PW Enclosure within sight of Paris. From that point forward our ranking noncom and my close friend, Kurt Jasen, took over our fate. By flashing our identity cards as intelligence personnel, he got us into Paris; we were among the first US soldiers to enter after the liberation. He had also spread out a magnificent lunch before the three of his teammates at a prestigious restaurant and, as a seasoned man of the world, he had secured four single bedrooms at a reasonably prized hotel for himself and us. No small feat in overcrowded Paris!

But that afternoon was no time to spend indoors. Paris, the City of Lights, was aglow. Its citizens had taken to the streets, singing, dancing, embracing and kissing total strangers, overwhelmed by freedom restored, paradise regained. Toward evening Kurt introduced us to his favorite bar. A singer was standing on a slightly raised platform, giving her all as her salutation to "Paris Libre." The love songs of Charles Trenet and Edith Piaf enveloped us, spelling out unalloyed bliss.

I was carried away, all the more so because I am a rather disciplined person. "I've got to get some air," I said to my comrades in arms. They were similarly gripped. I walked fewer than two blocks—and saw her. She resembled the girl of my dreams. I, the young man from provincial Hildesheim, walked up to her and simply said: "Un jour magnifique!" She seemed utterly delighted to find an American with whom she could share her feelings in her own language. But in that evening of feelings, exploding like fireworks, few words were needed. Our arms interlinked.

"Je suis Guy," I said, pronouncing my name the French way. "Dorette." she said simply. And then a torrent of words, after all. She was a year older than I and was engaged. With liberation at hand, she rejoiced, she could now continue her studies. They had been interrupted by the hated German occupation. She had to earn a living; her preoccupation with Greek Antiquity had to yield to cooking in a Greek-style restaurant.

"But now we all have a new start," she exalted. "C'est un jour de fête," I agreed, bursting forth with a Piaf signature song I had heard moments ago in the bar. "Not a bad voice," she applauded. Our steps had taken us close to my hotel. There was no demurrer on her part. We found ourselves in my small room. In a spirit of exuberance she took off her red hat and tossed it ceilingward. She began taking off garments. I lagged behind; awkwardness had taken me in its grip. She laughed—and helped. "You are my first woman," I whispered. She did not respond. All of a sudden the lights gave out. Our room, all of Paris, was bathed in darkness. But I was prepared. I had confiscated an ever-ready flashlight from one of our prisoners, for use at nighttime interrogations. I successfully groped for it in my musette bag. I turned the small wheel that operated it. A soft light suffused the room. I turned it on her and gasped at beauty.

Then we were lying side by side. "I am so happy that I am your first woman—on this night of all nights." Unlike me, she did not whisper, but audibly proclaimed her response. I could say it was a night of utter fulfillment, but that would not describe this apogee of emotions. The feelings of all that had happened on this day and a half, the ecstasy of an entire city lived in us as body met body.

In the morning she was dressed before me. She bent over, kissed me, and softly closed the door behind her. Still half asleep my reaction was far too slow to stop her. I never saw her again. I passed up a chance of returning to Paris after V-E Day. I knew no visit would equal that night. In the course of time I looked up the meaning of her name. Dorette, I learned, is derived from the Greek and means "a gift."

CHAPTER SIX

Postwar

My Life as a Student and Beyond

🜏

THE MEDAL THAT WAS bestowed on me by Courtney H. Hodges, Commanding General of the First Army at our last outpost in Germany, had a direct effect on my personal development. It removed some of the lingering doubts I had about my self-worth, which had been diminished as a result of my father's admonition to resemble invisible ink. Ever since I was appointed to head the Survey Section, I felt competent to handle any set of questions posed to us. I was satisfied with the job I was doing. It was coupled with another recognition by one of my superior officers. My own returning self-esteem was bolstered by a highly ranked officer whom I greatly respected. The two testimonials, one officially bestowed on me by our commanding general, the other by a leading US journalist, who had been able to observe me closely throughout the war, reinforced my ambition to become a newspaper reporter.

I had met Major Shepard Stone upon several occasions during the war. I knew that in civilian life he was the editor of the Sunday Supplement of the *New York Times*. Our exchanges had always been limited to line of duty. One day, however, when he came to our interrogation enclosure, he congratulated me on the medal and then, to my surprise, asked me what I aspired to after the war. "I'd like to become a journalist," I answered.

"That's what I heard," he said "I have written a letter on your behalf to David Joseph, city editor of the *Times*. Here's a copy." I have kept that letter all through my life and will immodestly share it here with my readers:

13 September 1945

Dear Mr. Joseph:

    This will introduce M/Sgt Guy Stern, who was one of the chief
interrogators at the First Army Prisoner-of-War Cage. Sgt. Stern's
ability to extract information from tough Nazis was one of the wonders of the First Army's War. He showed considerable ability in
piecing together information and his special surveys were of great
value to G-2.

    Sgt. Stern wants to be a newspaper man. I think he might be a
good one. I've seen him under pressure, and at times when life was-
n't very healthy. He always came through. I'd like to recommend
him to you. Perhaps you can steer him on his way.

                                    Best regards,

                                    SHEPARD STONE
                                    Major, AC
                                    Chief, Intelligence

Mr. David H. Joseph
City Editor
The New York Times
Times Square
New York, N. Y.

I was looking forward to my discharge with a sense of elation. It seemed
that Major Stone's letter would directly open the door for me to the offices of
the *New York Times*. A troop ship brought hundreds of GIs, my Ritchie buddies and me, to Newport News, Virginia. A small band greeted us, and a bevy
of young Southern ladies had apparently charged themselves with meeting
incoming troop ships. One of the young ladies fell into a stimulating conversation with me, but finally I gave up because my German accent, incompat-
ible with her Southern dialect, was preventing the more subtle parts of our
remarks to be understood. Also, our encounter was brief. I was off that same
afternoon to St. Louis via a passenger train of the C&O Railroad.

    When I arrived at my old home after almost three years, my aunt and uncle
were there to greet me. I bear-hugged the couple that had seen me through
my adolescence into adulthood. Gratitude overwhelmed me. Within their
capacity, they had tried to truly be substitutes for the parents I missed. Aunt

Ethel was untiring in correcting both the English slang I had picked up in our neighborhood and the antiquated English I had learned in my German high school. Uncle Benno, in recalling his own childhood, reconnected me to the stays at my grandparents' home. With those thoughts I went into my old bedroom; it seemed to have shrunk.

The next day I looked up all my former schoolmates, many of them still living in the same neighborhood, some of them also returned veterans. Several would never return. I stayed in St. Louis less than a month. It wasn't only that a feeling, condensed in a popular song echoed by returned veterans, affected me as well: "How Ya Gonna Keep 'Em Down on the Farm (After They've Seen Paree?)." Also, Shepard Stone's letter was burning in my breast pocket.

A telephone call to the venerated city editor of the *New York Times* assured me that Mr. Joseph would see me if I were to come to New York. Prior to taking that train ride east, I informed my buddy Fred Howard, still on active duty in Europe, of my plans. He wrote back that I could stay initially with his mother and stepfather, living right in the heart of Manhattan. Paula and her husband, Jim Erickson, night manager of a Manhattan hotel, proved to be most gracious hosts, and I finally got to meet Fred's mother, our link to that fateful meeting with Marlene Dietrich.

Two weeks later I stood in an impressive office of the *New York Times*, convinced I would leave with a lifetime contract from my favorite newspaper. Mr. Joseph's opening remarks did nothing to discourage me: "We have been expecting you. We consider you a good prospect. You see, Shep rarely writes such letters." But then came a cold shower. "We are not hiring anyone at this time. In fact, we are double-staffed. Our correspondents are coming back from their wartime service and we don't want to lay off the substitute staff that did such an able job during these war years." Yet his final words returned some hope. "I would say, stick around New York and come back about once a month." That was a most generous offer, and it showed once again the weight he was attaching to Shepard Stone's letter. I ended up meeting with Mr. Joseph three or four times after our initial interview.

So I settled in New York, and when Fred returned from the war and to his room with his mother and stepfather, I found myself a cheap hotel. I had my union papers as a waiter transferred to the local chapter in New York, and I procured a job at a Broadway restaurant.

I looked up my friends from my Ritchie Boy days, many of them living in New York. One of these friendships was to give direction to my life and my career. Karlie Frucht, a writer in civilian life, had joined our team toward the end of the war. Despite the brevity of our acquaintance, he became a close friend because the stories he had to tell fascinated me. In that brief period before Austria was also taken over by the pernicious Nazi government, many German writers and artists fled there. Karlie and his admired friend, the author Hertha Pauli, opened a literary agency and were able to place quite a few refugees into professional jobs. In New York Karlie discovered many of his old clients and connected with their friends and acquaintances as well. He renewed his friendship with Pauli, who had become a close friend and then the wife of another refugee writer, E. B. Ashton.

Meanwhile, I had met a prominent exile writer while training at Camp Ritchie. Stefan Heym had written his first American publication prior to being inducted. His novel *Hostages* became a bestseller. He started his second novel, *The Crusaders*, while a trainee at Ritchie. He frequently asked his fellow soldiers for an English word. After the war, *The Crusaders* became a highly acclaimed semifictional war novel in both parts of divided Germany. One evening Karlie called me: "Hey Guy, Pauli and Ashton are having their monthly open house in their apartment at the Park Plaza Hotel. Would you like to come along with me?" It was an irresistible invitation. As we arrived, I spotted a whole galaxy of the well-known German-language writers Karlie had spoken of during our chats in the closing days of the war. Now they were engaged in fascinating conversations right before my eyes, and I, who had only reached the level of college sophomore, at least had the wisdom to listen rather than break into their remarks. At any rate, I was completely ignored.

Yet I was invited once again and I found a key to Hertha and Ashton's hearts. Their relatively small apartment appeared even smaller because they shared it with their dog Bambi, who had recently whelped and increased the population of the apartment by seven puppies. When I was invited for the second time, I came prepared. I had tipped the dishwashers at the Broadway

Lobster Pond, my place of employment, to make up a hefty bag of choice bits of leftover meat—fine steaks among them—and brought it along for the dog population of the Park Plaza Hotel. My hostess gift hit the mark. Such packages became my *entre billet* to the monthly get-togethers, which became my education in contemporary German literature.

So while I continued to hope that the *New York Times* might still be beckoning, I was by no means stranded in New York. Through my former Ritchie buddies I had a wonderful social network, enjoyed the heady atmosphere of those super intellects among the exiles, and could easily live on my earnings as a waiter at various Broadway restaurants. But of course, that was not what I pictured as my destiny in life. I needed to complete my education, arrested at the sophomore level. I started to apply to various New York–based universities. It did not take long to find out that the delayed quest for admission sought by veterans had already caused an overabundance of eligible applicants. All of us were encouraged by that wonderful gift of a grateful country, the GI Bill of Rights. But colleges were not looking for more enrollees and certainly not for transfer students who would only remain on their campus for two years or less and would then depart, causing under-enrollment in the foreseeable future at the upper-class and graduate level. The only positive response I received came from Fordham University. Since I was a former student at a fellow Jesuit university, the college was prepared to give me preferential treatment. But I thought that after studying at Saint Louis University, I should try a four-year liberal arts college. Not only did several ones in the East already have a very fine reputation, but also their surroundings seemed to evoke a sense of calm and an atmosphere of rigorous learning and, if movies were to be trusted, romantic opportunities.

Friends told me of a newly founded college that seemed to approximate my expectations. Hofstra College, which had severed its connections to New York University, was conveniently located in nearby Long Island and was still accepting applications. I took the train to Hempstead and was immediately given an interview by the chief academic officer, Dean William Hunter Beckwith, who accepted me on the spot. I was exuberant. The campus looked bucolic; only later did I learn that it also could evoke wartime memories. Some of the classes of an expanding campus were held in Quonset huts, resembling army installations. When a plane came in or took off from adjacent Mitchell Field, the professor simply stopped proceedings until a happy landing (or takeoff) had taken place. I met another Ritchie Boy within the first couple of weeks and had an immediate friend in former Staff Sergeant Felix Strauss.

I loved Hofstra. I was able to pursue a fairly light academic program: the college helped by having some of my classes at Camp Ritchie counted as equivalence. For example, our army course on terrain intelligence was deftly turned into the college equivalent of geology. Hence I could keep up my residence in New York, my waiter's job, and my expanding social ties, while making good progress toward graduation. Hofstra had much to offer. Its president, John Adams, was a Shakespeare scholar, and he had seen to it that our huge gymnasium could be quickly converted into a replica of the Globe Theater, if a Shakespearean play was to be performed within its walls. The performances, if not reaching the thespian heights of Stratford-on-Avon, were superb, with a beautiful leading lady and fellow student by the name of Aphrodite Stevens (optimistically bestowed by her parents). I also found myself suddenly catapulted into the chair of the features editor of the Hofstra *Chronicle* and the associate editor of the college yearbook.

I have looked back on those two years at Hofstra, 1946–1948, with both pleasure and amazement. What drove me to that ceaseless activity in both Hempstead and New York? The answer was not hard to find. The news from Germany and the demise of my entire family was descending on me with disturbing frequency. All those campus activities, though valuable in themselves, also served to drive away the demons. I had a need to suppress my sense of loss. Many of the classes had been most imaginatively staffed. For art history the college had imported a scholar from the Netherlands. He traveled on both his comprehensive knowledge of art and his imaginative assignments—he once sent his entire class to New York to see a highly praised exhibit on "Hogarth, Constable and Turner" at the New York Art Museum. But Professor Constant van de Wall also inserted the vivid memories of his homeland into his classroom lectures and made the campus aware of Holland's cultural tradition. In short, he brought a projection of the Netherlands with him. This was much needed by a college (later to become a university) that prided itself on the Dutch origin of its founder and on the name of its athletic teams: "The Flying Dutchmen."

Then there was Doc (not doctor) Reynolds. President Adams, who made all the decisions for the college, had the insight to hire a superbly qualified teacher of political science, who had never gotten around to writing his dissertation. He gave me a most creative assignment for my term paper: "Explore the political workings of the counties on Long Island." I asked him if I could write a paper in greater depth than expected, as a team effort with another student. He consented, and I enlisted a classmate with the traditional US name of Frank Roy Lee. We decided to delve into the political history of our county, Nassau. We asked ourselves by what means had a certain political machine managed to win every election ever held there? The coat of arms of Nassau County is a lion. So our paper, titled "Lion Marries Elephant," displayed the two animals embracing on its cover. It received a very good grade. I began to feel that a college campus fitted me like a tailor-made suit. During the next fifty years, I was able to verify that feeling.

Another political science professor, born in Czechoslovakia, was, to put it mildly, a warmonger. He would harangue his classes with the emotionally argued proposition that it was time to drop the atom bomb on the Soviet Union before our Cold War foe hurled it at the United States. I felt a counterstatement had to be made, especially since I had given myself the task of writing a column each week with the heading "Or Else." Its underlying philosophy was implicit: unless we found a diplomatic solution to the Cold War, we might well have a third world war, with the weapons this time being chemical and atomic. So I unleashed my satiric barbs at the bellicose professor, of course, without revealing his name. That did not deter him from tearing down every administrative office door in his quest to silence his critic. The results were mild. The dean of students called me in and asked whether I could not moderate my criticism, while the colleagues of Professor R. threw me knowing smiles when they passed me on the quad. At any rate, my journalistic crusade did not seem to have hurt me beyond redemption. Many years later my alma mater graced me with an honorary degree, as Doctor of Humane Letters.

My rejoinder to the warmonger took yet another form. Or I may have used this form of response prophylactically. The United Nations, long before it took up residence along the East River, was housed in the Sperry Corporation's offices in Lake Success, New York, in Nassau County on Long Island. Without prior announcement visitors were welcomed into the stands overlooking the hall of the Security Council. One day my friend Lee and I ventured there without worrying much about what was on the agenda. Our spirited article published in the Hofstra *Chronicle* concentrated on US Delegate Warren R. Austin and on Andrei Gromyko, his Russian vis-à-vis. We described Gromyko as iron-willed, but not necessarily set on yet another war. We accompanied our text with pictures we had taken during the proceedings. In reading this, my audience may well ponder how fraught with security measures our attendance and picture taking would have been, had we entered the holy halls of the United Nations twenty years later.

Though academically I was thriving during this time, one expectation of my postwar college days did not come to pass. I had no romantic life to speak of. What I and many veterans had not taken into account is that we hit college campuses with, on the average, three years' delay. Our female fellow students were three years younger, and separated from us by our war experience. They were not eager to hear our tales of combat and thus were disinterested in dating us old men. Laurie, a young lady in my fine arts class, found elaborate excuses for refusing my invitations for a date. We met again fifty years later at the fiftieth reunion of our graduating class. (A year behind me at Hofstra, she apparently had caught up by taking summer school courses.) We were both there with our spouses. "Laurie," I said, "I have waited for this dance for fifty years. Will you give it a twirl?" If at first you don't succeed. . . .

Fortunately my quest for romance was eventually fulfilled from an outside source reaching back to my Ritchie days. While I had lingered in St. Louis, my friends—at first three, then four Ritchie Boys—had lost no time in New York getting their romantic lives going. Kurt Jasen, he of the razorback pigs, had become engaged to his childhood friend Roe (for Rose); both came from well-to-do families. Karl Frucht was about to marry Lucy, a well-regarded film cutter. At an earlier stage of his life, she had been one of his rescuers when he was fleeing Europe and was attempting to gain passage from Lisbon to New York. Flamboyant Fred, who swelled our ranks upon his return from Europe, was matched up with a beautiful redhead named Fay, and Johnny Kirsners, our expert for Russian language and culture, with Sigrid, a serious student of psychiatry from Austria and Israel. Coming to New York I felt alone, even though Fred's mother and his stepfather, Jim Erickson, had taken me under their wings while I stayed with them. And then Jim took more direct charge of my life. During the summer he was doing double duty at a hotel at Jones Beach, Long Island, beyond his steady job in Manhattan. He found an intelligent, attractive young lady among his hotel guests and invited me for a swim at the beach and a stay at the hotel to subtly introduce me to his discovery. He could have had a career as the manager of a dating service. The right sparks flew. We shared an interest in literature, theater, and modern dance, and together we attended one of the early appearances of Martha Graham at Hofstra. My Ritchie friends delighted in advancing our romance. Johnny and Sigrid had acquired a motor boat and took us along on a crossing from New York to Connecticut. Karl and Lucy invited us to their parties. My new girlfriend was impressed by the exiled writers who opened another world to her.

Taking a lead from my fellow Ritchie Boys, all happily married within half a year, I proposed to Faye. "I thought you'd never ask," she answered. But her parents vehemently disapproved. They liked me well enough, but because Faye was ten years older, they foresaw marital troubles when we reached our middle and older years. I suspect they projected upon Faye and me their own, quite similar marital issue based upon their significant age difference. Their arguments prevailed. I was crushed.

Perhaps this disappointment and the loneliness that followed led to one of the most injudicious decisions in my life. I met Margith at a dinner party held by Fred and his new wife, Fay. Margith was a close friend of Fay's, who praised Margith in exuberant terms, which I accepted at face value. But while Fred's stepfather had led me to a fulfilling and exciting relationship with my girlfriend Faye, Fred's wife would never have made it as a marriage broker.

In 1948, my attention was divided between our courtship and final exams prior to the graduation exercise. It was probably the last time that the majority of graduates didn't march to the leisurely steps of, say, Elgar's "Pomp and Circumstance." Since so many of us were veterans, we assumed once more our military strides. One or two of us graduates responded to President Adams, who was handing us our diplomas, with a snappy salute. It was apparently easier to get us out of the army than to get the army out of us. When Hofstra presented me with an honorary doctorate in 1998, I could finally approach a college president with the customary grave gait of a senior academic.

One month after receiving my degree as a bachelor of arts, I lost my bachelor status by marrying Margith. Perhaps the example of my wartime buddies motivated my rush into marriage. Today I ask myself: Where was my astute ability to correctly assess people? Margith turned out to be, in time, the most difficult person I had ever encountered. But "Of the dead, (say) nothing but good," so I will largely confine myself to her redeeming virtues.

We married in June 1948. Our wedding was a dismal affair. The completely Orthodox rabbi, picked by my in-laws, wasn't at all to our liking and our antipathy for him grew during the wedding day when he showed up two hours late for the ceremony (he had squeezed in another wedding prior to attending to ours), trying the patience of our guests, to our utter dismay. My usually mild manners gave way to insulting barbs thrown at the rabbi. I greeted him by observing that he had arrived with an unwashed neck. My aunt and uncle, who had taken the train to New York, said they hadn't thought such an outburst of temper dwelled within their nephew.

Within a week of our wedding, I also entered upon my career as a graduate student by attending summer school classes at Columbia. I still felt I needed to catch up on my education. As Andrew Marvel expressed it in a poem, "But at my back I always hear Time's winged chariot hurrying near." I had applied to Columbia during my senior year at Hofstra and found out that I hadn't handicapped myself by only applying to one institution. Today such single-mindedness would appear almost reckless.

When I was getting ready to plan my professional career, I could not suddenly erase the past, certainly not the most immediate past: the Normandy Invasion, the liberation of France, the freeing of the surviving inmates of Buchenwald, and the fall of Nazi Germany. I felt conflicting impulses. My affinity for the cultural heritage of Germany was in conflict with the warning of friends. My own instincts to enter the field of German Studies would inevitably reopen my German past—and very deep old wounds. Hence, I thought of a compromise. During my graduate studies, I would acquire an M.A. in Germanic languages, followed by a Ph.D. and (I hoped) a professorship in comparative literature. But matters turned out differently. I discovered—or rather rediscovered—my affinity for German literature and culture, which was over the years nurtured by a committed and inspiring department. With a position in German possibly attainable after the doctorate, I stayed with Germanistics. That sounds straightforward and uncomplicated. But it wasn't.

The chronicle of my years at Columbia, 1948–1955, plus five more years as a guest instructor or professor in summer school, inextricably (if modestly) parallels the history of its German Department. They were years of transition both for me and for the unit—a facile statement, as it applies to all but the most hidebound years in history. Those postwar years were anything but hidebound. For me they meant the growth of a conviction concerning Germany, and for the department, a gradual sea change.

Shortly before my graduation from Hofstra, I made my first foray to Philosophy Hall, then the seat of the German Department's graduate division. In the hallway I met an incredibly youthful-looking gentleman. He turned out to be Henry Hatfield, who by his personal appearance and professional outlook embodied the transition from an emphasis on the literature of earlier centuries to up-to-date treatment of postwar German authors. He was the son of a respected but utterly conservative Germanist, James Taft Hatfield. Having served during the war in the Office of War Information side by side with Klaus Mann, Henry had become the champion not only of Thomas Mann but also of his far more "socialist" brother, Heinrich. Hatfield spearheaded a counterforce to the entrenched old guard, which coalesced around Frederick W. J. Heuser, the director of the German House.

To give him his due, Heuser saw to it that the hand library was well stacked. Both graduates and undergraduates could use it as a study hall and the department's ancillary organizations could hold their meetings there as well. I spent many hours in its comfortable setting. And Heuser had the good sense of hiring the wife of one of our instructors, Mrs. Scott, who made us forget that the "master of the house" harbored pent-up anti-Semitic feelings.

On that first day, Henry Hatfield exuded friendliness and steered me to Carl F. Bayerschmidt, the head of the department. He told me that I had been accepted into the graduate program; a clerical mistake had delayed my letter of acceptance. Only one more perfunctory hurdle had to be passed:

a sort of qualifying exam in which the entering student was to record his past knowledge of German literature. Henry Hatfield graded these bits of expository writing. He thought well of my essay. That summer in 1948 two graduate courses were being offered. Professor Bayerschmidt introduced us to the mysteries of the history of the German language, and Professor Puckett, borrowed from Barnard College, gave one of the most up-to-date courses on German literature—one that stopped midway in the years of the Wei-mar Republic. He stressed Frank Wedekind but mentioned Kurt Tucholsky only en passant, though both had been pioneers of German modernism. He dwelled on Carl Spitteler, "the only Swiss to gain a Nobel Prize for literature," but had scant words for the poet Rilke and none for Kafka. During my years at Columbia, the slow department transition meant a Thomas Mann Sem-inar taught by André von Gronicka, one on the nineteenth- and twentieth-century lyrics by Jack Stein, and then, by Henry Hatfield himself, a survey of modern literature. Except for those breakthroughs, tradition prevailed. We students had hoped for an advance into internationalism through the de-partment's invitations to guest professors from abroad. But those "imports" tended to reflect the dialectic between a largely still prevalent tradition and innovation or, worse, their need to hide their past sympathy for the Third Reich. For example, Emil Staiger, the renowned Swiss scholar, confined him-self to the classics for his seminars and never let his past admiration for Ger-many's Nazi past slip out. Curiously enough, despite his politics, I became (or so I believe) one of Staiger's favorite students.

But one guest professor became the harbinger of change. Mostly at the urging of Hatfield, Professor Barker Fairley was imported from Canada and held a riveting class on Heinrich Heine, with pointed references to his post-humous treatment in Nazi Germany. We graduate students admired Fairley, especially when he, in the era of the House Committee on Un-American Ac-tivities, went to a left-leaning meeting of writers and intellectuals at the Wal-dorf Astoria, where reputedly Thomas Mann and Reinhold Niebuhr were among the speakers. Only the active intercession of Henry Hatfield prevented Fairley's mid-semester expulsion back to Canada.

The winds of tradition also coursed through the reading lists, although the storm left some vestiges of the past untouched. There was, for example, the incredible retention, post-Holocaust, of some of the most egregiously anti-Semitic German literary works. Alongside new histories of literature, we were asked to read the prejudiced Emil Ermatinger, who applied Goethe's term "forcierte Talente" (labored talents) with palsied erudition to Heinrich Heine. Even more remarkable, there was scarcely an exile who made it into our classes or our reading lists, with the exception of Thomas Mann. I learned of celebrated exiles such as Paul Celan, Nelly Sachs, and the philosopher Walter Benjamin after graduate school, or as they entered via a back door, the Society of Graduate Students. The exiled literary scholar Kurt Pinthus, who had landed a job in the Theater Department but not the German Department, was invited by Walter Sokel to one of our meetings. I invited the poets Walter Mehring and Hertha Pauli. My collaborator Gustave Mathieu brought in Rudolf Hirsch, a former assistant of the world-famous theater director Max Reinhardt. A fellow graduate student, Joan Merrick, became a friend and then the wife of the Kafka scholar Charles Neider and infused us with her and his enthusiasm for the German-Czech writer. I gloried in meeting my cultural heroes and, in later years, would become a champion of their lives and works by teaching about them in my classes and by taking on the role of cofounder of the Society for German Exile Studies.

At times the readings in the advanced undergraduate classes were more progressive than those in some graduate courses. Jack Stein, my mentor and model, selected textbooks featuring short stories by the anti-Nazi Wolfgang Borchert, by members of the newly founded authors' association, Gruppe 47, and by Bertolt Brecht. At the undergraduate club, Gus Mathieu, as a self-appointed disc jockey, played Weill-Brecht's *Threepenny Opera.*

Yet I cannot recall a single mention of Holocaust literature at either level of instruction. But in this and in all the other curricular practices, we were probably no different than the other Ivy League universities. I don't think a course on the Holocaust, per se, was introduced at Columbia prior to the late fifties.

Perhaps one incident will illustrate the sense of unreality that suffused our instructors about the unredeemed past. A representative of the German government named Gerhard Seeger gave a public address on the New Germany, focusing on the postwar Adenauer era. He mentioned the West German policy of paying reparations to Holocaust victims. I walked out of the lecture with Jack Stein and had one of my few disagreements with him. I termed the restitution for the horror inadequate. Jack, not yet cognizant of the full extent of the Holocaust, thought it was, by its voluntary nature, a generous act.

At Columbia College, this all-male undergraduate school, the fair-mindedness of Jack Madison Stein, a non-Jew who earlier in his career had doubled as a church organist, but was perceived by many as Jewish (perhaps because of his name), did much to counteract resentments against anything German. For example, he introduced a textbook edition of *The Diary of Anne Frank*, published under his general editorship at W. W. Norton, into upper-division classes. Also, the pervasive presence of German-American Jewish graduate assistants attenuated the widespread (and understandable) Germanophobia of our Jewish undergraduates.

Returning to a more general analysis of the department: What marked departmental policies? Carl Bayerschmidt, a decent, rather conservative person—he supported me warmly, even enthusiastically for several positions, in fact making personal contacts on my behalf—was in favor of innovation, but he had no intention of offending the old guard. Two examples of antediluvian attitudes come to mind: Professor Emeritus Alfred Remy frequently extolled Richard Wagner, but termed both Weimar art and music aberrations. Professor Henry Schulze, the past departmental undergraduate representative, occasionally offered graduate courses that I avoided. They culminated in four questions on the final: Write down (that is, regurgitate) one poem by Theodor Storm and one by Gottfried Keller, two nineteenth-century writers, then narrate their biographies. At one time Schulze turned down a master's essay on Kafka: too trivial an author, he found, if compared with Storm.

Hence, Bayerschmidt had to maneuver between such fixtures and his department's need of Columbia-level graduate students. He realized that the department was all of a sudden blessed by an influx of second-generation exiles from Germany and Nazi-dominated countries. In later days many of them would enrich the profession: Peter Heller and Walter Sokel (both two years ahead of me), Gustave Mathieu, Inge Halpert, Ursula Jarvis (later, Ursula Colby), and Peter Demetz (who in midstream transferred to Yale). Two others would also distinguish themselves: Dr. Kurt Lubinski, contributing reporter of the exile newspaper *Aufbau*, and Fred Wolinsky, working later in counterintelligence in Paris. Fred, one of the most gifted explication-de-texte experts among us students, could have been a great Germanist. He foundered on his perfectionism; he never finished a seminar paper. His story is worth telling because it illustrates the humanity of some of our faculty members. One day André von Gronicka called him in: "I know that you have mastered this subject backward and forward. Just tell me about your findings and insights and I will jot them down and consider that your paper." Wolinsky, true to his character, answered that he couldn't accept the offer.

A different type of encouragement emanated from Henry Hatfield. During a stay in the hospital, he entrusted me (I had just garnered my MA) with the conduct of his Lessing pro-seminar. I was intensely proud. It was seminal for my enthusiasm for Lessing, which in later years would inspire me toward founding the Lessing Society and the *Lessing Yearbook* at the University of Cincinnati. Lessing represented to me the breakthrough of tolerance and an appreciation of Jewish intellectuals during the eighteenth century.

But the influx of incipient scholars from abroad didn't sit well with the conservatives. Years after the days at Columbia when Henry Hatfield and I had become friends and colleagues, he confided to me that our resident Deutsch-Nationaler, Professor Heuser, would periodically lambaste Bayerschmidt with the warning: "Too many Jews are getting in!" Bayerschmidt listened, kept on admitting them, and added some Jewish women to his staff as well. But we knew of Heuser's predilections and prejudices even while we were at Columbia. I found, in his beloved German House, an early exposé of I. G. Farben, the world's largest chemical concern, or cartel, and its iniquitous complicity in the "Final Solution." Lo and behold, the author quoted a letter of Heuser's from the early years of the Third Reich. He was soliciting funds for the German House. The contribution, he argued, would help to dispel the "distortions" about the New Germany by means of a more positive image. And yet when I, one of only two students, enrolled in his last Hauptmann seminar, he showed no bias. He lauded my seminar paper on Hauptmann's philosophy of history and made me the generous offer to accept it, with just two chapters added, as my dissertation. I refused, giving some plausible or implausible rationalizations for my refusal. Had the winds of change surging around the department touched even Frederick W. J. Heuser? Of course I knew that, when it came to dissertation writing, I wanted to work with Professor Hatfield.

As I was beginning my dissertation, Henry Hatfield did me the courtesy of telling me confidentially that he would be leaving for Harvard at the end of the year and that he could only be my principal advisor if I finished within this time span. In retrospect I still don't know how I did it. Well, yes I do. I lived a cloistered existence that year, leaving the typewriter only on the first day of Hanukah and on New Year's Eve. My subject, suggested to me by Hatfield, involved exploring the impact that the innovative novels of Henry Fielding had on his German contemporaries and successors. It was a fascinating investigation how the flowering of the eighteenth-century novel in England brought forth an equally impressive creativity in Germany. My dissertation committee, beyond its chairman, included representatives from the English, French, and Spanish departments. I successfully defended my thesis just a month before Hatfield's departure for Harvard. At the time Columbia didn't require that we pursue publication in book form, and I was content to cannibalize my thesis for articles.

Much later, in 2003, a colleague of mine, Leo Fiedler, told one of his publishers behind my back that my dissertation had never been published. Surprise! The publisher offered me a contract. That same year my scribblings saw the light of day. I went to my friend and department head, Donald Haase, and told him the good news. "Congratulations, Guy," he answered. And then he added, as he would to any young graduate student: "Good luck in your search for a job!"

My years at Columbia reaffirmed and justified the decision I had arrived at early in my studies. I had decided to accept and build on my patrimony by entering the field of German Studies and staying with it. To do otherwise, because of the Third Reich, I felt would have come close to performing an act of self-amputation or cooperating with the enemy. I also determined (though this came later, after I had joined the Leo Baeck Institute, with its mission of preserving the German-Jewish heritage) that I would promulgate and teach the works of German-Jewish writers of the past, and particularly those of contemporary authors killed or driven out of Germany during its darkest hours. Exile and Holocaust literature would become part of my repertoire. Several of my professors had told me that I would make a place for myself within the profession; Carl Bayerschmidt even predicted that I had the qualifications of a department head.

In short, my professional life seemed to be built on a sound foundation.

But my personal life didn't match that promise, as the mistake of my marriage became ever more evident. Margith's unenviable flaw, whispered about by her acquaintances, and even by her closest relatives, was that she had the ability "to lose friends and alienate people," to quote a satire of the famous Dale Carnegie book. Margith accompanied me through my years as a graduate student at Columbia, when she met with my professors and fellow students, merrily making enemies and scattering faux pas. Margith insisted that her opinions of whatever were the only ones that were correct and she would persist until her self-righteous behavior had silenced all opposition. In time I would find a modus vivendi: "You may have a point there," I would respond, even if she were to say that the globe was square and made of blue cheese.

I also hadn't realized, until enlightened by her sister a few years into our marriage, that Margith preferred spreading a favorable image of herself, even if that presentation veered widely from the truth. For example, she gave a grandly exaggerated picture of her past college studies until the official transcript from her college, which a dean from CCNY shared with me, shrunk her alleged credits into insignificance.

As our marriage went on, we failed to start a family. Margith had a series of miscarriages and carried one almost to term, only to end up losing the child. This last one ended traumatically for both of us.

To tell that tragic story, in 1960 Margith got pregnant again. This time we did not entrust her care to our general practitioner in Granville. We sought out the leading gynecologist in Ohio. Dr. Ullery, renowned far beyond the Midwest, practiced at Ohio State University Hospital in Columbus. He rarely accepted new patients but made an exception when he heard Margith's dolorous case history. He dispensed advice, foremost forbidding her to smoke. When I caught her disobeying the rule, she rationalized that she always used the latest model of a cigarette holder, guaranteed to filter out all the nicotine.

She carried longer this time. We became hopeful. But again, the baby was born premature. "We will do the best we can," Dr. Ullery promised. And he and his team must have. The child lived for three days. I intuited the worst, when he entered Margith's recovery room the following day. "I am so sorry," he said softly, "your baby died."

He had scarcely left the room, when Margith broke out in screams. Time and again she shouted, "Heidi, Heidi," the name she had picked for the baby. With great determination she walked to the large windows. "There is nothing left," she said to me. "Let's end it!" I took her away from the windows, then pushed the emergency button. The nurses sedated her.

She came to in the evening. She was calmer—but still set on suicide as before. I had to act. In our luckless years we had occasionally discussed adoption. In fact I had once inquired about that feasibility. "The chances are slim," a representative of the State Adoption Agency had told me. Another failure, this time a thwarted adoption, would provide Margith with another motive for self-destruction. I was desperate. Did I have any influence in Ohio beyond the official channels? I called the office of our Congressman Robert W. Levering. I had vigorously campaigned for him. I got him personally; I stammered out our crisis. "I think I can help," he said without further explanation. We signed the papers for a month-old Mark and he filled the cradle intended for Heidi. Within a short time Margith spread the legend that her child had made it and coerced me to join her deception. I have reason to believe that our closest friends, Janie and Jim Gordon, never believed her story.

Margith showed little aptitude as a mother. Her behavior grated on both Mark and me. Throughout his life, he could cope even less than I with his mother's eccentricities. Mark was an average kid in the classroom. He loved and extended his wingspan in the outdoors and eventually decided to learn about the construction trade. But Margith wanted to make an intellectual genius of him. She would insist on his reciting poetry with a highly stylized interpretation of her choosing.

One example of my exasperation during his childhood has especially stayed with me. Mark and his babysitter Nancy (a student of mine), Margith, and I were on a trip through Scandinavia, where I was interviewing surviving contributors to a literary and political journal that had flourished during the twenties, in the process of writing its history. Coming back from one of the interviews, I found my wife standing in front of the hotel entrance, her temper barely under control. I asked her what was wrong. "Our hotel has overcharged us. I ordered a pot of coffee and I was charged more than yesterday. I just called the police for foreign visitors and they should be here any minute."

"Well," I said, soothingly. "How much was it?" The sum seemed trivial to me, but that didn't appease her. In fact, my point of view further enraged her. "I will stay here until the police arrive!" she declared.

As I had expected, the gendarmes never turned up. She returned to our room and instructed Nancy to pack our suitcases for the next morning's departure. There were further instructions. "Pack up the silver coffee pitcher, the tray, and the spoons to make up for that unconscionable overcharge!"

My attempted persuasion to let the whole thing rest—I reiterated my point that the so-called overcharge was trivial—availed me nothing. I foresaw horrible consequences. "American Fulbright professor arrested for larceny" was a headline I anticipated. What was I to do? I mulled it over during sleepless hours. Finally I grabbed a German book that I had just acquired: Alexander Spoerl's *Recollections of a Mediocre Student*. His infectious humor diverted me for part of the night.

In the morning my wife urged me to get ready. It was time to leave for our next interview. Suddenly my mind started to function. I responded by telling her that I would not leave the hotel until her ill-gotten gains were placed back on the credenza. She admitted defeat by simply telling Nancy to take out the silver tray setting. I was glad that everything had been returned, or so I thought.

When we arrived at another of our destinations in Denmark, she triumphantly showed me her stolen goods. "These two teaspoons provide me with some measure of revenge," she said.

Having laid bare one of the numerous follies of my first wife, it is only fair that I also expose a bit of stupidity of my own, committed during that same time period. It's the only time in my life when I got absolutely and totally drunk. During one of the summers of our troubled married years, we decided to spend a few weeks at a fabulous vacation spot at Saint-Jean-de-Luz on the Basque coast. Mark was having a wonderful time discovering his prowess as a swimmer. But he discovered something else as well. He was told by a playmate that underground caves with prehistoric drawings had just been discovered in Limoges, France, and he urged us to visit these caves immediately. We looked at a map. Limoges was 275 miles away. We found out that in the city of Vare, quite close to our temporary residence, underground caves also existed. Even though they had no cave drawings, Mark was satisfied. We arrived in Vare around noontime, and I, the eternal optimist, stood ready to commandeer a cab to take us to the caves. But, alas, Vare didn't boast of a taxi company. Rumors told us that a baker, as a further source of income, would take tourists around town. We hastened to the bakery and were greeted by the baker's wife in a language we failed to understand. It was Basque. When we finally arrived at a lingua franca, Spanish, she told us that her husband was out taking another tourist to the environs of Vare. She suggested we have lunch at a five-star restaurant, which lived up to its reputation, and as a bonus, numbered two prominent people among its guests. We were in the presence of Brigitte Bardot and her fiancé, Gunther Sachs, and we got our fill of gazing at them.

Back at the bakery, the baker was very willing to take us to the caves, provided he could bring his seven-year-old son along on the trip. The boy turned out to be the perfect playmate for Mark, even though a language wall stood between them. They raced around the caves several times. We later learned from our driver that during World War II, those caves had served as assembly points for German refugees in flight, prior to their attempts to cross the Pyrenees and the French-Spanish border. I felt greatly obliged to our good baker and suggested that we stop at a bar for a drink.

"Well," he said, "if we cross the border into Spain, my cousin, a farmer, also operates a makeshift bar where we would be served drinks at very reasonable prices." He brushed aside my reservation that we didn't have our passports along. "We're driving across the fields to his farm. There is no checkpoint."

When we arrived at the farm, a whole clan was assembled, eating dessert on an improvised table. I looked at their fare and was appalled. There, at a countryside abounding in orchards, they were partaking of an imported delicacy, cans of Dole's fruit salad. The male members of the clan and I gathered around the bar al fresco. I ordered a round for everyone, a glass of port for myself. And I thought this would be the end of a small-scale drinking bout. But that was not to be. An elder member of the Basque clan immediately called for a reorder just moments after we had drained our glasses. I told our kind driver that I had had my quota. "Oh, but you can't do that. Once you have extended your hospitality to all, each one in this round will now take his turn at ordering."

I have no idea how my wife and son got me back into the baker's car, nor into the bus taking us back from Vare to Saint-Jean-de-Luz, nor from the bus stop to the hotel. I awoke a few hours later, alone in our hotel room, and knew that the intake of some food had become imperative. I dragged myself to the dining room, long after lunch, but a merciful waitress brought me a large portion of paté. I survived and was nearly a model of sobriety again the next morning.

Margith had some positive points that allow me to retain some kind feelings toward her, including rescuing me during this episode of inebriation, though I scarcely remember it. She was the excellent manager of a print shop. Margith successfully continued my program that introduced foreign languages into the curriculum of an elementary school. She could exude at will the charm of an Austrian operetta star. Also, her exquisite baking betokened her Viennese origins. In fact, this skill catapulted her to local fame!

If I look back on my first marriage, I try to remember the moments of pleasure that dispelled the gloom. I felt thoroughly at home on campus and less and less at home within my own four walls. Margith and I weren't meant for each other. I should have realized my lack of judgment much earlier, but I wasn't comfortable with the idea of a divorce after a short-lived marriage. The conservative customs of my childhood persisted. People didn't get divorced often among my parents' generation. We stayed together past the twenty-year mark. The photos of the last years still show me smiling. That was more of a mask than a reflection of my true feelings.

Beyond the satisfaction that my profession yielded during the difficult years of my marriage, Mark and I had fun together outside of the house. Hiking became both a pastime and an escape—before the legal escape of divorce.

We received joint custody. I would have preferred being the sole custodial parent. During my time with Mark, I took him to science museums, here and abroad, on long nature walks that he looked forward to, and on summer trips in pursuit of natural beauty, in Washington State, in the forests of Ontario, and around the San Diego coastline. I also functioned as his swimming coach. At age twelve he became the leading backstroker on his team, the Tiger Sharks, who won the regional finals, one of the happiest moments of his life. After the victory ceremony, barrels of ice cream were wheeled in, and like champions, the Tiger Sharks won the battle at the dessert table as well. I rarely saw him so happy. He enjoyed the moment of victory during which his mother didn't have the opportunity to belittle him. I shared his triumph and three of his ice cream cones.

He graduated from high school, but only through an equivalency procedure that involved passing the graduate requirement exam. He wisely didn't try for college but got himself a job in construction instead. Later he became a partner in a small company. He had acquired a girlfriend and a reasonably satisfactory lifestyle.

And then, at age forty-five, he died far too early. Neither we nor he realized that he suffered from some kind of heart disease, and death struck suddenly when he was home alone. Under different circumstances, a defibrillator might have saved his life. My grief at his death, attenuated only by time, has turned into lasting regret.

CHAPTER SEVEN

Teaching

E VEN AT THE DANGER of inviting guffaws, I will maintain that my career as a teacher began while I was a senior in high school. It antedates by decades my official entry into the profession. As Shakespeare does not say, "some are born teachers, some achieve being teachers, and some have teaching thrust upon 'em." I will say, somewhat immodestly, that all three conditions, to various degrees, apply to me. My uncertain beginnings as a tutor-teacher reflect the third scenario. I had been in this country only a year and a half, when, at sixteen years old, I received an unusual message from the employment office of the high school where I had registered. The parents of a precocious piano prodigy, about five years younger than I, wanted their Mozart-in-the-making to have German lessons, so that he would know how to pronounce German song titles and to glean the sentiments pouring out of the lieder and arias he so nimbly performed on his grand piano. I presented myself at an opulent manor house, not far from the high school grounds, and for the next three months taught my pupil, quite successfully, the content of Schubert and Schumann lieder, but failed dismally in my attempt to get him to properly pronounce Wagnerian arias such as "Winterstürme wichen dem Wonnemond," with its difficult pronunciation of Germanic Ws.

After that I went into temporary retirement until pressed into service by the US Army. In Bristol, England, in 1943, while we were feverishly preparing for the invasion of the Normandy beaches, an inventive colonel decided that our frontline troops should come prepared with some basic German commands at their disposal such as "werft die Waffen weg" (throw away your weapons). I thus toured a good part of the British countryside going to different units for intense, sometimes hilarious teaching sessions in military German. I felt that we supplied our "students" not only with some useful phrases but also with some comic relief. On one occasion, the corporal of a battle-ready infantry outfit challenged me: "Hell, Sarge, we won't be that polite to those bastards!"

"You are right, corporal," I said. "So here are some words you might want to add." I taught them the German slang equivalents for "posterior" and "rectum." Bursts of laughter and perfect repetition greeted the vulgarisms. For the moment anyway, humor had dispelled their (and my) anxiety about the impending invasion.

I was propelled into genuine teaching seven years later when I found myself standing before classes at Columbia that featured a healthy sprinkling of hard-boiled discharged veterans, most of them only slightly younger than I. Hence, my initiation into teaching, at first with only a few orientation sessions under my academic gown, was, because of my audience, perhaps more dramatic than the situation facing almost all graduate teaching assistants, past, present, and future. I quieted the volcanic veterans by coming to class one day bedecked in my Eisenhower jacket, complete with the stripes of a master sergeant and some sundry decorations, and shouting "At ease," perhaps for the first time in the classroom history of Columbia College.

Until I had my master's degree firmly in hand, I continued working as a waiter, a somewhat fail-safe activity that had sustained me during my days as an undergraduate. When I finally turned in my uniform at the Broadway Lobster Pond, the waiters' union newspaper headlined the event alliteratively, "From Lobsters to Languages." I came to one insight early on during that sink-or-swim emergence as an instructor: you become an effective teacher by modeling yourself on a personality that closely resembles your own temperament. In the course of my career, I have had the good fortune of encountering several such models. At Columbia I conjured up Father Steven J. Reeve, the Jesuit priest who had been one of my teachers when I was a lower-division undergraduate at Saint Louis University before the war. He was strict and demanding but also showed kindness to his students when a softer approach was in order. Also he had a mordant sense of humor. He apparently surreptitiously supported the theory of evolution. When one student claimed that he believed literally and unalterably in the Genesis version of the creation of the world, Father Reeve answered, "Well, you can as easily believe that the world was created yesterday, that we all have the same memories, and that today most of us need a haircut."

I also modeled myself on Professor Jack Stein, the department representative at the undergraduate Columbia College. He held high expectations of his students, but when a student failed to meet his standards, he studiously refrained from putting the student down. In his meetings with graduate teaching assistants, he repeatedly stressed the fact that a superior or supercilious attitude was out of place in the classroom: "Those students in front of you," he would say, "don't know as much yet as you do—or the roles would be reversed—but it figures by the law of averages that a good many of them have better brains than you. Respect that!"

Stein was untiring. He would remind us that if we came into the classroom with droopy eyes, our students would be all too happy to join us in a prolonged session of dozing. This advice stood me in good stead when I was asked to undertake a three-week teaching marathon during Columbia's so-called Summer Interim Session. The work of a full semester was to be covered in less than a month. The five-day-a-week rhythm meant three hours of teaching, interspersed with three hours of supervised studies and a communal lunch in the Kings Crown Cafeteria, where the patter of stereotypical German phrases was accompanied by the ingesting of equally humdrum meals. While this was the most strenuous teaching I endured at Columbia, the most challenging and stimulating experience came my way for three years straight in the form of a wonderful invitational conference called "Forum on Democracy." Promising young instructors (a dizzyingly high rank, which I attained after receiving my master's degree) were asked to participate. High school student leaders and editors of high school newspapers were invited (with free room and board) to this forum of lectures and discussions on a topical sociopolitical subject. It was always keynoted by some of the nation's finest minds, including luminaries of our own faculty, such as Gilbert Highet, Lionel Trilling, and Mark Van Doren. We young instructors, touted as Highets or Trillings in the making, led smaller breakout discussion groups.

I doubt I attained the Olympian heights of those vaunted older colleagues, but I have it on good authority that I did not entirely fail either my students or American democracy. Let me explain: More than thirty years ago, in 1985, I was present in Jefferson City, Missouri, during the inauguration of the legislature and the new governor, John Ashcroft. A cousin of mine, Bobby Feigenbaum, was also sworn in as an incoming state legislator. At an informal, post-inaugural luncheon, my cousin introduced me to Missouri's Republican Senator John Danforth. "I remember a high school student by your name," I said. "That young fellow gave brilliant answers during one of Columbia's Forums on Democracy. Might you be related to him?"

His face was all smiles; he looked as pleased as if he'd won a close vote on the Senate floor. "Yes," he said, "that was me. And you were a damned good discussion leader!"

In recent years I received an accolade from Senator Carl Levin, Democrat of Michigan. As a speaker at Wayne State, he had talked to some of my students and heard favorable comments about the lectures in my German Cultural History classes. I therefore feel proud that my teaching has received bipartisan support.

During those years Columbia College attracted many Jewish students. They were not, for the most part, from the upper echelons of society. One student came to me after class, nearly in tears. He had torn his pants on a nail in his chair and had ruined his only presentable suit. The next day I slipped him a smallish parcel. I had correctly assessed that he was of about the same size and build as I. I had remembered that one of my suits came with two pairs of trousers.

Generally among the students there was little suspicion of postwar Germany. In an ahistorical age, a war that had ended ten years previously seemed already a conflict of long ago. With their parents, however, it was a different matter.

One of my Jewish students who was all fired up for German literature was particularly good at his studies, and I had secured a small outside scholarship for him for summer study in Germany. Both of his parents came to my office hour. "What have you done?" they reproached me. "We escaped from Germany; many members of our family died there, and you are sending our son back among the Nazis!" I told them a bit about my own tragedy, about my initial aversion to all things German, followed by the recognition that to make a mass judgment about a group of people was shortsighted, particularly if it involved new generations. My counterargument in their son's case—it was his decision after all and he would meet students of his own generation and not former members of the Hitler youth—only partially assuaged their dismay. Yet the story had a happy ending. The student, occasionally given to bouts of drinking, reformed under the lasting impact of his studies in Freiburg. After his return, his father, the owner of a jewelry store, came once again to my Hamilton Hall office and presented me with a tie pin.

Some Jewish students, like their parents ambivalent toward Germany and courses in German, became inordinately conscientious after enrolling in them. Mrs. Rose, a Barnard student, had gotten special permission to enroll in my advanced conversation course at the all-male Columbia College. She came to me around midterm: "Could I take my final ahead of schedule? The regularly scheduled time is my due date." But on the agreed-upon early spring morning before our class, Mrs. Rose, who had a perfect attendance record, did not show up. Half an hour later her husband called: "It's a boy," he said. She had attended classes right up to the last minute. My squeamish stomach was very relieved that I didn't have to contemplate how to attend a delivery in my office.

A telling symbol of a department in transition was our Columbia College German Club. In retrospect, it was fusty, with the meetings a watered-down replica of Old Heidelberg and its beer-filled romanticism. The student president, Ernest Leo (later an instructor at the City College of New York), wielded a saber or sword instead of a gavel, and we sang boisterous songs, such as "Krambambuli," printed in the ancient copies of a "Kommersbuch," a collection of student songs. We drank weak beer in copious quantities, encouraged by toasts straight out of the repertoire of old German dueling fraternities. Midway through our meetings, there would be a series of modern presentations given by faculty and graduate assistants. Jack Stein talked about the beauty of words and music in German songs; Hugo Schmidt (later department head at the University of Colorado) compared the national characteristics of Germans and Austrians. I talked on Wilhelm Hauff as a precursor of the modern historical novel. My friend Gustave Mathieu spoke on Brecht; the exiled poet Walter Mehring gave a reading; and a guest speaker from the Music Department played Impressionist music on an out-of-tune upright piano, a performance that made me a lifelong enemy of Claude Debussy. In my last year at Columbia after I received my Ph.D., I became faculty advisor to the German Club.

The department's classes in German literature, as well as the club—with all its outdated claptrap—formed bonds among our students. It was obvious there was no division along religious lines. It now puzzles me why our Jewish students flocked to those meetings. One of our officers, Yale Meltzer, was Jewish. Even more startling, a refugee economics professor at Brooklyn College, Dr. Garbuny, graced our bibulous meetings, impeccably dressed. Relationships were also cemented by various other departmental activities. Barnard College women recruited two of my students from my class "Introduction to German Literature" for a Goethe celebration. Both young men put on eighteenth-century court costumes, one of them—a recent arrival from Germany—playing Goethe, and the other—a diminutive student—playing Goethe's secretary Eckermann. A large group of Columbia College men joined together with Barnard women to celebrate classical German literature.

Drawing on my acquaintance with Ms. Beasley, then the executive secretary of the Metropolitan Opera Guild, I acquired affordable tickets annually for performances of *Don Carlo* as a supplement to our reading of the Schiller play, which was the inspiration for the Verdi opera. One student, seeking perhaps a greater recognition for Jewish achievements, pointed out that the two protagonists of the opera, Don Carlo and Rodrigo, were routinely played by Richard Tucker and Robert Merrill, two Jewish opera singers. Perhaps he, like I, felt the last vestiges of Columbia's biases. Our bookstore, for example, displayed advertising brochures supplied by hotels and travel agencies with the telltale epilogue. "Churches nearby," a euphemism for "Jews, please go elsewhere." I took one of the brochures and showed it to the clerk who had waited on me and told him about my concern. He wasn't authorized to remove any display, he told me. I asked to see the manager, who first explored my standing in the Columbia hierarchy, probably found it wanting, and talked down to me. He dismissed me by saying he found "nothing offensive" in those brochures. As to other vestiges of anti-Semitism, I'd heard of the Fascist predilections of some of the former, and not yet inactive, faculty. I should emphasize once more, however, that our students seemed virtually untouched by the virus of prejudice, at least when it came to Jews. One year I placed third in the annual student popularity contest, which for mysterious reasons—unknown to me then and now—was dubbed the "Ugly Man Contest."

On the other hand, the student body at the time contained only a sprinkling of African American students, and that meant an even more minute number in our German classes. In fact, I can recall only two. One was an older student, who had performed in German cabarets and spoke German almost without an accent. The other one stuttered, but as he became more fluent in German through conversation classes and steady attendance at our Kaffeestunde, another department activity, this speech defect disappeared completely when he spoke German instead of his native English.

I was lucky landing my first professorship; even then jobs did not grow on trees—or in the foliage of ivy-covered walls. There were only two such positions open in 1956, and the competitors, as I found out later, included the young teacher-poet Richard Exner and the subsequently preeminent scholar Walter Sokel. I got the job at Denison University in Ohio aleatorily, or vulgo, as a fluke. The interviewing Denison department head, Walter Secor, also a Columbia Ph.D., consulted a Columbia French professor, Otis Fellows, one of his former teachers. The latter knew and endorsed me because he had been on my dissertation committee.

Early on during my nine years at Denison, I discovered a model that became a lifetime inspiration. Paul Tillich (a Protestant theologian this time rather than a Catholic like Father Reeve) came to Denison and held an entire campus in thrall. I have told this story previously in the Millennium Issue of *PLMA*, the journal of the Modern Language Association, but I think it bears repeating. In 1957, Tillich, theologian, philosopher, historian, art critic, and humanist, burst upon that small liberal arts college like an intellectual pyrotechnist. He held forth on religion, art history, philosophy, music, and history, before steadily growing crowds of students and faculty. Finally, only the auditorium could hold the retinue of this benign Pied Piper.

Our German students, the last group to meet with him, came to sit at his feet in one of the sorority houses. He began with a short, jargon-free discussion in German about the need for a greater emphasis on ethics in the curriculum, and then encouraged questions. He listened intently to each question, no matter how naïve or linguistically imperfect. He rephrased and polished it till it glowed. Then he answered it at length, turned to the student with a thoughtful mien, and added by way of a compliment: "Thank you for that question; it truly gave me a good deal to think about." The thirty to forty students, as I observed in the weeks ahead, changed during that encounter with a great personality and teacher. They had been uplifted by his respect and his responsiveness. In short, if Jack Stein had taught me never to put down a student, Paul Tillich taught the even greater lesson that good teaching consists in uplifting students and thus inspiring them. I have, in all the years afterward, at least strived for that goal.

Denison, of which I think fondly, inculcated me with yet another fragment of pedagogical know-how on which I, needless to say, have no monopoly. Variety, I learned, is the spice of teaching. Of course with the technological aids we have now, that aim is attained with far less physical effort. I still see myself lugging a record player to my classrooms to present to my students the musical numbers mentioned in a story by E. T. A. Hoffmann about a protagonist who might be the composer Christoph Willibald Gluck, returning to earth as a spirit. My 78-rpm recording made it happen! Another valuable adjunct to teaching was a custom called the Weekly Language Table. Each language area reserved a room at the campus cafeteria one night a week and gathered its students for a joined meal where only the target language was spoken. I introduced a cultural program each week, ranging from an operetta recital by our music professor Dale Moore to films. Or I disc-jockeyed the records of Marlene Dietrich, who induced wild enthusiasm among our students and, conversely, indignation at her risqué repertoire from a stiff-collared professor from Germany and now a member of the Denison faculty.

The most singular extracurricular learning experience for the Denison students and me would be hard but not impossible to replicate today. I learned that the renowned Gustav Gründgens Theater Troupe, starring Gründgens himself in his famous role as Mephistofeles, was coming over from Germany in guest performances of *Faust* at Carnegie Hall in New York. I corralled the college's transportation officer and asked him how I could get my students to New York. "We could charter a bus," he replied, in the unbureaucratic manner of yesteryear. Not a seat remained unsold. Faculty from other departments joined us and we witnessed one of the most memorable *Faust* performances, I exaggerate not, of the century. We'd arranged in advance to meet with the cast after the performance. Finally, we topped off our New York adventure with a reception at the Goethe House, where the poet Hans Egon Holthusen gave us a private poetry reading. A busload of Denisonians, heady with excitement, returned to small-town Granville, Ohio, the following day.

Frankly, I was the initiator of that teaching experience but did little teaching myself. I had planned to give forth with a post-performance commentary on the bus's intercom system during the return trip, but my students were either asleep or had, on the spur of the moment, discovered or rediscovered a romantic interest in one of their fellow students. But on another occasion, skills hitherto slumbering inside me were demanded. On the last day before the Christmas break, I decided that we would treat the campus to German Christmas carols. I ordered multiple copies of a brochure of seasonal German songs. The day before the holiday break we went from building to building, with me conducting the carols in the happy-go-lucky style of a cheerleader. Our lively event became a campus tradition for a while, but with more skilled conductors leading the chorus.

I truly liked the campus atmosphere and experience at Denison in picturesque Granville, despite the fact that during my first year there I taught eighteen credit hours, and when I left, I still was only down to twelve each semester. When I started, I was teaching at every level from beginning German to senior-level literature courses. Finally, our department head realized that the teaching of such an avalanche and variety of courses would make me look for greener pastures, and on my recommendation hired a German-born Yale graduate to ease my load, which included a course for which there were, at the time, few precedents or guidelines. It was called German Area Studies, the precursor to German Cultural History. I must confess here that I drew heavily on some of the materials about Germany that had been distributed to intelligence personnel during my years in the service. They had been developed, as I found out later, by those highbrow intellectuals known as the Frankfurt School, while its members were working as civilians for the US Office of War Information. Whole sections of their writings could be adapted for classroom lectures. For example, they had brilliantly analyzed the propagandistic means that had undergirded the Nazis' rise to power and that proliferated during the years of Hitler's dictatorship. Their demagoguery gave me a chance to show how critical thinking could have exposed the deceptive methods of Germany's Ministry of Propaganda. I also confess that I obtruded my own army experiences upon my classes. I felt at times that we, the Ritchie Boys, had entered history.

This course on Cultural History became part of my repertoire until the day I retired. Toward the end of my career, at Wayne State, I was able to add a new feature to my teaching of German culture. During visits to Munich I had made the acquaintance of a member of the Cabinet of the State of Bavaria. Dr. Otto Wiesheu was then the Minister for the Interior. I noticed during our friendship that he and his wife, Roswitha, née Sprenzinger, were masters of communication. A thought struck me. Wouldn't they be a wonderful team of visitors to my classes on German Cultural History? Of course, that was easier thought than done. They weren't about to visit America. Fortunately, a presentation I attended on the latest advances in teaching technologies informed me that you could now have a two-way conversation with people in a faraway country. Today, of course, such communications are commonplace, but back then it seemed a stunning development.

I phoned the Wiesheus' home to ask if they would be willing to come to Wayne State's Munich Office, which housed our Junior Year in Germany program, and from there speak to my students. They agreed, and my students greeted the possibility to ask direct questions of a German government official. The former director of our Language Lab, Farouk Alameddine, and Sangeetha Gopalakrishnan, director of Faculty Development and Instructional Technology, made it all happen. The reception was perfect; the students had well-thought-out questions at their fingertips, and our Bavarian friends told me later that they felt challenged and rewarded by being quizzed by our Wayne State students. It was a hit!

But I have raced the clock. Still to be told is the story of my change of universities, from Denison to the University of Cincinnati, and from there to Wayne State. After nine years in Granville, and after a taste of invigorating contact with graduate students during guest lectures at the University of Munich (where I had spent a year and a half as a Fulbright Research Professor), I felt the need to teach in a German or Comparative Literature graduate department. I applied for and secured the position of professor and department head at the University of Cincinnati, a quick promotion even in those halcyon days for a teacher.

The experience I had assembled at Denison stood me in good stead at the ten times larger municipal University of Cincinnati. I only had to apply the microstructures of a small liberal arts college to the macro infrastructure of a huge university. The socializing of the German table became an activity of the German Honor Society Delta Phi Alpha. The informal collegiate conversations in the Student Union took on the formal structure of scheduled programs: one for undergraduates, one for graduate students and faculty, both on a once-a-month basis. Would you believe that we had Kathleen Battle, later an opera diva but then a music student at the University of Cincinnati, give a recital of lieder for our German club? Or that we were able to corral Günter Grass and Uwe Johnson, Germany's most eminent authors, for a reading on the same evening? Or that Lotte Lenya consented to head a cast of our Theater Department for an unforgettable performance of "Brecht on Brecht"? Or that a German theater group would twice give guest performances in our theater building? Those then were the new dimensions of learning and teaching beyond the classroom.

But again classroom teaching was paramount, and I introduced and participated in some experiments. Knowing that beginning teachers, including graduate assistants, have a penchant for using extended grammar explanations as a security blanket, I banished grammar lessons from four out of five days of our multiple-section beginning and intermediate courses and had them congeal on Fridays into two to three master sessions with an experienced professor, including me, purveying all the grammar for that week. Halfway through the semester, we turned that task over to some of the most promising graduate assistants, who had in the meantime observed the experienced teachers. My credo of model setting was once more in full operation. As a corollary my credo also argues for the efficacy of the Equal Opportunity Act.

A diverse faculty will set exemplars for various distinct groups within the student body. With some gentle chivying of our administration, our German Department was one of the few with an African American professor, Alfred Cobbs, coming out of the ranks of our graduate students.

I introduced a course on exile literature, one of the few to be on the curriculum of American universities in those early years. Also, the new theories of literature were making their way on our campus as they were across the nation. In 1975 when I was granted a yearlong National Endowment for the Humanities seminar on the German novel, I had the crazy idea of trying theories which, at first glance, would seem all but inappropriate for a given text. With varying success we tried a sociological approach to Goethe's Werther (*The Sorrows of Young Werther*), forced structuralism on Hilde Spiel's exile novel Lisas Zimmer (*Liza's Room*), and imposed deconstruction on a Zeitroman (*Novel of Contemporaneity*) by Barbara Frischmuth. I stretched a course on the works of Bertolt Brecht across an entire academic year and team-taught a course on German literature with Professor Fishbein of psychology. This adventure in team-teaching also gave birth to the not entirely welcome side effect of being psychoanalyzed by a colleague. "You are guilt-ridden," he said after one seminar. "Curse the Nazis, not yourself!"

Sometimes these seemingly inappropriate approaches can reveal hidden aspects of a work of literature. For example, in *The Sorrows of Young Werther*, the sociologists tell us, the character's suffering springs not only from a thwarted love affair but also from his frustration with a calcified social hierarchy. I enjoy these insights, but I must also admit that I remain committed to my earliest approach to literature: "explication de texte," meaning: Let the text speak for itself! But these pleasant professional concerns were overtaken by the need to arrive at a decision that was certainly not an easy one.

I was well liked at Cincinnati and had made an easy transition to a vice-presidential level under a new president, Warren Bennis, a well-known specialist in management. I got along with him, because we were kindred minds who strongly favored the humanities and the arts. Our close relationship also allowed me to make a significant appointment on campus. As university dean of graduate studies and research, I was still allowed to teach one graduate-level course. I felt comfortable in my position but also learned my limitations. I realized I was sorely in need of the assistance of an academician with an educational background in the natural sciences, in order to help me with decisions such as the consideration of grant applications. I met with Warren to make a request for the appointment of an associate dean with a specialty in the sciences. I also told him about my concerns that our university's administrative structure needed to be enhanced with minority members. He readily agreed.

Among the many applicants the most qualified was Albert C. Yates, who was African American. He was a magna cum laude graduate with a B.S. in physics, chemistry, and math from Memphis State University and a Ph.D. in Theoretical Chemical Physics from Indiana University, where he was then a professor of chemistry. Dr. Yates accepted the University of Cincinnati's offer to come on board. Albert and I worked well together.

Whenever we needed to attend meetings of the Ohio Board of Regents in Columbus, we would drive together. These hours in the car provided time for conversation and sharing of our life stories with one another. At the moment I am remembering one particular exchange, which makes me smile. In a restaurant at which we had stopped for a meal en route was a menu item that neither of us was familiar with. Albert inquired what it was. The waitress's answer didn't really clarify it, but Albert, nevertheless, said to the waitress, "I'll *try* it." It was the perfect moment for me to rejoinder, "Now I know, you really *are* an experimental scientist!" We could relax and have fun like this, although, of course, the majority of our time spent together was involved with the serious matters of our positions as dean and associate dean.

One of our mutual successes was in winning the approval of the Board of Regents for the University of Cincinnati to add a degree in Medical Communications to the curriculum of the School of Medicine. This was a blossoming new digital age arena, which enables physicians to confer through internet channels instantaneously—even in the operating room.

Sadly, as so often happens in life, we lost touch because of the demands of our professions and our families. In a recent phone conversation renewing our too-long-neglected friendship, I discovered Albert had gone on to become the chancellor of Colorado State University, from which he retired in 2003. We reminisced for a moment and then he said, "I'm so glad to hear from you. You opened the door for me." Since his retirement Albert has remained very active, and he has received awards for his continuing contributions.

Albert advanced diversity at both the University of Cincinnati and Colorado State University. In addition to many other programs at Colorado State, he was instrumental in developing a leadership institute, which was named in his honor. He opened the doors for many.

Shortly after my divorce from Margith, I found that our mutual town of residence became a pretext for Margith to join me in various campus activities or to initiate a meeting, ostensibly to discuss Mark but in reality to attempt a reconciliation. "Guy, Mark is bored to tears. He's got to do something. You know, a movie just opened, *Star Wars*. That would interest him. Why don't we take him to that movie?" In time her maneuvers became, by their frequency and intensity, utterly unbearable. I decided that I had to move. Several offers came my way. I thought that the University of Maryland at College Park would make for a seamless transition of my teaching assignments, especially since the provost for humanities offered to have me straddle two departments: German-Slavic on the one hand and Comparative Literature on the other. My dreams of being a comparatist might still see fulfillment. Also, I felt that my acquaintance with Walter Hinderer, one of the luminaries of German Studies at the University of Maryland (and now one of the leading scholars in our field), might be the beginning of a wonderful friendship.

All the information pointed to a satisfying career. But the only expectation that came to full fruition was an enduring friendship with Walter Hinderer. When Dorothy and I—more about her later—first came to Washington, DC, Walter and his wife, Dietlinde, immediately offered us their guest room until we could find a suitable residence.

But portents can be deceptive. Provost Corrigan had alluded to the fact that there was "internal strife" within the department but had predicted that my experience as a department head and dean would make this a trifling obstacle to success. Well, it wasn't. My time as a fireman, counteracting the havoc brought about by some skilled academic arsonists, consumed much of the moments I had set aside for scholarly activities. I found that the ethics of one member of my department rarely interfered with his quest for professional aggrandizement. Loud warning signs came early. He had published a scholarly article and a colleague in Europe had republished whole paragraphs of it, accompanied by corresponding passages of his own, earlier published article. The excerpts were identical or nearly so. As another indicator of his character, my colleague had broken library rules. As department head I should have taken additional action beyond reprimanding him. My words apparently didn't upset him greatly.

I was dissatisfied with my position, and my personal life also lacked the complete fulfillment that I had hoped for. To be sure, I approached my post-divorce relationships with more caution than I had exercised in my first marriage. During the next few years, I dated several women, all of them talented, with admirable professional aspirations. One of them became more than a conventional date. Dorothy, also divorced, and a former graduate student and successful Ph.D. candidate of mine at the University of Cincinnati, came to neighboring Washington after landing a job with the National Endowment for the Humanities. We went to the theater together, never missing a performance at the Arena Theater in Washington; collaborated on a scholarly article; shared trips to conventions; and moved in together. This might have lasted. Then came a flattering but portentous telephone call: an offer to me from Thomas N. Bonner, the incoming president at Wayne State University in Detroit, to become his senior vice president.

Dorothy and I sat down one evening to ponder options. We considered a joint relocation to Detroit, with Dorothy relinquishing her job with NEH, or we could both stay in Maryland, where I might escape the civil war in my department, but that also meant turning down the chance for a major advancement. Two mature adults—Dorothy was one year older than I—addressed a decision at a crossroad of our lives. But the very fact that we could discuss our dilemma so dispassionately told us that whatever existed between us was simply not enough to sustain a long-term commitment. Passion, to be sure, was not lacking in our relationship. But after we returned from a party one evening, she repeated a remark she had overheard. We were tagged as "the odd couple." And she agreed with that characterization. To me she typified the restrained, self-controlled Brit. She saw me as the extroverted, spontaneous continental.

Also, a remark she once made had stuck with me. I had repeated a question posed by a close friend: "Could you two ever contemplate marrying and, even at this later age, starting a family?"

She reacted rather brusquely: "I *have* a family." That reinforced my perception that her highest priorities were clearly the daughter and son she had from her previous marriage. I rarely met them—and never became part of what she called "the inner circle." We parted as friends, and I went to Wayne State and stayed there for twenty-five years.

Teaching and administrating at Wayne State bred different problems than I had encountered during my halcyon years at Cincinnati. The differences are easy to point out: Like virtually every municipal or state university, Cincinnati had financial problems. But then, at an opportune moment, a friend of the university would step in and during a fund drive would surpass everyone's expectations by lifting the university out of the pit of deficits. Money in Detroit was harder to come by. Not that the alumni at Wayne did not have an equal aggregate of postgraduate success stories, but people tended to be far more cautious in making large-scale contributions. Another difference: in Cincinnati, a college or a professor might encounter opposition from the board of directors, but most of the time the objecting board member would be impelled by his conservative convictions, reinforced by his belief that Cincinnati and its university had attained a golden age and that any large-scale innovation would cast us down from that pinnacle. Frankly, I had no great quarrel with that comfortable attitude. I was still recuperating from the fractiousness at Maryland. In short, a sort of golden atmosphere hovered over the campus, and one event that happened at UC probably could not have happened at Wayne State.

University of Cincinnati had a very prestigious music department. When it appeared that the department's strength and growth would stretch the seams of its facilities, the dean of the College of Music approached two of its most generous patrons. Patricia and J. Ralph Corbett had come into sums of money beyond avarice. Ralph's company had invented a new type of doorbell, Nutone, which played popular tunes upon being activated. It sold millions. So Pat and Ralph Corbett, who became my friends during my time in Cincinnati, were petitioned to help with the needed expansion of the music department. They had a better, more ambitious idea. "Why don't we simply raze the old buildings and put up a new music campus?" Exactly that happened. I was there as graduate dean for Graduate Studies and Research when the new campus was inaugurated. In preparation for that event, Ralph's generosity climbed to yet another dizzying height. "Why not have a rarely performed opera be the touchstone of the inauguration and draw on top talents?" he asked. He managed to import the entire cast, plus costumes, sets, and other niceties, from that season's showing of *Prince Igor* by the New York City Opera. Every luxury hotel in town soon resounded with the voices of the leading performers. I can still hear the baritone belting out "Oh, give me back—Oh, give me back my freedom" during a lunchtime visit to the Vernon Manor Hotel. I was charged with escorting the charismatic star and subsequent director of the New York City Opera, Beverly Sills. As a symbol of our matchless collaboration, Diva Sills and I shared an oversized, quickly devoured salami sandwich en route from the Vernon Manor for a dress rehearsal on campus.

The Music Department at Wayne State was no less blessed with talent and outstanding instructors. But when we found that it also needed expanded facilities, the solution was to overhaul Old Main, the oldest building on campus. It was imaginatively done and, voilà, the Music Department had a new home, if nothing as spectacular as the brainchild of Mr. and Mrs. Corbett.

When I assumed my duties at Wayne State, I knew from the start that the combination of teaching and administering would not be my duty from here to eternity—or retirement. As many others have learned to their chagrin, professional skills in a specialized discipline can atrophy very quickly. Teaching one course each semester turned into my inviolate routine; burning the midnight oil became my guard against professional obsolescence.

I will not dwell overly long on my work as provost. Some of the problems that faced an administrator at Wayne were endemic to its location and mission then, and, to some extent, now. Detroit is divided by the so-called 8 Mile Corridor. To the north the population is largely white, to the south largely black. Often resources are unequally divided, so that schools and supportive institutions in the black sectors receive less and the students are disadvantaged. As a result, many undergraduates from the poorer neighborhoods are inadequately prepared for a college career, and hence do not finish their education or take inordinately long, dropping in and out until they have acquired a degree or certificate.

Wrong inferences are often drawn from the disparity in precollege education. As a language professor of fifty years, I can say with conviction that there is no difference in mental endowment because of race or ethnic background. Damn the so-called bell curve! I have seen cases where a certain shyness holds back an American student when talking or writing in his native English. But then a miracle occurs: the same American student finds that acquiring a new language becomes a liberating launching pad toward speaking without inhibitions.

My three years as provost will not go down as a hallmark in academic leadership. Yet I look back on them because they gave me the opportunity, when the right moment came along, to become administratively creative. Those memories I cherish.

First of all, there was a chance to solve a controversy among a segment of the African American population who contributed a significant tributary to our student enrollment. At the end of one academic year, the African American Lawyers Association of Michigan, called the Wolverine Society, protested that a much higher percentage of African American law students than white students were terminated by the law school faculty after their first year. The faculty explained that the gateway to a law degree was a course in legal writing. Only those students who passed that course were admitted to further study. And the final examination in legal writing, the professors argued, was standardized and submitted pseudonymously. Hence the grades were arrived at completely objectively. The Wolverine Society responded that due to the current university practice, they could foresee a shortage of black lawyers in Michigan and beyond, much to the disadvantage of African American citizens who would be deprived of getting legal assistance from an attorney of a similar background.

The two positions appeared to be irreconcilable, neither side willing to desert its point of view. Finally a solution occurred to me. To be sure, the law faculty had balked at the idea of reexamining students who had failed the first time, but in collaboration with the dean of our Graduate School I proposed a variation short of an immediate reexamination. What would the law faculty say if we did not terminate the students who had failed the legal language examination, but instead transferred them to the Graduate School with a one-year tuition-free enrollment into our Advanced Writing Program? Much to my relief, especially after some sharp exchanges on the floor of faculty meetings, both sides found this to be a reasonable compromise. At the end of the year, several of the discontinued African American students presented themselves for a re-examination in legal writing. More than half of them, about six in number, then passed that requirement, and, for all I know, are now active attorneys in Michigan.

The other memorable mark I left as provost was not entirely original. At the University of Cincinnati there existed a society of outstanding scholars of all disciplines, the Graduate School Fellows. No similar recognition existed at Wayne State when I became provost. I looked at the vitae of notable scholars, writers, and artists at my new university. Colleagues of great merit, recognized nationally and internationally, graced our faculty. No further incentive was needed. In the spring of that year, I approached President Thomas N. Bonner during the first year of his presidency with the idea for an academy. Its main purpose was to raise the scholastic prestige of the university by bringing the most prominent academic experts to campus under its aegis and to create a community of scholars from among its most celebrated researchers. The Academy of Scholars, as the organization was ultimately called, was founded in 1979 with the enthusiastic approval of Wayne State's faculty, administration, and board of governors.

During its entire history, the Academy of Scholars has lived up to its charter. The drafters of the charter accorded equal acknowledgment to distinguished scholarship and creative achievement. As the highest recognition the university can bestow, the Academy was instructed to choose for membership "the most productive and widely recognized" members of Wayne State University. It defined the functions of the Academy as promoting and recognizing creative achievement in scholarship and providing incentives. The Academy would also serve to attract young scholars of outstanding promise by bringing to the university distinguished experts from other institutions, sponsoring meetings, stimulating interdisciplinary intellectual activity, and promoting intellectual interchanges at all levels.

It also envisioned that the Academy, as a whole or through a committee, would advise the university in intellectual and artistic concerns, act as a scholarly resource, and sponsor lectures by distinguished speakers from the WSU campus and beyond. The charter outlined the internal method of nominating, electing, and inducting new members and the procedure for electing its president. It stipulated that election was for life. The most gratifying development in the Academy's history has been the constant addition of further enterprises by its successive presidents.

President Bonner's endorsement had been immediate, and after his retirement as president he was to become one of the chief benefactors of the Wayne State Academy. He established a book prize in his name and charged me with the implementation of his idea. The biennial Bonner Award, given to the best treatise of the combined benefits of scholarship in humanities and the natural sciences, was established in his honor in 2000.

It was also my sad duty to be the main speaker at a Wayne State memorial service after his death in 2003. I praised both his scholarly accomplishments and his administrative leadership. But I think he would like to be remembered most for his character. This is what I said:

> Tom never surrendered his principles. At WSU he faced financial crises matching those of today. But, he was buoyed in all his struggles by an unquenchable faith in the validity of American democratic education, born of his own background. All that he had achieved and would achieve, including a nomination for the National Book Award, came mostly by dint of his own efforts. Hence he wanted each American, no matter what his or her background, to have an equal chance. Wherever he could exert his influence, he promulgated a fair, unbiased admissions policy.

Finally, in my role as provost, I had a chance to stimulate cooperative learning experiences between our colleges within the university. I have always felt that C. P. Snow's distinction between the humanities and the sciences represents a false dichotomy. In Snow's *Read Lecture* of 1959, he argued that a precipice had opened between the natural sciences and the humanities.

There have been plenty of days when I have spent the working hours with scientists and then gone off at night with some literary colleagues. I mean that literally. I have had, of course, intimate friends among both scientists and writers. It was through living among these groups and much more, I think, through moving regularly from one to the other and back again that I became occupied with the problem of what I christened in my mind as the "two cultures." For constantly I felt I was moving among two groups—comparable in intelligence, not greatly different in social origin, earning about the same incomes, who had almost ceased to communicate at all, who in intellectual, moral, and psychological climate had so little in common that instead of going from Burlington House or South Kensington to Chelsea, one might have crossed an ocean.

At times in my work I was able to push through the walls that separated the two disciplines and create departments that could further the philosophy and practices of both. In retrospect, both the University of Cincinnati and Wayne State, each in its own way, proved to be the most rewarding chapters in my teaching career. In addition, Cincinnati provided me with some of the closest friendships of my life and Wayne State with a wonderful wife. As to the former, my initial suggestion of converting an existing vacancy into a continuous guest professorship greatly contributed to the well-being and harmony of our department and provided me with a new friend, Heinz Starkulla Sr. Heinz became a close friend on and off campus until his death in 2005.

His classes were so stimulating and good clean fun that students enrolled in every one of his course offerings. One of my students excused himself from a meeting by saying, "I am in Dr. Starkulla's class and I don't dare to show up tomorrow without being familiar with every German phrase he has assigned for his conversation class."

And his charisma didn't stop there. Heinz Jr. was of high school age when he accompanied his parents to Cincinnati, where he attended a magnet school, one of the most demanding in Cincinnati. He was very appreciative of that opportunity. After his father died in 2005, he slowly grew into his father's role in relationship to me. We became friends. Even today the friendship and collegiality continue. He is also a communications expert at the University of Munich. When I was a guest there, the two departments that had engaged me realized they had both signed me up for a full program for communications and Germanistics. When the departments realized they couldn't do that even to a sturdy character like me, they offered to ask Heinz to join me in all my responsibilities of that year. I accepted with alacrity. The fun of it became apparent in the first week of that hectic academic year. We rarely agreed on anything, but our students fell in love with the sparkling debates that we spread out before them.

Hence, the steady insertion of another guest professor in Cincinnati proved to be a boon to our program. But one of them was marred with a tragic ending. Hans-Georg Richert came to us from the University of Uppsala in Sweden. He became not only a trusted colleague and collaborator but also a fellow participant in leisure activities. Both of us were dedicated swimmers, rivals at the Ping-Pong table, and each other's confidants. I advised him to hold on to his admirable wife (this advice didn't prove successful), and he advised me to run, not walk, to the nearest exit from my marriage. He also played locus parentis to my son when obligations took me out of town.

But Hans-Georg was bedeviled by an unwarranted guilt feeling. As a German he assumed the guilt of his countrymen in relationship to the Holocaust and felt that I and my fellow survivors were constant reminders of his people's complicity, which, of course, didn't apply to him at all. He was only a youngster when the Nazis came to power. Occasionally he would return to that self-imposed burden in his conversations with me.

Yet our first meeting started beneath a cloudless sky. Hans-Georg had been recommended to me by Dr. Fritz Schlawe, his predecessor as visiting professor. "He has an unquenchable sense of humor and a foible for practical jokes," Fritz had told me. Guided by his friend's characterization, I came up with my own version of a reception marked by high jinx. I wrote Hans-Georg that he and his wife would be picked up by a university car and taken directly to his campus apartment. I didn't tell him that I would be awaiting him there. The couple arrived on time to find me in their apartment and I introduced myself with a gross bit of deception: "You must be Mr. and Mrs. Richert. They told me to meet you here and lend you a hand in your move." They gratefully accepted. When the task was completed, Hans-Georg pulled out his wallet to tip the handyman. That was the moment to drop my incognito. There were startled looks, then unrestrained laughter. My prank set the mood for our relationship.

His divorce, which took place about three years after our first encounter, didn't appear to change his behavior. In fact, after his wife's departure, Hans-Georg had no trouble finding solace with one of our graduate students. But then his guilt feelings took over at an ever-increasing rate. When he first threatened suicide, I reminded him of his Christian faith: "You Christians are told that Jesus died for everyone's sins." My exculpation didn't hold for long. As his determination seemed to grow, I appealed to his friendship with me. "I want you around when Ambassador Pauls comes here to give me an award. You must be one of the speakers at that occasion!" He promised and kept his word. But a few months later, a similar appeal failed. My department lost an inspiring teacher. I lost one of my closest friends and confidants. I believe Hans-Georg Richert could be considered yet another victim of that indescribable evil that was the Nazi regime.

Hans-Georg's death increased my sense of loneliness, especially since neither Cincinnati nor Wayne State helped me to break down the walls that restrained a president or vice president in his explorations of social contacts. Dating a faculty member was encumbered by a code of do's and don'ts. Nevertheless, it was through Wayne State that my future wife Judy and I met. On a wintry day I received a call from one of the university's trustees. "Could we have lunch today? There are a few things I'd like to discuss with you. We could drive to the German Club. Good German meals there!" I accepted with alacrity. The promise of a good German meal would mean a most desirable change from my amateurish self-cooked meals.

I also had a commitment later that day. Lillian Genser, the director of Wayne's Center for Peace and Conflict Studies, was giving a dinner at a local Italian restaurant for a dignitary from Washington, DC. As provost, I was to extend the greetings of the university. But when my luncheon host dropped me off on campus after a meal "both good and plenty," I felt that another copious meal, Italian this time, would disable me. I called Lillian and made my elaborate and lame excuses; but as the time of the meeting approached, conscience made a coward of me. What I had done reminded me of our army's definition of "dereliction of duty." I called Lillian and agreed to attend after all.

Much later I found out that my vacillation had saddled my good colleague with a major headache. She had given my "seat of honor" to another university official; what to do now with me? She asked one of her board members, a charismatic teacher, to sit next to me. "No way," Judy stormed. "I came here to see old friends. And what the hell is a provost anyway?"

"Someone you don't want to offend!" Lillian said. She won out. So did

I! Judy and I sat next to each other at dinner, and I felt I had never met a more dynamic, independent personality. I thought I heard a line from a well-known musical invade my brain. "Someday she'll come along, the girl I love." (I have a penchant for Old Tin Pan Alley songs.) Judith Owens, née Edelstein, was the jewel her maiden name signified in German, a determined woman, yet with infinite kindness and humanity. Imposing and attractive, she proved her mettle as early as childhood. She and her younger brother Sol were the offspring of deaf parents; both had lost their hearing due to accidents early in their lives. Judy became her parents' guides through a bewildering city, their purchasing agents, their interlocutors, and in some respects, their teachers. And some of those functions she also assumed for her brother. Yet her parents did get by and were able to provide for their children. Judy's father was a skilled mechanic and held a lifetime job with one of Detroit's auto manufacturers.

In a world of silence at home, she became an inveterate reader and radio listener. She excelled in high school and acquired three degrees from Wayne State University. The last one she earned, a doctorate of law, can stand as a symbol of her resolve and idealism. As an undergraduate, she had majored in history and political science. I have never seen her stumped by any question about US history and government. Then she acquired a master's of education and a job at a high school in suburban Royal Oak, which she held for forty years. (Inevitably, at our outings to restaurants in Royal Oak, admiring graduates at various stages of adulthood would surround our table and cause our meals to grow cold on our plates.)

In the suburbs and in municipal Detroit, Judy joined social causes, such as Model Housing, and movements against war and racial discrimination. At times she would integrate her extramural causes into her classes. She took classes to local court sessions and to the state capital in Lansing. She helped organize trips to Washington, DC, for her seniors, with built-in attendance at sessions of the House and Senate, followed by meetings with elected members. As a one-time member of the Fulbright Screening Committee for Germany, I marveled when she received three successive Fulbright Summer grants to different countries in Southeast Asia. She would pass on the insights she gained to her students and enlivened her classes by showing them photographs of her meetings with Madame Ghandi or of her group of Fulbrighters as they, on her initiative, crossed the Khyber Pass from Pakistan to Afghanistan. Judy had guts. I urged her, in my strongest voice, to come home at once when riots broke out in Sri Lanka. She brushed me off.

One curious episode during our courtship had sped us along on our way toward marriage. Judy was visiting me in my campus apartment. We both knew, of course, that we were twenty years apart in age—which had not bothered my young future wife. We were talking about the signs of the zodiac, in whose predictions she believed and I did not. "When is your birthday?" Judy asked, pursuing her astrology. "January 14," I answered. She first looked at me in astonishment, then burst out laughing. "You sly fox. You must have looked at my driver's license," she concluded. Even though I was a nonbeliever, the fact that we shared a birthday and were both born under the sign of Capricorn greatly advanced our romance.

We were married on July 19, 1979, in front of the botanical conservatory of Belle Isle, where Detroiters of all backgrounds would congregate, especially during the summer. When choosing the site of her wedding, Judy wanted to set a symbol of her dedication to the City of Detroit. As a further symbol she asked her favorite rabbi, Dannel Schwartz, to officiate along with Damon Keith, a frequent and admired professor of hers during her studies at Wayne Law School, as well as Head Judge of the Ninth US District and one of the highest-ranking African Americans in the legal profession. Judy had planned everything. But our wedding, as my Associate Provost E. Burrows Smith put it, turned into a happening.

Rabbi Schwartz, who had never been to Belle Isle, had apparently lost his way. Our numerous wedding guests, smoldering in the hot July sun, were getting restive. Judy took command. "Damon," she addressed her former professor, "there is no sign of the rabbi. You will have to marry us."

"But I have never done that," he protested.

"All you have to do is to ask us whether we want to get married and then pronounce us man and wife."

Judge Damon Keith took his stand on the balustrade. As if in a rehearsed drama, Rabbi Schwartz entered at that exact moment. Helping hands catapulted him up the balustrade. The rabbi and the judge were now collaborating.

The rabbi named the team Schwartz and Schwartz, making a pun of the basic German meaning of the latter term (it means "black"). You might think the ceremony now proceeded without interruption, but it did not. Halfway through the proceedings, a beautiful young African American lady, formally attired, was climbing up the slope, bearing a large, unwieldy picture frame. "Your Honor, Rabbi, Ladies and Gentlemen! I am here on behalf of the Michigan State legislature. Its members heard of this event in advance. By these greetings they extend to you, Judge Keith, the right to confer marriages for half a year."

Both the learned judge and Judy, the legal scholar, were dumbfounded. They did not know or did not recall that the right to marry people at that time belonged to the states and not to the federal government and its judiciary. With that additional document in hand, our marriage was legal!

The marriage, so dramatically launched, soon turned into a pleasant routine. Family ties as well as higher education and social problems were our continuing topics of conversation at home. In the evenings we often sat side by side, correcting tests and students' papers and moaning in unison. But we became by no means sedentary. The trips Judy planned took me on new routes: a cruise circling the Greek islands and another to Jamaica; a visit to Crested Butte, Colorado; and overseas trips to China and Japan. We did crazy things together. When an airline offered a bargain on a flight from Detroit to New York, we booked an early flight to the city, returning that night. In between we burst into the birthday party of Jonathan Dudley, a former student of mine at Denison and now a successful composer—it was probably just a pro forma invite—but we thought it would be fun.

From the peak of mixing with delightful and sophisticated friends, new and old, during that weekend, we tumbled, like all Americans and international well-wishers of our nation, into a tragedy.

September 11, 2001, started like any other Tuesday in my office at Wayne State. I was reviewing my notes on the paintings of the Romantics, updating them a bit; a wonderful new study had appeared since the last year, and my student assistant was preparing some handouts. No problem. I had an hour and a half before my sixty-odd students, enrolled in German Cultural History Part II, would begin to arrive for class. The telephone rang and I heard the frantic voice of my wife on the line: "Guy, I'm rushing to an unscheduled high school assembly; something horrible is occurring in New York. Turn on your radio!"

Across the hallway of Manoogian Hall, I already heard the blaring of broadcasts. As the coverage of the attack on the Twin Towers continued—the horror of lives lost, the cries of the bereaved muting the announcers—I said to myself that to walk into that auditorium with replicas of serene Moritz Schwindt paintings would approach a travesty. And to dismiss the class? That would be cutting a bond between me and the students. My mind went to wondering how my friends and colleagues, here and abroad, were reacting to the disaster. Cultural history was in the making.

I rushed down to our language lab, laudably up-to-date with the most technical innovations for the pedagogy of ancient and modern language departments. I found its director, Dallas Kenny, immediately. "Dallas," I said, "would it be possible to pipe the German coverage of this horrific event into my classroom?" "No problem, Guy. I can do that in an instant." And he came through.

We witnessed how our national mourning was shared by an allied nation whose leaders expressed their sympathy and outrage. We had the feeling that we Americans weren't alone in our grief. And then came a tangible reinforcement of that sentiment. The city of Frankfurt designed an artistic poster expressing sympathy. A colleague of that city's university, whom I'd informed of my classes watching the event on German national TV, sent me a copy of the poster by Federal Express. Before mounting it, I had each student sign it, and then made copies for them as a memento of a national tragedy experienced in common. The poster carried the message: "Americans, the City of Frankfurt stands with you."

I reported all of this to Dallas and thanked him for making such a meaningful contribution to my classroom via his up-to-date expertise. "Technology," he said, "can help you teachers in the classroom. And you did the right thing by your students on that day."

I like to think so, because on another occasion, in my penultimate year of teaching, I truly failed them. My class in German Cultural History, Part I, began as all those many ones before. My students and I had reached the necessary comfortable feeling with one another. But then one of my female students came to my office hour, scheduled right before the lecture running from 6 to 8:30 p.m. on Tuesdays and Thursdays. The late hour accommodated that large cohort of working students who could only attend the university after work. "I am troubled," she said right at the start of our meeting. "Perhaps I can help you," I offered. "I don't know," she answered. And then her story came out. One of the male students in that class was stalking her, following her at the conclusion of each session. "Professor Brostrom, whose Russian class ends at the same time as ours, and I will walk you to your car," I offered. "Perhaps that will discourage him."

But she was back again when my next office hour came around. "He's still at it?" I asked. "Yes, in fact it's gotten worse. He found out where I work. I'm a waitress in a restaurant at the Oakland Shopping Mall. He came there and asked the headwaiter to be seated at my station. Fortunately when I told him the trouble I was having, my boss asked one of the other waitresses to serve him."

Wayne State had evolved the right procedure to deal with her concerns on campus but had no tool to deal with the rogue student at her place of work. He must have sensed that I had a hand in protecting his intended victim and gave me a hateful look when by chance, we passed each other. I was but just one example of a bystander to an incident involving inappropriate behavior toward an innocent young woman, and had become a further, if indirect, victim of his hateful behavior. My student evaluations from that class were the worst of my teaching career. The whole incident had gotten to me, and I was gripped with fear. I was afraid each time I came to campus that the obviously disturbed student might escalate his antisocial actions. My classroom presentations became uninspired. Was I still the same person who had dealt with 9/11? I had found a pragmatic and kind solution for one student and let down fifty-nine others. But finally, after talking to colleagues who had had similar experiences, I was able to put the incident behind me and regain faith in my teaching ability.

That opportunity to commiserate and consult with colleagues, and, more positively, to find inspiration in their work, gave me unalloyed pleasure. Year in and year out I could be found at one or more gatherings of our clan of academics. I have never lost my zest for them. All our conventions had an unwavering purpose. In addition to being a job market (we called it a slave market), it allowed us to acquire expertise beyond what we learned in class-rooms and seminar rooms. At MLA conventions I learned of the various new approaches to dissecting literature, gaining further insights into fiction I previously felt I'd fully understood. I also learned new methods of peda-gogy, particularly in relation to the technology that was becoming important to the profession.

I will cite one example of my sink-or-swim approach to technology. It is, of course, an imperative of good teaching that you stay ahead of your students. But three years before my retirement in 2003, I noticed that the brightest of my charges were not lagging far behind. I went to see Amanda Donigian, the secretary of the German section of our department—and everyone's confi-dante. "Well, Professor Stern," she answered, barely able to hide her laughter, "your students have discovered the Internet." "Good grief," I said. "I'd better learn something about computers! I don't even know how to turn on that monster!" "That's easy to fix," she said. "They give lessons at our Office for Teaching and Learning." During my next semester's sabbatical I called the Of-fice for Teaching and Learning's director, Dr. Donna Green. I had had some contact with her in the past. "I need to become computer literate," I told her. "High time!" she cracked. "Let's make a date."

One week later at her office, she introduced me to one of the tutors, a graduate student a bit older than the average graduate assistants. "Karen Frade, Guy Stern," she introduced us. "But most of us are on a first-name basis around here. She can work with you all day."

She was unrelenting as a teacher, but used subtle psychology when my at-tention lagged after lunch. Good God, she complimented me more than my just deserts, when I discovered an alternate way to complete a procedure by twisting the wheel on my mouse. I pulled out of my slump.

The session ended at five. We went downstairs for a cup of coffee. "Karen," I asked her, "are you full-time at the Office for Teaching and Learning?" "No, I'm a part-timer," she replied. "Do you have another job as well?" I asked. "No," came the reply, "but I am married and have responsibilities at home. My husband is Peter Frade, the head of the Department of Mortuary Sci-ence." I looked at her through bleary eyes and quipped, "Karen, after this day of cramming a week's worth of information into one day, I'm ready for your husband!"

My wife and I occasionally ran into the Frades at faculty functions. As her obedient pupil, I told her each time of my halting progress on the computer.

The advance in technology was one of the reasons that made convention-going an essential part of my annual routine. A venerable German proverb tells us:

Meister werden ist sehr schwer,   To become a master is a chore,
Meister bleiben noch viel mehr!   To stay a master, even more!

Convention halls were also fabulous meeting grounds with old friends and, as the years progressed, for reunions with my students and former colleagues.

Sometimes I made a revealing discovery about hidden agendas, for example, the propagandistic efforts of another country trying to influence us Americans, even down to the visitors at a local conference. In 2012 I was asked to give an address and to receive an award at the annual meeting of the Michigan Council of Social Studies, held that year in the medium-sized town of Kalamazoo. I went through the exhibition hall, and lo and behold, a certain foreign country had mounted more bookstands than any American publisher. Obviously that country, the People's Republic of China, was trying to get its Communist doctrine to all high school and college students via its books in English.

It would be impossible to chronicle all the conventions that I enjoyed (and occasionally abhorred) throughout all the years, but there are some that have stuck in my mind, possibly because they became the catalyst for surprising discoveries. So it was with one of the annual Kentucky Foreign Language Conferences held on the campus of the University of Kentucky. I'd given a paper on a topic related to my favorite subject, the writings of exiles from German-speaking countries. The ever gracious German Department head, Paul K. Whittaker, had invited out-of-town professors of German to his home for a reception. In the course of the evening, he soon found out that I had been one of the Ritchie Boys. But that didn't elicit any revelations about his own participation in World War II. Nor did he say anything during the subsequent years when I was repeatedly invited to his house.

Finally, the reason for his secretiveness became clear: He had been not only an officer in military intelligence, but also an "Ultra-American," to borrow the title of a 1986 book by Thomas Parrish. In short, he had contributed as a skilled translator to arguably the most spectacular piece of intelligence work during the war: breaking the top-secret German code called Enigma. Paul had waited at least forty years before going public with his ultra-secret role in the war. Without our becoming closely acquainted, I would probably not have learned, even at that stage, the connection between that fine gentleman, fastidiously dressed like a Southerner, and his role as an American translator, borrowed from the US Army by our British allies. He had been at Bletchley Park, a site commemorated in *The Imitation Game*, an award-winning 2014 film.

Another meeting evoked a similar excitement that took me back to my days as a Ritchie Boy. I served for many years—more than fifty, in fact—as a board member of the Leo Baeck Institute. The organization, as one of its goals, preserves evidence of the symbiosis between Jews and non-Jews, right up to the time when that mutually beneficial relationship was ripped asunder by the Nazi barbarians. The meetings took me from my home campus—wherever that happened to be—to the LBI in New York. Once, when addressing my fellow board members, I referred in passing to my role in World War II. Right after the meeting a relatively new board member, John Weitz, stopped me in my tracks. "So, you were at Camp Ritchie?" I reaffirmed that fact.

His response surprised me. "Well, so was I!"

He had by now sat opposite me during several meetings; I was delighted to suddenly encounter in him a comrade in arms. "And what was your assignment?" I asked.

"Hold on," he cautioned. "Are you free for about an hour?" We ended up at a coffee shop across the street.

"I didn't stay long in military intelligence. OSS wanted me," he said.

"Oh so secret!" I punned, winking an eye at an inside joke of World War II, often applied to the initials of the Office of Strategic Services.

"I can say without exaggeration that my German has stayed flawless. Also, with all due modesty, I looked at one time like the prototype of a Nordic superman. And I had command of all the Jewish chutzpah to carry out the very mission for which I had been selected. OSS put me in the uniform of a German officer of high rank and dropped me behind the German lines, equipped with foolproof faked documents, which gave me a new identity. I was to ferret out the new German battle plans after the Battle of the Bulge."

"You fooled those Krauts?" I asked, lapsing back into my army jargon of a long time ago.

"Damn right!" he answered. "I attached myself to several German units, got the info, and got out in a bit of a hurry—or I would have occupied a piece of our fatherland for all eternity."

When he ended his incredible story, I stared at him in silent admiration. Once I was able to speak, I asked a rather mundane question. "What is your present occupation?"

"When you get home, look at the shirts in your wardrobe," he said.

I did that the moment I got home. "John Weitz" is what it said on the label of a couple of my shirts. Before we parted, he had also told me of his leisure activity: "I have just finished writing a book, the first biography of Joachim von Ribbentrop." Of course I knew the name of Hitler's Minister for Foreign Relations, who finished his dubious career on the gallows, hanged as a war criminal after the Nuremberg Trials. There now was an added reason to look forward to the meetings at the Leo Baeck Institute because of the charismatic presence of John Weitz.

Few of the meetings I attended sported such dramatic highlights. For better or worse they were entirely scholarly, but not unrewarding. I was a featured speaker at a SAMLA meeting (South Atlantic Modern Language Association) in Atlanta. I had been billed as a comparatist and keynote speaker on Henry Fielding's novel *Tom Jones*, which had been the mainstay of my dissertation. Now I was asked to provide further insights on the work. I foolishly agreed without knowing whether I had anything original to say about it. Thousands of treatises had preceded my investigation. I found one unexplored item. In one of his famous introductory chapters, Fielding had preached that perfect characters, either as exemplars of goodness or of evil, were unrealistic. And yet, scholars argued, he had created such a character in *Tom Jones*: Mrs. Miller, the widow of a clergyman, who befriends and advises the title hero. I went through the novel for every mention of this paragon. And I found what I was looking for: Separated by miles of text, Fielding subtly supplied all the information necessary to show us a flawed Mrs. Miller.

The diligent reader could deduce that her first child had been born out of wedlock. Fielding had practiced what he preached. And I had advanced scholarship not by a milestone but by inches.

One might think, based on some nasty accounts of our meetings in newspapers, that we professors were a stodgy and dour bunch. At the beginning of my career I shared that view, especially when I encountered the esteemed leaders in our specialty fields. At another conference that took place in 1972 in Atlanta, with the American Council for Teaching Foreign Languages (ACTFL), I had reason to shed that prejudice. Charles Osgood, the journalist and media personality, was the keynote speaker of the conference. He didn't confine himself to the usual entreaties for more language studies and a salute to us toilers in the field. He dared to be shamelessly entertaining, spicing up his talk with anecdotes about growing up during World War II and relating some choice bits of army humor. (I later learned that Osgood, at the time of his Atlanta address, was preparing an entire anthology on the same subject, *Kilroy Was Here: The Best American Humor from World War II.*)

In his book he explained why soldiers had to have recourse to humor during some of their most desperate experiences. I think it applies just as much to the lives of professors. Osgood argues that all of us can profit by a sense of humor:

> But humor and laughter are a part of life, a part of being human. Even in the grimmest of times, people find things to laugh about . . . there's a fine line between tragedy and comedy, between tears and laughter . . . the more fearsome and threatening the situation, the more we need a sense of humor to keep going and hold on to our sanity.

His speech lightened up the atmosphere at that convention, as if it were lit by a galaxy of chandeliers. There were many veterans in the crowd who, following Osgood's performance, dared to share their own brand of army humor, some of it quite raucous. He encouraged all of us academics to become equally loose-lipped. "Share your favorite jokes with your colleagues," he admonished.

Of course, more staid colleagues reminded us of the seriousness of our undertaking at that meeting and beyond. I still recall incidences from those more conventional conferences. But I must confess that the hook that makes

me remember things is frequently not scholarly at all. Why do I recall a meeting of our group of American students taking part in a work-study program
in Germany, conceived by my colleague, Professor Helga Slessarev, and me?
It was planned to take our students from Hamburg to a spectacular heath
near the city of Lüneburg in northern Germany. I was scheduled to be the
speaker at this get-together. The forgetful professor, I mean me, arrived in
the city and found to his chagrin that he had forgotten the location of that
specific-youth hostel where the retreat was to take place. There were many of
these hostels, spread across a huge territory. I had no idea where to meet my
supposedly eager audience. I sat down in the town's market square, reproach-
ing myself and clutching at straws. At the very last moment, praise the Lord,
inspiration struck. I bought a telephone card and started calling all bus com-
panies advertised in the Yellow Pages. The telephone card was nearly used
up when a gruff voice answered that yes, they had taken that unruly group of
Americans to a youth hostel earlier that day. I arrived there by taxi at the last
possible moment. Breathing more easily now, I confessed that frequently the
Prussian in me was in conflict with the "forgetful professor."

A more recent conference afforded me a welcome chance to broaden my
involvement in current affairs. The meeting of the 39th Annual Symposium
for German-American Studies came in October 2015, not too long after
riots erupted in the suburban town of Ferguson, Missouri. Led back to my
American roots, to my early years in St. Louis, I felt duty bound to present
a paper that would set a positive example for conflict resolution. My intention was advanced by the fact that a reporter for the St. Louis *Post Dispatch*
approached some of us speakers in advance of the meeting. I told him, "I'm
glad you contacted me because my most recent interview by the *Post Dispatch*
lies more than seventy years behind me. That was right after the Normandy
Invasion and your star reporter, Virginia Irwin, interviewed me at our prisoner of war enclosure in Fourcarville, France. Does your paper always space
interviews at such immense intervals?"

He laughed and said, "I have unearthed a story about a St. Louis boy beyond all expectations." I gave him all the background information he asked
for, but what was important to me was to link my paper to the contemporary
events in Ferguson. The reporter wrote, "For his presentation Friday morn-

ing at the symposium, Stern will try to do his part to bridge a small piece of the racial gap that the Ferguson saga laid bare. His paper is titled: 'German-speaking Refugees in an Afro-American Setting—Afro-American Poets in a German Setting.'"

I was pleased that this advance notice probably swelled the audience attending my presentation. Of course I stressed how, via the material I presented, the meeting of two different cultural backgrounds led to greater harmony and understanding. I was gratified that I had fulfilled my purpose of linking a scholarly paper to a civic cause. Whenever I had a chance, I used this example to reinforce the idea that we must retain our obligations as citizens even while discussing some seemingly unrelated scholarly subject.

Overall, the conferences I attended were carried out in a spirit of collegiality and mutual respect. Alas, there were occasions when that good-natured spirit didn't prevail. I recall those incidents because once or twice I was the victim of, let us call it, collegial rivalry. The initial such criticism occurred after my first scholarly presentation. As I was congratulated by some of my colleagues and fellow students, a professor from a small and less than distinguished college threw a barb at me: "Dr. Stern, after hearing your paper, I don't understand why my paper was rejected." This kind of crossfire followed a predictable dialogue. Today I find those somewhat catty exchanges largely amusing. Yet as I wrote at the outset of this chapter, I was more often enchanted than cast down by our meetings, even when incidents like that one occurred. I have come to understand that many fellow attendees used these break-aways from their daily routine to bolster their wounded egos. As to my reflecting on my history of attending conferences, it is a way to measure how far I've come. When my friend and frequent collaborator, the late Gustave Mathieu, and I planned to be in New York for an MLA convention in the mid-fifties we had one concern: We were just out of graduate school and felt the need to save our nickels. (We were both newly married and needed to be extremely prudent with our funds.) Even at reduced convention rates, the hotel costs in New York made us decide to live for three days as cheaply as possible. We ended up sharing a stamp-sized room at a nearby YMCA, along with many other young conventioneers and a few homeless or destitute people. At the last memorable meeting we attended together, again at the MLA in New York, we two were treated like honored guests to a truly sumptuous reception. We had authored, in collaboration, a textbook reader for undergraduates. It was a success, and after several years, W. W. Norton presented both of us with a leather-bound copy of our textbook. In further appreciation we were invited to a cocktail party, synchronized with the conference, where the food and the drinks were exquisite. Gus and I used the occasion to recall our humble beginnings during our fledgling flight to an MLA meeting. Being wined and dined was to us a barometer of progress. We relished it as though we had been invited to Buckingham Palace.

On the campuses of the University of Cincinnati and Wayne State University, I was blessed by the cohesiveness, harmony, and abundant goodwill that pervaded there. I had no fears in helping to introduce new courses, though knowing full well that experiments, as is the nature of the beast, frequently court failure. Our departments brainstormed and came up with such courses as "The Changing Face of Europe" and "The European Immigration to the United States." My flexibility was tested when I became involved in a new arena of teaching started by Wayne State. One of the counselors there felt that the university needed additional outreach to an underserved population, retirees. He proposed the founding of such an outreach program. The university administration endorsed his proposal and allocated space and resources at its Oakland Center branch in the suburbs. The response of the Greater Detroit community far exceeded the modest expectations of the founders. Today it has a constituency of more than five hundred participants and has spawned courses ranging from semester-long offerings to single presentations.

SOAR, an acronym for Society of Active Retirees, relied for its initial leadership on a distinguished English professor and successor to me as provost, Marianne Wilkinson. Most of the guest lecturers are former professors from Wayne State or other neighboring universities. When I was asked to become one of the presenters, I immediately joined the staff of the new undertaking. My very first lecture demonstrated to me that the enrollees were highly sophisticated men and women from all walks of life. I was able to present my latest research—augmented by some needed background material—for the SOAR audience, at the same level (or nearly so) as for a graduate seminar. I must have given nearly twenty of such presentations, ranging from an analysis of Jewish conceptualization of the Messiah to masterly works of children's literature composed by exiled writers. During this latter lecture, I had the satisfaction of teaching parents and grandparents who had regaled their off-spring with the saga of *Curious George*, without realizing that two exiles from Germany had created this American classic. Emboldened by these successes, I distilled my latest research on World War I and its literature, a topic suggested by the centennial anniversary of the beginning of the Great War, as a team-teaching effort with a distinguished colleague from the WSU Humanities Department. As an indication of the advanced level of that course, I can report that I had given the same presentation before the Michigan Joint Social Studies Conference, which, on the strength of this lecture, awarded me the Terry Kuseske Memorial Award. It worked just as well as at SOAR.

As a department head, I had given newcomers to the profession of teaching a set of guidelines: "Respect your students! Don't put a student down! Remember, they are probably as smart or smarter than you, only less knowledgeable in your discipline or the roles would be reversed. Don't mistake the excitement and love of learning on a student's part for a sign of personal affection. Don't play favorites with students." I also frequently said, "You learn while teaching." For me, walking into a classroom was a simultaneous exchange of ideas.

It is my conviction that one of the most effective ways of teaching is to bring the subject into the off-campus lives of students in a manner that is not banal. This truism was brought home to me as early as my army career, when we Ritchie Boys, during our preparation for the invasion, were instructed to teach our front troops some commands in German. The GIs listened closely. They knew that the enemy was deadly serious; many of the troops we would encounter were seasoned veterans. So in German the command "lay down your arms" might become a verbal weapon on which their lives depended.

Throughout my career, I continued to reinforce this belief in useful knowledge, even when the stakes weren't so high. At the University of Cincinnati we brought German culture to the campus when we invited a different guest professor from Germany each year. Our first choice was the aforementioned Heinz Starkulla Sr., a specialist in communications and media. He introduced the up-to-date language into our classes and social get-togethers, bringing colloquialisms into his class on German conversation. I remember him teach-

ing our undergraduates the phrase "das schnall ich nicht," which translates to
the English colloquialism, "I can't wrap my head around that." It's an expression the students learned very quickly.

Heinz Sr. had an incredibly easy way to get to know the townspeople
of Cincinnati. One of his new fans was a certain Stearns, an internationally known manufacturer of mattresses and other bedroom-related articles.
Knowing of my ambition to make culture accessible to students, Heinz persuaded Mr. Foster Stearns to sponsor a huge German Fasching (carnival) on
campus. We knew we had made a campuswide impression when John Major, our staid dean of Graduate Studies, and his wife showed up in vagabond
costumes.

My career as an occasional professor in Germany ran parallel to my days
as an educator in America. My first stint as a guest research professor in Germany was only sporadically conducive to encounters between a German-
Jewish-American professor and new generations of German students. In
1962 I was awarded a Fulbright Research Professorship at the University of
Munich to complete a history of a defunct German literary magazine once
published in Munich. I had no teaching obligations but was occasionally
sought out for guest lectures, since in contrast to my German colleagues, I
had introduced up-to-the-minute texts into even my undergraduate courses
on Modern German literature, especially of Die Gruppe 47 (Group 47), a
postwar writers' coalition. Similar courses and seminars at the University of
Munich—hard to believe—stopped with Gerhart Hauptmann and the pre-
war Thomas Mann. Professor Hermann Kunisch, my Fulbright-appointed
liaison colleague, was already occupied with writing and editing the first
handbook to include the postwar generation of writers. In the meantime he
asked me to step into the breach with his seminar schedule. He scheduled
my first lecture, a survey of texts just published, at the university's huge auditorium, where about a thousand students— more than I had ever enjoyed
before—showed up. Among them were two young journalism students: Peter Glotz, in years to come a breath of heady intellectual air to waft through
the Social Democratic Party; and Wolfgang Langenbucher, today the head
of the Journalism Department at the University of Vienna. In later years, the
two would collaborate on a pioneering study, *Versäumte Lektionen* (Missed
Object Lessons).

During a subsequent chance encounter, the two young men introduced themselves to me and I listened to their polite plaudits and liberal sentiments. Then I did a double-take on the name Langenbucher. My mind had dredged up memories of a loathsome, fascistic, anti-Semitic history of German literature published in 1939. I had sampled it, with growing revulsion, during my time as a graduate student at Columbia. "Are you related to Helmut Langenbucher?" I asked.

"Yes," Wolfgang answered, "unfortunately he is my father."

"How do you communicate? You seem to stand at completely opposite ends of the political spectrum."

"We meet from time to time," the son answered, "but we have nothing to say to each other."

That same year I met Emil Pretorius—artist, stage designer, art historian, and art collector. A whole gallery in the Chinese collection of the Neue Pinakothek in the Schwabing artist district of Munich is named after him. I had sought him out because he had been a friend of Efraim Frisch, the editor of the *Neue Merkur* (the object of my research), and an occasional contributor to the journal. Especially after it emerged that I, like Frisch, was Jewish, my interview with him turned into a lengthy attempt at exculpation on his part. "No," he declaimed in righteous indignation, "the photos taken of me with Hitler in front of my Bayreuth stage designs were falsely interpreted as my approval of National Socialism." As his expiation continued, I began to realize that in his eyes I had become the alter ego of Efraim Frisch. His implied confession delivered to me might have been the words he would have spoken to his friend, if Frisch had not died in 1942 during his exile in Switzerland.

This kind of encounter with a person with a sullied past repeated itself several more times. Following my Fulbright year, I served three successive summer lectureships at the Munich Goethe Institute. After a concurrent lecture at the America House, arranged by its then director, James Fifield Crane, I made the acquaintance of a young woman, an editor at a Munich publishing house. She and her escort invited me for dinner. During our lighthearted dinner conversation about books and music and art, I innocently asked whether her father was in the same publishing profession.

"That Nazi swine is dead to me," she answered. Apparently he had held a high position in the Reichssicherheitshauptamt, Germany's feared Central Security Office, headed by SS leader Heinrich Himmler.

"And your mother?" I interjected in an awkward attempt to change the subject.

"I don't talk to her, that Nazi!"

A dramatic tale of a generational divide unfolded. Her brother, equally repulsed by his parents' abject role during the Nazi years, had one day broken open a locked drawer in his father's desk. He found stacks of incriminating material. Without hesitation he sent it to the head of war crimes prosecution in Israel. He received a quick answer: "We know all about your father's activities. We do not plan to prosecute."

Nothing approaching that level of drama happened in my Goethe Institute seminar for in-service professionals in the Kaulbach Strasse in Munich. Rather, what stands out is the fact that I was handed a very practical lesson in reception theory. We were analyzing Heinrich Böll's short story "Mein trauriges Gesicht" ("My Sad Face"), a tale of the protagonist's torture by the police of an unnamed dictatorship. He had displayed an unhappy visage on a day when, to the contrary, he should have been overjoyed, because it was the day of the week when he had the privilege of partaking in the pleasures provided by the state-administered bordello. "Böll," I lectured, "has invented a perfect symbol to show how dictatorships control us even down to our most elemental drives." A teacher from Taiwan raised his hand. "I disagree. That is not invention. I fled to Formosa after serving in the army of Communist mainland China. That's exactly how the army bordellos are administered. Böll drew on reality."

My first university guest teaching assignment took place at the University of Freiburg. The overwhelming majority of my students during that short Freiburg summer term were students from abroad. My assignment consisted of a Vorlesung (lecture class) on the reception in the US of postwar German writers. It was a time, the late seventies, when the German political cabaret had regained much of the luster it had attained in the twenties. Despite my demurrers, pointing to Tom Lehrer and Second City, the students astutely noticed that an appreciation of political satire, imported or domestic, is not our American strong suit, with some notable exceptions as of this writing.

My guest professorship at the University of Frankfurt was a semester-long love affair. Rarely have I felt the eros of teaching and learning more as a force in my career. For the most part the explanation for that intellectual bonding resided with the subject matter. Four hundred students participated in a course titled "Introduction to German Exile Literature," very rarely taught before at German universities. The students told me they felt they had embarked on a journey of discovery. Also, about fifty students took part in a seminar on postwar German-Jewish authors; they all produced reports and seminar papers. Because of rather forbidding prerequisites, a smaller group of only about a dozen enrolled in my third course, a Thomas Mann colloquium.

A whole bevy of subsequent M.A. and Ph.D. theses emanated from those classes, with several published afterward, which also happened after my later guest stints at other German universities. I took this as an indication that Exile Studies were making their way in Germany. I can also recall two cheering incidents: As best I know, Daniel or Danny Lieberberg was the only Jewish student in my seminar, or at least the only one who openly made reference to his religion. He was both bright and voluble. Occasionally he would assume that he was privy to superior knowledge because of his background. But that did not save him from rebuttals by his fellow students. The dialogue grew into informed spontaneous debates, with my moderation almost uncalled for. I compared them with discussions that followed after those early guest lectures in 1962 in Munich. The contribution of a Jewish member of the audience had induced deference in earlier days by the non-Jewish discussants. I found the free-and-easy debate following Danny's remarks to be a healthy step forward.

As to the second cheering episode, Nora Müller (I am using real names in these remarks) was the heroine of this extraordinary occurrence. When I gave out the assignments for oral presentations in my seminar, I suggested Rafael Seligmann's novel *Die Jiddische Mamme* (*The Jewish Mom*) to Nora, but I warned her that the text contained quite a few risqué passages. As an adult person, she told me emphatically, she was prepared to deal with that. A week later I asked her to come to my office. Would she be willing to postpone her presentation by one week? Rafael Seligmann, I explained, had accepted my invitation to come to our last session. She could give her paper in front of the author himself. "Please give me time to think that one over," she answered. She returned two days later. "I will never have an opportunity like that during my entire years of study," she enthused, "to be critiqued by the author himself. Yes, I will do that!" Nora brought her boyfriend, an economics major, along for reinforcement, but she needn't have. Her paper was her best performance to date. And she had the gumption to say in front of Seligmann that some of his passages had veered into pornography, others into Jewish anti-Semitism.

I won't dwell on his counterattack on the pornography issue, but I was absolutely stunned by the give-and-take regarding anti-Semitism. Here was Israel-born, dyed-in-the-wool Jew Rafael Seligmann, pitted against Nora Müller, born near Frankfurt, Germany, a Christian whose knowledge of Judaism stemmed almost exclusively from books. And she held her own. The story had several happy endings. Rafael Seligmann, usually prickly and contentious, inscribed one of his books to her, lauding her paper, and she showed it off during a sort of farewell party. Later, after receiving her degree, Nora sought and obtained a job at the Fritz Bauer Institute for Holocaust Studies and ultimately gained a position with a Frankfurt newspaper.

My Frankfurt semester also afforded me an unusual chance to apply my theory that a classroom should be a clashroom, because controversy is the lifeblood of an academic environment, as it is of a newspaper. One of my favorite paradigms of exile literature had been challenged by a fellow specialist, Helmut Müssener, of the University of Stockholm. Helmut, a good friend, was unable to accept my invitation for a debate before my class. And so I hit on a (rather ingenious I thought) substitute scenario. My greatly gifted student assistant Martin Spieles, then in his last semester at Frankfurt and shortly before joining the S. Fischer Publishing House, assumed the role of the absent challenger. He immersed himself in Müssener's counterargument and we clashed point-counterpoint fashion. Soon my students entered the fray on either side, tremendously enjoying themselves by testing their own acumen against ours and exercising their cerebral matter to the fullest.

I don't remember much about a lecture I gave that semester at the newly built Jewish Community Center in Frankfurt. But I remember with utmost clarity an absolutely brilliant presentation a few weeks later. The speaker was Dr. Salomon Korn, the Center's architect and a member of the jury to select the best design for Berlin's Holocaust Memorial. He spoke on that aspect of

his career, about the design selection for the memorial. "Why is it so devil-
ishly difficult, apart from the politics of the task, to come to a satisfactory
resolution?" he asked. "Throughout the history of memorials, all monuments
were erected in celebration of a public figure or as an expression of a group's
or nation's exaltation or sorrow. But never before was one planned as the confession of national shame." His remarks went to the very core of the problem
of erecting a Holocaust statue in Germany. To that I can only add that I am
quite unhappy with the Peter Eisenmann Memorial in Berlin. He erected
rows upon rows of massive rectangular stone slabs (stolae). Their symbolism,
to me, is ambiguous or elusive.

What followed in the adventures of the itinerant and peripatetic Professor Stern were two invasions of the defunct German Democratic Republic.
Unlike the previous guest professorships, both were launched with the co-
sponsorship of Jewish organizations. The New York Leo Baeck Institute,
a well-known repository of German-Jewish history and culture, received a
major grant from Germany to send a Jewish-American professor to a former
GDR university, in order to help such institutions during their process of
transition. I was selected as the second of its emissaries and joined the German Department of the University of Leipzig in 1992. I accepted with a sense
of excitement and apprehension. Excitement, because I would be one of the
first Germanists to teach in the Eastern part of the newly reunited Germany,
apprehension because I wasn't sure how I would be received by the East German students. I feared that I would not be able to duplicate the rapport I had
enjoyed in Frankfurt.

Neither my expectations nor my fears were entirely matched by reality. The
students did not object to me at all; the eager debaters of Frankfurt had been
replaced by rows upon rows of zealous notetakers. During my second lecture
on exile, I decided to address the problem head-on. You are too goody-goody,
I thundered. And I presented in English my favorite adage about a classroom
being a clashroom. The god of teaching—I guess it is Mercury—be blessed,
it worked. Then my clarion call had an echo. The next day, my call for a more
rambunctious attitude appeared verbatim, amid nice comments in a daily, the
Leipziger Volkszeitung. A woman reporter had sneaked into the lecture hall,
together with the students, in order to take the measure of the exotic import
from America. The article by Claudia Würzburg was titled "A Provocateur

with a Sense of Humor," and it also called me "a professor with rolled-up shirt sleeves" who "spices his lecture with jokes [and] challenges the students to ask questions and to contradict him."

As my Leipzig semester unfolded, I learned that my guest department was deeply divided. On the one hand there were colleagues who had become willing or unwilling supporters of the Communist regime during the time of the rule of the so-called German Democratic Republic. After the reunification of Germany, they were told by the new democratic rulers that they could continue as professors for a short period (say, three years) and then would be retired. They obviously resented their pending dismissal. On the other hand, vacancies in the various departments were filled by arrivals from the former Western part of Germany, who were criticized for a lack of experience— start-ups, the Easterners called them, because of their deserting the Leipzig campus for the West even during brief national holidays. As an American I wasn't personally involved in the enmity of the two parties. But the peacemaker in me told me I should try my skills at this seemingly unsolvable conflict. I shared my thoughts with one of my colleagues, the late Professor Eilers. She jumped at the suggestion of easing tensions in the department. "I am on board!" she exclaimed. "I'm going to give a departmental party. East and West shall meet!"

She set out a buffet, which in reality was a feast. I was charged with contributing a humorous interlude. Virtually every member of the department streamed into her apartment. They provided, in microcosm, an image of a country in transition. The situation also indicated to me how a relatively short period of dictatorial rule can leave its deleterious imprint long after its demise.

Details tell the story. When Dr. Eilers urged her guests to take second portions, the "Westerners" accepted her invitation with alacrity and gusto. The "Easterners" had to be encouraged several times. After a polite period of hesitancy, they also succumbed. The informal dress of the "Wessies" stood out in contrast to the shirt and tie/blouse and skirt of their Eastern neighbors. About forty years of separation had allowed different manners and customs to bloom.

The contrast was emphasized again when I took on my assigned duties as entertainer and told a tall tale. I pretended that I had been at an archive in Düsseldorf devoted to the life and work of one of Germany's immortal authors, Heinrich Heine, and asked for the last edition of his poetry under his personal control. It was delivered to me, but "the binding," I said, "felt swollen. My curiosity was piqued." I continued, "I took out my trusted Swiss Army knife, opened the binding, and extracted several handwritten pieces of paper. They contained further verses of Heine's masterpiece, *Journey through the Harz Mountains*." A shocked silence all around! I started to recite, apparently from the manuscript pages. In Heine's style I produced satiric verses, each one mocking the foibles of one of my listeners.

What surprised me most about my experience in Germany at the time was the fact that the so-called Jewish question, despite my Leo Baeck sponsorship and despite the Jewish authors we were reading, rarely surfaced. I believe that in those first years after the fall of the Wall, a certain awkwardness vis-à-vis a subject so long ignored in the GDR still prevailed. My assumption was supported, certainly not entirely proven, during the one occasion when my Jewishness was catapulted into the realm of public consciousness. The university decided to designate a public address by me as its contribution to the Leipziger Jüdische Woche. My lecture on "Being Jewish in Today's Germany" went well enough; it was subsequently printed in a university journal and the first couple of questions, less than searching or profound, passed without a ripple. But the next one was unexpected. "How do you explain Jewish self-hate?" Fortunately I had read Sander Gilman's book on the subject, and I explained at some length that pariahs in all societies tend to absorb the calumnies of the majority and to apply them frequently to a subgroup within their own ranks. Yet the question attested to the poser's awkwardness when dealing with the Jewish experience. My impression was reinforced afterward by two West German colleagues, recently appointed to the department. "Die Frage paßte wie die Faust aufs Auge," one of them said. "That question was off the wall."

One more experience during that Leipzig week appeared to reify my impression of the East's slow learning process about Jewish matters. As its contribution to the Jewish week, the Gewandhaus (Orchestra Hall) featured a concert by the synagogal choir of Leipzig. The Hebrew melodies were flawlessly, even inspiringly sung and the house was filled to capacity, but I found out afterward that the synagogal choir did not number a single Jewish member among its singers. In all probability, Leipzig no longer numbered Jewish singers among its current inhabitants.

Concurrently with me, but exceeding my stay, the University of Leipzig invited the Austrian writer Joseph Haslinger as guest professor, arguably the most eloquent anti-Fascist in Austria and beyond. Hence the invitation carried with it a liberal commitment; his 1995 novel *Opernball* is a merciless dissection of Austrian flirtations with right-wingers. I first met with Joseph Haslinger in Chicago during an AATG meeting; the Austrian consul walked out on his lecture. We renewed acquaintances in Leipzig. "Here it is easy," he told me, "to rally students to squelch rightist demonstrations." Obviously neither he nor I was an infallible prophet.

The following year found me at the University of Potsdam. The Moses Mendelssohn Institute, one of the university's subsidiaries, was my sponsor—and Professor Julius Schoeps, the director of the program, became my boss. But our connection became much stronger through our lunchroom discussions. We felt at times like the successors to the age of Lessing and Mendelssohn. I wish I had a transcript of our lunchtime talks. One of his forefathers, a battle-scarred and -starred medic during World War I, had been rewarded by having a garrison in my hometown of Hildesheim become the bearer of his name. Of course, that name plaque was forcibly removed during World War II.

The same rapport marked my association with the "second in command" of the Institute. Professor Wolfgang Hempel kept my senses ever active. Our discussions had mostly to do with the future of a new Germany. But he played a far more important and personal role in my life—as he did for so many others. At least half of the new acquaintances and friendships I struck up in Germany were of his making! I joined a team determined to devote a Festschrift (a commemorative publication) to him subtitled "A Weaver of Nets." He had brought many people together. He even played a vital role in the introduction to my third wife.

From my base in Potsdam I was occasionally removed upon instructions from the head of the Kurt Weill Foundation, Kim Kowalke. I made frequent side trips to Chemnitz as a consultant to that city's opera company. I was lend-ing a hand, as I have detailed elsewhere, to the revival and German premier of Weill/Werfel's biblical drama *Der Weg der Verheißung* (*The Eternal Road*).

Also, I was invited, as a sort of an appendix to my guest professorship, to give one of the dedicatory speeches for the new synagogue in Dresden on November 9, 2001. The community leaders and the city fathers had scheduled an open house after the official opening. Judy and I could not believe what we saw. Propelled by curiosity, civic pride, and—as newspapers reported—the desire to counter recurring signs of prejudice, the line on that cold November day stretched from the synagogue and community-house complex to the River Elbe. The average wait, it was estimated, was two hours. And I lectured to a full house at a nearby art gallery.

In many respects my semester at the University of Potsdam replicated my Leipzig experience. Yet it produced one of the most emotional moments of my teaching career. I had arranged for our seminar on postwar German-Jewish writers to visit a dramatization of the memoirs of Inge Deutschkron, titled *I Wore the Yellow Star*. By way of preparation, I had asked Mrs. Deutschkron to guest lecture to our students. In an hour and a half she won our hearts with the recollection of her flight with her mother from one hiding place in Berlin to another to escape deportation to the Nazi death camps. Shortly afterward, we went to the Grips Theater, the most prestigious youth theater in Germany, where a superb actress played the adolescent Inge. The students saw an individual fate, a mother and daughter belabored and persecuted right within their own neighborhoods. After the play, as arranged, we stayed in the theater to meet Volker Ludwig, the play's director. He did all the talking. The students and I were too busy using Kleenexes and handkerchiefs.

I should like to conclude with a report on my hitherto last guest professorship, years ago at the University of Munich. It constitutes a kind of musical coda, in which, fleetingly, the old themes reemerge. Two departments, Germanistics and Communications, had joined forces to get a grant from DAAD (Deutscher Akademischer Austauschdienst), roughly comparable to an NEH grant, for my services. When a prestigious Mercador fellowship came through, both departments claimed their hold on me. Not to dwell too much on that toilsome semester, let me just mention that I taught a full program for both of them with huge enrollments: before being split up with my colleague and (occasionally combative) friend Heinz Starkulla Jr., one seminar numbered ninety students. Again, a plethora of master's and doctoral theses grew out of those courses. And then again, one of the authors under discussion, Arno Reinfrank this time, attended a seminar. My seminars usually concluded amid wine and pizza at an outdoor restaurant. At the end of the semester, Dean Hans Wagner asked me to hold a student-faculty colloquium and, as a final gesture, issued an invitation to repeat all that in the following year. I was asked to give the major address at the Colloquium of the Social Studies Division of the University at the end of the semester. As my subject I chose "Nichtjüdische Deutsche von heute im Dienste jüdischer Anliegen" (Non-Jewish Germans of Today in the Service of Jewish Causes). I ended my speech with a lyrical commendation of all men and women of goodwill, words borrowed from a poem by Hilde Domin.

Wer den Hund zurückbeißt	The one who bites the biting dog
Wer auf den Kopf der Schlange tritt	The one who crushes the snake's head
Wer dem Kaiman die Augen zuhält	The one who blindfolds the caiman
Der ist in Ordnung.	That one is on the right side.

With Mom (Hedwig), 1922

With Grandfather Israel
Silberberg, 1926

With Werner (younger brother), 1927

With Werner, 1928

My parents, Julius and
Hedwig, with my siblings,
Werner and Eleonore, 1938

Cousin Marianne and Grandmother Rebekka Silberberg, around 1936

At far left wearing a vest, with my fellow members of the youth group of the Hildesheim Jewish community in 1936 on a bicycle tour

Far right with my fellow members of the youth group on a hike, including Cantor Cysner (third from left under the tree) and Gerda Schönenberg (standing on the left), early 1937

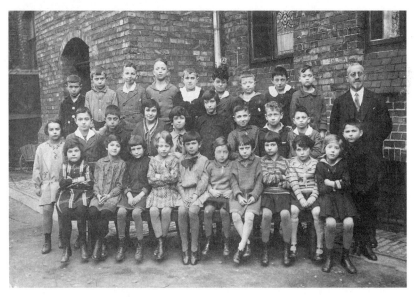

Oskar Stern, teacher at Jewish Elementary School in Hildesheim, and Werner Stern (top row, second from right)

On the far right, at the Picadilly Room at the Melbourne Hotel, 1939

My naturalization document

Entering the Army
at Fort Leavenworth,
KS, Fall 1942

Camp Ritchie entrance, 1944

Interrogation in Belgium,
Winter, 1944

First Army Headquarters Interrogation Teams, 1944

As an accordion player, 1945

The Ritchie Boys: Guy Stern (left), Lt. Walter Sears (middle), Fred Howard (right), Victory in Europe Day, 1945

After homecoming in St. Louis, 1946

On the day of my wedding to Margith (1948), with
Uncle Benno and Aunt Ethel

University of Cincinnati, 1981 costume ball. Second from the left is Heinz Starkulla Sr. I am third from the left.

German Embassy, Washington, D.C., 1972, when I was awarded the Order of Merit of the Federal Republic of Germany, shaking hands with Ambassador Rolf Friedemann Pauls

2nd Festschrift in Munich, 2005, with Professor Barbara Mahlmann-Bauer and
Professor Konrad Feilchenfeldt, Germanists and editors

WSU members of German Slavic Department. Alfred Cobbs, me, Marvin and
Roz Schindler, Mark Ferguson, Donald Haase (back row)

At the Aspen Institute as a participant

At the Chemnitz Opera House (Germany), 1999

The growing WSU Academy of Scholars, 2010

My son, Mark, around
three years old

My wedding to Judy, July 19, 1979, with Rabbi Dannel Schwartz and
Judge Damon Keith

With Mark at my wedding to Judy

With Judy in Italy, 1990s

With Judy at the premiere of *The Eternal Road*, 1999

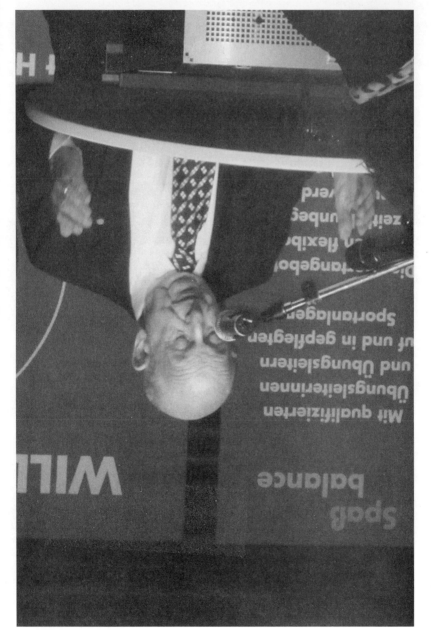

In Hildesheim, celebrating the Annual Festival of Eintracht
(and my honorary Eintracht membership)

With prominent German authors Günter Grass (right) and Uwe Johnson (center) at the University of Cincinnati, May 1965

With Christian Bauer, Toronto Documentary Film Festival opening of *The Ritchie Boys*, 2004

Fellow Ritchie Boy Fred Howard, video producer Sabine Anton, Christian Bauer, and me at the opening of the film, 2004

With past director Stephen Goldman during the Ritchie Boys Exhibit at the Holocaust Memorial Center, 2011. Photo credit: Holocaust Memorial Center

With Susanna on our first vacation together. Recloses, France, August 5, 2004 (photo by Ingrid Fiedler)

Attending a wedding with Susanna, July 25, 2009 (photo by Joshua Nowicki)

With Susanna in a typical "winter picture," January 2016 (photo by Karen Melaas)

At the Eisenhower Library, Abilene, KS, for Victory in Europe Day, 2014

Same time and place as above, but only army officers and guards are shown

In Germany with high school students, 2018

With Poet Laureate Rita Dove and her husband, German author Fred Viebahn, at the Holocaust Memorial Center, July 2017

University of Michigan Homecoming Game, Veteran of the Game, October 2018

Le Professeur Guy Stern
Visite en Normandie
Le 25 Mai 2016

Visiting Normandy, May 25, 2016 (photo by Sabina Lorkin)

CHAPTER EIGHT

Research and Scholarship

AS I WAS CLIMBING the rungs of academia, moving from undergraduate instruction to a combination of graduate and upper-level undergraduate teaching, I had a chance to carry my insights gained from scholarship into the classroom. To me that is one of the main reasons for staying active as a scholar. It is fair to demand of a professor that he/she be a competent teacher, a role model and mentor, and a publishing scholar. The adage "Publish or Perish" is often shamefacedly owned up to as an incentive to activate pen, typewriter, or computer. I gladly confess that though I have been mostly self-propelled, the "P or P" warnings of my professors also reverberated in my mind upon occasion.

I need no epiphany to realize why I am a self-motivated workaholic in my research. There, as in so many other activities, I have the survivor syndrome. As I have defined that characteristic elsewhere, it means that the survivor of a catastrophe feels the need to justify his or her continued existence. In my research I have been allowed to pursue two specialties in my field that combine my intellectual, professional, and personal interests. In part they define who I am. I think of myself as a "descendant" of the Age of Enlightenment. In the eighteenth century, European thinkers, writers, and artists were convinced that rational thinking could advance human progress. By virtue of reasoning and "humanitas," we could walk from darkness and delusion to humane morality and behavior and intellectual insights. Among many others Voltaire in France, Hume and Locke in England, and Lessing and Mendelssohn in Germany were the initiators and promulgators of that philosophy. In graduate school I read their works, enrolled in seminars on the Enlightenment, and started explicating their theories and creative works. Several chapters in my dissertation dealt with Christoph Martin Wieland, one of the German pioneers of the movement. When I became a department head and dean at the University of Cincinnati, I used my prerogatives as an administrator to create a monument to the most distinguished representative of German Enlightenment, Gotthold Ephraim Lessing. I convinced the academic leaders of my university and of the Cincinnati University Press to authorize and partially finance the publication of the *Lessing Yearbook*, as of this writing in the fifty-third year of its publication. I found a collaborator among the colleagues in my German Department. Gottfried F. Merkel, our director of Graduate Studies, became the cofounder of the *Yearbook* and the Society.

It was a happy collaboration and an exciting time for us all. Merkel had become an aficionado of Lessing primarily out of local patriotism. He gloried in the fact that both he and the philosopher had grown up in Saxony and had studied at the University of Leipzig. As for me, an exile from Germany, I had turned to Lessing at a time when his message was being howled down by Nazi barbarians and his drama *Nathan der Weise* (*Nathan the Wise*) banished from German stages. Later I had rejoiced when I, a Fulbright professor in Munich in the early 1960s, saw the play's resurrection in a deeply moving, exhilarating performance by the German-Jewish actor Ernst Deutsch in the title role. Although traveling different paths, Gottfried Merkel and I had arrived at the same destination as admirers of one of our cultural heroes. Yet a project such as ours required, of course, many fostering parents. If Gottfried and I were avowed disciples of Lessing, so were two of our American-born colleagues, Jerry Glenn and Edward Paxton Harris. But they were imbued with the spirit of Lessing's American contemporary and think-alike, Benjamin Franklin. As the masterly managing editors of the early volumes, their enthusiastic ideas, together with those of other members of the department, including our guest professor from Freiburg, Wolfram Mauser, became invaluable.

I tried to recapture that creative spirit when I was asked to chronicle the *Yearbook*'s first ten years. In his foreword Wolfgang Mauser supplied a summary of the *Yearbook*'s achievements, and I brought in those of longtime editor Richard Schade.

The impeccable scholarship of the *Yearbook* helped solidify the reputation of Germanistics. It would be too facile to say that German, Austrian, and Swiss schools at one time had a "colonial" attitude toward scholarship from abroad. But the assumption that colleagues in other countries were but the younger siblings of the older European brothers and sisters persisted for a long time. With the continuity of the cutting-edge Enlightenment research of the society and the equally distinguished work by other American societies that the Cincinnati model sometimes spawned, it has become increasingly difficult to maintain a superior attitude.

The Society and the *Yearbook* also became a bridge-builder through the various symposiums it sponsored; Cincinnati became a vortex of eighteenth-century studies for scholars from three continents. Through those initiatives the severed ties between Lessing's home country and those of his worldwide admirers became refashioned.

Our department sponsored several conferences on Lessing that engendered their own brand of excitement. We were surprised and elated when our invitation to a Lessing expert from East Germany was accepted. He later told us that he ran a gauntlet of initial bureaucratic objections, all of them rooted in the Communist reluctance to deal with those capitalists across the ocean.

Four colleagues from West Germany had no such difficulties, of course; but they created their own. We had advised them that the papers to be presented had to conform to the time constraints we had set for each speaker. Apparently they had paid little heed to that admonition, which became obvious on the second day of the conference. Our East German guests had been able to observe our strict enforcement of the time limitations. The next morning the West German crew appeared early, ensconced themselves in the rear of the lecture hall, and began to eliminate major portions of their planned readings. We couldn't resist a pun. We called them "The German Streichquartett," which on its obvious level means string quartet but also can suggest four string players striking away at excessive verbiage.

At the end of the conference, we organized a party in the faculty dining room. I was to give a speech, but I thought that wouldn't really project the abundance of ideas that had sprung up during the preceding two and a half days. I knew our scholarly president would show up and so I gave a speech called "A Report to Our President," in which I gave a thumbnail sketch of all the papers offered at the conference. Warren Bennis, with his vise-like mind, surprised our audience with his reaction to some of the papers whose synopsis I had presented. He also termed my report a new form of nonfiction writing. Of course, he made every participant at the conference feel like a pioneering intellectual. For a while I was similarly deluded.

Even our undergraduates caught the Lessing bug. Jan Unna, one of our majors, returned from a trip to Europe, and on his first day on campus he headed straight for my office, holding a mysterious package. He ceremoniously peeled off the covers and unveiled a plaster cast of a famous statue of Lessing. He had spotted it in an antique store. A photograph of his discovery graced the cover of the first twenty or so *Yearbook*s.

I was in Munich that summer of 1968 and decided to visit Ernst Hueber, the second-generation owner of the Max Hueber Publishing House and an old friend. Ernst combined in his character a kaleidoscope of contradictory traits. He was a devout Catholic and also a staunch supporter of the Social Democratic Party and other liberal causes. He made all major decisions on his own but was one of the first businessmen to build a worker's health facility at company headquarters. He cultivated all the "right" people while building his rather small firm into one of Germany's largest textbook houses. Nevertheless he would readily invite a struggling young instructor from Poland or an ancient refugee intellectual who had returned to Germany to his informal dinner parties. He hated all wars. Small wonder that he loved Lessing.

Aaron Salomon Gumperz said of Lessing that he brought clarity to every branch of knowledge. That illumination, I believe, benefited all those who have tried to preserve Lessing's legacy, from the early progenitors to those who are his current champions at the Lessing *Yearbook* and the Lessing Society. The spirit of Lessing left its mark on all of us.

It is scarcely surprising that over time my second field of specialization was to become the study of exile and of exile literature. My time in uniform and my unplanned relocation to New York in search of a post with the *New York Times* had been my passport to a different world, a world in the making pastiched with "unfinished stories," to quote the title of an exilic drama by the playwright Sybil Pearson. Through my assignment to Ritchie, I had met

Stefan Heym, a German author in exile; through my friend Karl Frucht, I had met a whole bevy of artists and writers, such as the painter George Gross and the writer Walter Mehring. And then I looked in the mirror and asked myself, wasn't I one of them, my fate with a double dose of hubris, perhaps by potential?

Unfortunately, I must recall that the hubris was deftly extinguished by a one-sentence book dedication by my friend Hertha Pauli. Having risen to the heights of feature editor of the Hofstra University *Chronicle,* I had been feeling my oats. Vanity beckoned and I started to write poetry and had the temerity to show the results to Hertha. She did not comment but went to a bookshelf for a copy of one of her publications. She scribbled a dedication for me: "To a very gifted editor." I got the message.

I did not fare much better when she allowed me to escort her to a concert featuring her uncle, the legendary pianist Artur Schnabel, at Carnegie Hall. I had lobbied her to introduce me to Schnabel; I wanted to include remarks by him in a term paper for my music appreciation class. Before the concert I researched Schnabel to a fare-thee-well. Finally, I stood with Hertha before greatness. I felt I had to ingratiate myself. "If I may," I said in German, "I have one or two questions. I know your background, of course, maestro. You come from the Steiermark in Austria."

I got no further than that. "Hold on, young man. Bad research. You, as many others, are the victim of a name confusion. I come from Styria in Galicia, a city which American biographers confuse with Styria, Steiermark. In Styria the people yodel. We don't." The great man had a sense of humor, even if it was at my expense.

These and other small revelations about the exile writers and artists, though not published, became the spice of my exile courses and seminars here and abroad. It was also a way to personalize the study of exile literature, to wed research and teaching. To my mind such a personalized approach is indicated, since the individual travails of flight and exile were so often the catalysts for creativity. Furthermore, when teaching in Germany, this personal approach was also the key to a more perceptive reception on the part of my students.

I began asking myself why many of the exile writers, whom I met through my new contacts, were scarcely mentioned in American publications, and I became convinced that it was our task to keep alive the writings of those who tried to rekindle the past German cultural tradition in their country of asylum. When I entered Columbia as a graduate student, I made the first deferential suggestion that the department might wish to introduce a course on exile literature. Henry Hatfield liked the idea. As I mentioned earlier, his seminar on the exile writer Thomas Mann had drawn a record number of students, many of them from beyond the German Department, and had he not left for Harvard, he might well have followed it up with a class on Brecht. The textbook production at Columbia's German Department—for example, those by Jack Stein and by the collaborators Gustave Mathieu and me—also sparkled with the texts of exilic writers. As I learned quickly, we were by no means the first ones to champion this novel field of research. The exiles themselves had broken down some of the doors that routinely opposed innovations in the once super conservative field of Germanistics.

Those early proponents and we, their successors, persisted. However, the motives of us younger scholars were more diverse. Having accompanied my fellow scholars on their scholarly journey, I can, with a reasonable hope of success, guess at their individual motives, which I believe were widespread. For example, I infer from his writings that my colleague John Spalek was motivated by the exile fate of his Polish countryman, Jan Wittlin. Wulf Koepke, dedicated to restoring the wholeness of German culture while a department head at the Goethe Institute, gained a further incentive through his friendship with a Jewish Holocaust survivor, who would become his wife. Egon Schwarz could not and would not accept the forcible severance from his Austrian cultural heritage. Oskar Seidlin became a devotee of a single great exile author, Thomas Mann. Similarly, Harold von Hofe became a scholar and advocate of Lion Feuchtwanger; Dagmar Barnouw and, later, Dagmar Lorenz highlighted the creative works of women writers in exile. And some—like Käte Hamburger—let it be known that they resented the slighting of the exiles by the first German postwar literary historians and therefore doubled their efforts on behalf of the refugee authors. But we all felt that it was our task (and continues to be so) to keep alive the works of the exile writers. They had stood up under the most adverse conditions, as defenses against the debasement of the German cultural tradition.

I have also come to reexamine my own attraction to the oeuvre of a younger generation of exiles. Some of them, like me, felt like exiles when they visited or returned to their hometown in Germany. A gradual estrangement had set in. Or, put differently, the world in which we had grown up and had loved had left us rather than the reverse.

My past vision of a yearlong course on exile writing didn't come to fruition until I became "the boss" of a department at the University of Cincinnati and could bring along the standard definition of the subject. That was easy. Exile literature, I repeated, is the literature written by writers driven out of their native countries by tyrants and dictators. At first this umbrella definition was applied solely to those men and women who were persecuted by the rule of the Nazis. Later we would add the definition globally and include as well those in hiding or still tolerated because they were exercising self-censorship. We are still in the process of thinking through whether to include some expatriates and "internal exiles" in that honorary fraternity of "exile writers." The thought struck me after a conversation with the African American writer James Baldwin. He rejected the label "expatriate," applied to him after his move to Paris. "I was driven out," he said. "A minority of racists deprived me of my creativity while I was in the US." The tyranny of a fraction of ideologues can cause a creative person to seek a place of asylum.

Some colleagues, no doubt because of my somewhat advanced age, have labeled me "the Nestor of Exile Studies." I must reject that appellation, not only because the Nestor of the *Iliad* is afflicted with logorrhea but because my colleagues and I did not "invent" Exile Studies. Not surprisingly, the first interpreters were the exiles themselves. They explicated not only their own works but also those of their fellow exiles. When I started upon my investigations and attended forums and conferences, established writers, exiled from German-speaking or Nazi-dominated countries, were present—an added bonus for attending. At a conference in Stockholm I got to talk to Carl Zuckmayer, the author of one of the most successful postwar dramas, a play about one of Hitler's acquiescent air force generals. I met Günther Anders, an avowed pacifist writer, in Vienna; Hilde Spiel, an eloquent novelist about the Nazi past, on my own campus in Cincinnati; and Wieland Herzfelde (Heartfield) in Copenhagen. The creative writers were followed by established scholars, often exiles themselves. One of the earliest advocates of Exile Studies was Walter Berendsohn, who had spent his exile years in Bromma, Sweden.

What then were the contributions of my generation of exile scholars? A group of three obsessed devotees found their way to one another and joined forces: John Spalek, a native of Poland; Joseph Strelka, an immigrant from Austria; and I, the refugee from Germany. We explored not only existing archives, such as the New York Leo Baeck Institute, but also private holdings. At a party I met a couple that in all innocence told me that they and their acquaintances owned whole bundles of letters from prominent exile writers. That correspondence became grist for my article-writing mill. John Spalek took the initiative of starting a series of volumes in which virtually every notable exile in the United States was explicated in article-length studies. He had little trouble attracting contributions. The excitement of being co-pioneers in a new sub-genre of literature was, I imagine, an irresistible attraction. We became the driving forces behind finding sponsors for conferences. We founded the American Society for Exile Studies. It still exists in full force and has spawned similar organizations in other countries.

When I am looking at some of the correspondence from that period—snail mail, of course—I recapture a sense of excitement. As with any new field, so many questions, so few answers. There were general concerns: when do the exile years of an author end? What are common themes in works born in exile, such as bemoaning a lost homeland? That latter theme accompanied exilic poetry from the times of the Jews' Babylonian captivity (example: "By the Waters of Babylon we sat and wept") till the modern, seer-like German writer Karl Wolfskehl, who exclaimed, "I am freezing somewhere in a far-off ocean." We wanted to delve into specific mysteries: Why did one of the most globally famous exile writers from Austria, Stefan Zweig, safe and appreciated in Brazil, commit suicide? Why did Joseph Goebbels order the kidnapping of one specific exile, a journalist, after he had reached asylum in France? Why was an exile novel by Salamon Dembitzer published only forty years after its completion? And how did courageous Martha Feuchtwanger manage to smuggle her husband, the novelist Lion Feuchtwanger, out of a French internment camp? We solved some of these knotty puzzles.

Forty or more years of Exile Studies now lie behind me. I have just proofread yet another article of mine about exile literature (this one about its future), part of an anthology. It is edited by Dr. Doerte Bischoff of the University of Hamburg, who belongs to a still younger generation of exile scholars. It is probably my last on the topic. At an MLA convention I had made a similar resolution after I had presented an analysis of an iconoclastic performance of Lessing's tragedy, *Emilia Galotti*, by the Deutsche Theater in Berlin. So far I have stuck to that resolution concerning Lessing and the Enlightenment.

As an illustration of my scholarly pursuits, I have lifted out two of my three favorite subjects. Occasionally, I have poached on the preserves of others. If I can blame anyone for that waywardness, it was the actress of stage and screen Lotte Lenya, the widow of the composer Kurt Weill and arguably the greatest interpreter of his songs. She drew me into her orbit, the world of music. My friend and colleague Gustave Mathieu and I had successfully turned Kurt Weill's correspondence concerning his composition for a music drama, *The Eternal Road*, into an adventuresome chronicle of the work's genesis. Lenya's new husband, the writer and editor George Davis, liked our chapter, "The Birth of a Broadway Play." The proof of his and Lenya's approbation came half a year later. Lenya had just returned from a trip to Germany; in her luggage she carried the first German recording of Weill and Brecht's polemical and satirical opera *The Rise and Fall of the City of Mahagonny*. Lenya had assembled a stellar cast in Berlin — with one of the leads, the prostitute Jenny, interpreted by her. Now George Davis was on the line. Lenya and he had selected me to write the first English translation of the work, which was scheduled to appear in an extensive brochure together with the 33-rpm recording by Columbia Masterworks. I was thrilled with the assignment, and also when the couple, shortly thereafter, commissioned me to produce a new literary translation of the earlier work *The Threepenny Opera*, also a synopsis, plus some rather scholarly commentaries on the work. I was no musicologist, yet I rushed in. Where I felt out of my depth, I harassed colleagues at Columbia University's Music Department for explanations.

Lenya, George Davis, and I became close friends, a valued friendship that continued beyond George's death and into Lenya's third marriage with the painter Russell Detweiler. She came to my son's Bar Mitzvah, visited FLES (Foreign Language in Elementary School) classes I had helped initiate at a

Cincinnati elementary school, and headed a local cast of performers when we, at UC's German Department, commemorated Weill's eightieth birthday in the largest campus auditorium. It was fun being with her. When we both found ourselves in the German state of Bavaria, we decided to visit the widow of Georg Kaiser, one of Germany's best-known dramatists prior to the Nazi takeover. She asked me to escort her to her performance at the triumphant opening night of the musical *Cabaret*, where I met several of her fellow actors. We met by chance in Vienna, where she confided in me that she had just consented to the marriage with Russell Detweiler. "Isn't that rather sudden?" I asked tactfully. Lotte replied, "Well, when somebody keeps after you night and day, what else can you say?"

During that stay in Vienna she also had her famous set-to with a female Viennese vegetable stand proprietor. When Lenya turned out to be rather choosy, the woman cursed her in a Viennese proletarian dialect inaccessible to anyone not a native, but Lenya heard and understood her. She replied in the same patois, retained from her childhood days. The woman apologized, "How was I to know that the lady in the fur coat was one of us?" At another time I took my advanced German class to Cleveland for Lenya's performance in the play *Brecht on Brecht*. She had my students in stitches when she added a line to the play at the end of one of her entrances, which was clearly addressed to her visitors from Cincinnati.

But the most palpable token of her trust in me came when she asked me to join the board of the Kurt Weill Foundation, which she had recently founded. She showed me a letter from her lawyer that described its goals.

"The purpose of the foundation will be to perpetuate Kurt's memory by promoting the use of his music and keeping alive an interest in his works. The foundation would have the power to exploit and publish Kurt's music, arrange concerts, award scholarships, give prizes, etc. In addition, I should think that the foundation might also have as one of its purposes the right to promote an interest in music generally."

Today the foundation has undertaken so many more activities, notably among them an annual Kurt Weill–Lotte Lenya Singing Contest, which has launched the careers of some outstanding performers here and abroad.

Judy and I visited Lenya during Lenya's final days. To our horror she was dying in the studio of a sculptress, one of her many friends and acquaintances. We also met her designated successor as president of the foundation, a young Weill scholar from Occidental College, Professor Kim Kowalke. He had concerns. He was being importuned by the new lawyer of the foundation, who had succeeded the author of the above-quoted mission statement. Kim needed an ally and asked me where we could counsel against the counsellor. In one meeting we learned to trust each other because our goals and ambitions were parallel to Lenya's.

Lenya's choice of Kim as a successor was inspired; her choice of me led at first only to my most ambitious excursion into autodidactisism—disciplined self-education. My education in Germany, high school courses in music and choral training in synagogal singing by Cantor Cysner, then classes in musical appreciation at Hofstra, coupled with frequent concert going, had lifted me a bit above musical illiteracy. But then, after Lenya's death, I attended my first Kurt Weill Board Meeting. I was surrounded by some of the most prestigious names in the world of music: Julius Rudel, conductor of the New York City Opera Company; Harold Prince, the producer/director of some of the best-known Broadway musical dramas; Kim Kowalke, later a department head at the famous Eastman School of Music; prize-winning musicologist Lys Symonette, Weill's rehearsal pianist—to give just a sample of the personages surrounding me and a highly abbreviated list of their achievements. I listened to their musical small talk. It was simply over my head.

My leisure reading turned to music. I learned how to read a piano vocal score, caught on to a "diminished fifth chord," and came to appreciate such experimenters as Stockhausen, Schönberg, and Glass. And then I dared write about some works of Weill, at first concentrating more on texts than notes. A few articles later, I wrote on some of Weill's musical offspring, for example the Belgian lyricist-composer Jacques Brel. When a French journal asked for permission to reprint the Brel piece, first submitted to a German journal, I knew I had arrived at the lowly peak of my musical expertise, but only by having Kim and Lys give my contribution a critical reading first. I quit writing on musical theater while I was ahead. Nowadays I am a most dedicated listener and still a devoted vice president of the Kurt Weill Foundation.

Perhaps in saying farewell to both research and teaching after fifty years of following their call, I feel I have erred on the side of self-congratulation. But then I checked with my bibliography to make sure I had omitted nothing vital. Any sense of pride vanished, drowned by the recurring question: "Did the world really need that article?" How could I have published a paper on an upstanding New England clergyman, but a decidedly lesser literary hero? In the files of a once prominent, now defunct Philadelphia publishing house, I found Charles Timothy Brooks's unpublished translation of poems of a scarcely more prominent German poet, August Kopisch. The poem "Blücher at the Rhine" is not far removed from the blood-and-guts variety of lyrics. I had traveled to Philadelphia in search of bigger booty. Now ill-placed persistence made me want to publish the Kopisch-Brooks "collaboration" as a poor substitute for my original treasure hunt. A dozen rejections did not discourage me. A new journal, probably in need of submissions, finally published it.

I also take no pride in an arch paper titled "How to Escape the Poorhouse. German among the Other Humanities: A Graduate Dean's Perspective." Had I, a mediocre manager, acquired the acumen of George Soros? To confirm that my financial expertise ranged somewhere between D+ and D–, I dredged up my first budget report as a department chair and submitted it to the dean of the College of Arts and Sciences at Cincinnati. "Professor Stern," Dean Weichert had said in a gravelly voice, "a budget report need not be poetic."

And why did I, of all people, decide to write a story about an important geographic discovery and illustrate it? With glee someone pointed out I had left the most important geographic feature, the McClure Strait, completely unmarked.

I have lifted out, in somewhat anecdotal fashion, some highlights that accompanied those fifty years of teaching and scholarship. Yet this chronicle is, of course, anything but complete. One omission is in my enumeration of my models. I should have mentioned my wife Judy as one of them. Occasionally, when I was teaching abroad, Judy would hop on a plane and surprise me by sitting demurely in my huge lecture hall. One time I turned the tables on her. I had accepted an invitation to speak to the joint English classes of my former high school in Hildesheim. Judy had arrived a few hours before and I

ter became, across the decade, a close friendship, and I considered myself almost a member of the family of Ute and Dieter and their three sons, rapidly
outgrowing adolescence. Now Ute and I were sitting across the table from
each other at a museum of arts and crafts she had initiated. We were enjoying
the obligatory German tea and coffee hour, replete with calorie-filled cakes
and cookies. "Ute," I said, confessing this feeling for the first time, "I have
mourned Judy now for about a year. I think I am ready for another meaningful and lasting relationship." I met Susanna the next day. And that calls
for another chapter, because with that meeting life and writing became one.

CHAPTER NINE

Susanna

I T WAS BASHERT," MY Yiddish-speaking friends would exclaim. As a devotee of American musicals, I would sing the familiar words from Rodgers and Hammerstein's *South Pacific* when recalling our first meeting. In our case, the crowded room was located in the Westphalian town of Minden, a city familiar to me since boyhood. It is only a few miles distant from Vlotho—my grandparents' home, my mother's birthplace. During my early years, my uncle Max had repeatedly taken me along on his business trips from Vlotho to Minden. At that time car rides were still a treat for a youngster, so I remember them well. Now my friend and colleague, Professor Wolfgang Hempel, who is also a native of Minden (the plot thickens), arranged for me to lecture before the Minden Literary Society as a way-stop on an ambitious speaking tour across Germany and the Netherlands.

The room was crowded; my subject, "The Image of Germany in Contemporary American Literature," apparently had appeal. In the second row, I spotted a very nice-looking lady, and I must confess that I addressed some of the choice passages of my lecture in her direction. She was all attention and, gratifyingly enough, joined unrestrainedly in the general laughter, provoked by my jokes. Some astute questions followed my lecture, one from the lady who had caught my attention.

The event's sponsor, a formidable persona and wife of a Protestant minister, met me at the lectern after my speech and supplemented her complimentary remarks with the expeditious presentation of a check. Then she added an invitation: A reception was planned in my honor at a local restaurant, just a small circle, and would I join? I knew the routine; it would probably be quite formal and stiff. Sensing my hesitation, she made an alternative suggestion: "It's such a lovely evening. Perhaps you would rather like to sit on our back porch and enjoy a Prosecco?" "Of course, let's go to your house," I replied.

To my utter delight, Mrs. Hirschberg had also invited the lady from the audience, who turned out to be a writer and had been invited to read from her short stories just one evening before. Soon after my arrival, snacks and drinks were served—and then fate proffered a hand! On the back porch, the writer was placed kitty-cornered to me at a table and introduced herself as Susanna. She had blond hair, green eyes, and a beautiful smile.

We started talking; the subjects were a potpourri. I mentioned Kurt Weill and she responded with an enthusiastic endorsement of the *Threepenny Opera*. She lobbed a reference to the Thomas Mann novel *Doctor Faustus* in my direction; I volleyed back with a quotation from the masterwork. And so it went the whole evening. We shamelessly monopolized each other. With every passing minute, I increasingly felt that something very special was happening.

When I asked Susanna about her professional background, she told me that she had studied law for some years but then had switched to researching language learning and teaching. Her minors at college had been American Studies and the History of North America—how convenient for making headway with her, I thought. After working and teaching at a university in the nineties, she attended a journalism school and became a broadcast editor. In her free time, she wrote a desk-drawer full of short stories and poems, many subsequently published in well-known journals. For her freelance work at a broadcast station, she had to write many book reviews as well, something that she even now loves to do.

Somewhere during that ebb and flow of conversation, I mentioned that I wore my wedding ring out of piety for my late wife. Susanna mentioned that she was divorced many years ago.

As I learned later, she had been a reluctant attendee at my lecture, but her good friend and host, Gottfried Weidelhofer, persuaded her to come anyway: that American professor might not be utterly dull.

At the end of the reception, we got up and hugged. Susanna offered to chauffeur Wolfgang Hempel and me to our hotel. On the way to her car, I started humming an aria from Mozart's *Don Giovanni*: "Là ci darem la mano" ("There we will give each other our hands"). Immediately, even though I was just humming the tune, Susanna remarked that this was a very nice song with especially beautiful lyrics. "I knew you'd understand me," I exclaimed happily and added: "I have to see you again! Can you come to my hotel tomorrow morning for breakfast?" With a big smile, she assented.

"How did you sleep?" I asked Susanna the next morning in the lobby. She answered with a German equivalent to our American "like a log." Suddenly she blurted out, "I have to make a retraction—I didn't sleep a wink last night. The evening was simply too exciting!" It made me happy to hear her say that. I complimented her for her honesty, took her hand, and led her to our table (or I should say, rather, to my table, since Wolfgang discreetly failed to show up for the scheduled breakfast). I didn't let go of her hand when we sat down but looked deeply into her eyes and joyfully made a confession that would change my life: "I love you."

She stared at me in disbelief. "You don't waste any time, do you?"

"No, not at my age."

She looked at me for what seemed to be endless moments before she finally said, "I love you, too."

"I am taking a train to Amsterdam this morning, but I will return to Germany, to Heidelberg to be precise, next week. Any chance of a further meeting?"

Susanna assented once more.

After dropping Wolfgang and me at the railway station, Susanna, as she was later to confide, had called her mother in Bochum, telling her that she had met the man of her life. Hinting at her daughter's former marriage, Ingrid had just one comment: "Again?"

A week later I met Susanna in Heidelberg, touted by many as the most romantic town in Germany. Two months later I visited Susanna again and this time had a chance to also spend some time with her wonderful mother, who had been a kindergarten teacher for some decades. We got along very well right from the start. When Susanna later asked her about her impression of me, she answered kindly but bluntly: "That's a very nice, likable fellow. But for me he would be too old."

Our first trip abroad led us to France, where we stayed with a friend of mine before we traveled to Austria. The board of the Kurt Weill Foundation had been invited to the Bregenz Music Festival, where Weill's early works took center stage. Neither Susanna nor I had ever been present at this, one of the most spectacular stages in the world. Enchantment gripped us as we viewed the open-air stage, which jutted out into the Austrian waters of Lake Constance. A recent travelogue by the Italian photojournalist Simone Zanetti expresses it all. It almost sounds as if she had seen the two of us sitting among like-minded concertgoers:

> Can you imagine spending a romantic warm summer night with your sweetheart listening to a beautiful performance of classical music like opera, operetta, or musical? If you have not experienced this yet, I urge you to do it at least once. Maybe you want to surprise your special one with tickets to an open-air performance this year.
>
> It is an unbelievable feeling to sit under the open sky not confined to an opera house or concert hall. Just visualize sitting under a blanket of stars, the moon is shining and you feel a cool breeze on your face and you cuddle with your sweetheart while taking in beautiful sounds—that is what it is like to be part of an open-air performance at the Arena in Verona, Italy, the Festivals in Bregenz at Lake Constance or at Moerbisch (Lake Neusiedl) in Austria.

As befitting me, then secretary of the foundation bearing Weill's name, I found the performance of his *Seven Deadly Sins* to be the highlight of the week of love and music. Susanna, who had seen Bernstein's *West Side Story* several times and had cheerfully "conducted" a recording of it since childhood, declared she would never see a more enchanting production than the one in Bregenz. The experience was complete bliss for us two music lovers!

This trip also provided Susanna with an opportunity to meet the few remaining members of my family. My cousins once removed, Mario and Claudio Stern, whose father, Heinz, and grandfather David had the foresight to depart Nazi Germany for Argentina, had found positions as physicist and engineer at the European Patent Office in Munich, Germany. They enjoyed the Festival in Bregenz along with us.

The adventure of mutual discovery continued to accompany our courtship. Each Sabbath back at home, I had been attending the same synagogue for discussions of biblical passages and their modern relevance. Those recurring Saturday morning gatherings were among the first activities to which I introduced Susanna on her three-week "getting better acquainted" visit in December 2004. As planned, we spent a few days in Greater Detroit and then embarked, via Miami, on a Caribbean cruise. On that trip we discovered not only the beauty of the Caribbean islands but also a great deal about each other. I found out that she is a marvelous dancer—her mastery of salsa brought forth some gaping mouths around the room. I also observed that she could talk to just about every fellow passenger and that on the land tours she would discover exotic flowers, aquatic life, native customs, and architectural sights to which I had been oblivious. She has a great sense of humor and could have become a comedian. What she learned about me was that I could identify every rare seafood item brought to the dinner table. (I told her only much later that I wasn't a connoisseur or bon vivant but rather had been a long-time waiter at a seafood restaurant.) To her persistent chagrin, she also discovered that I was a stentorian snorer, mostly in the key of C-major.

Also while we sailed the calm waters of the Caribbean or were in a submarine observing marine life, we learned of the shattering events following the most devastating tsunami in global history, taking place in Indonesia.

A new incentive had now been added to my flights to the Old Country. With Susanna, I was in the thrall of a chance encounter to equal all chance encounters of the past. I shared my feelings with my Detroit friends, and when I came back from Munich, where Susanna and I had last rendezvoused, I told my most intimate friends that they shouldn't be surprised if transoceanic wedding bells might soon ring out. Some friends applauded noisily; others opined that I had gone completely meshuga, completely balmy: "Marry? But she's more than forty years younger than you!" In April 2005, we started the application for a visa to get married the next year.

Shortly after applying, we had a most relaxing vacation during a trip to Slovenia. After some days in Ljubljana, the beautiful capital city, we spent some time in a seaside resort and went spelunking at a mammoth cave as Sigmund Freud had done long before us on a similar outing. We discovered that the country—also called "Prussia of the Balkans"—could produce incredibly tasty pastries, equaling everything sold in neighboring Austria. That summer we also visited Israel with my flamboyant friend, Fred Howard. Christian Bauer's documentary, *The Ritchie Boys,* was competing for the country's equivalent of an Oscar at the 2005 Jerusalem International Film Festival.

The evening started with a bang. Several persons associated with some of the films were invited to a garden party by Israel's acting Prime Minister Ehud Olmert. Two young Israeli women had volunteered to take us from our hotel to the party at the designated time. In their eagerness, they dropped us off thirty minutes too early. The two Olmerts were most gracious and unfazed. Until further guests arrived, we received a grand tour of their version of the White House and had a spirited conversation with Israel's first couple; we thoroughly relished our conversation with Mr. Olmert, a heady brew of laying out his peace plan; we also enjoyed the artworks of Mrs. Olmert and listened to the couple's sophisticated insights on world leaders. Then we shared Christian Bauer's triumph when his film won the Jerusalem Municipality Prize in the category of Jewish experience.

A further trip, one year later, led us to Minusio, near Locarno, in Switzerland. There my cousin's daughter Renée Gelfer invited us to spend some days in her apartment overlooking picturesque Lago Maggiore. As a child, Renée survived the Holocaust sheltering with a Catholic family in Belgium. We are very close to this day.

In December 2005 Ingrid, my mother-in-law-to-be, was diagnosed with cancer, after having battled with an autoimmune disorder for twelve years. When we finally got our fiancée-visa in April 2006, Susanna told her mother that she would not leave her but rather postpone emigration and wedding to stay with her in those critical times. Her mother, by then very weak, protested vehemently and told Susanna, her only child, that she had but one last wish: She wanted us to proceed as planned and that Susanna should return to be at her side after the wedding. With a heavy heart Susanna emigrated to the United States on May 11, 2006; we were married on May 15. Immediately she tried to get special permission to leave the country during the ninety-day period of the so-called advanced parole. It took us twelve days to get this permission. Too late, it turned out—her mother died on May 19. This loss and also the death of my son, Mark, two months earlier overshadowed the beginnings of our marriage and it took Susanna a long time to adapt to her new life.

Two years later, I visited Switzerland again without Susanna, and I experienced another chance encounter. I am glad to have witnesses; otherwise who would believe it? Upon my arrival, Renée's apartment was already stocked and stacked with visitors. But a solution for my housing was at hand: her life companion, Ernesto Moos, had retained his apartment nearby. It was situated just a ten-minute walk from Renée's spectacular apartment. I cheerfully took occupancy. One evening, spent at Renée's amid friends and relatives, I was ready for bed. Not known for an acute sense of orientation, I was given a key to Ernesto's apartment and elaborate instructions. I managed to get lost within minutes. I went forward and backward in vain attempts to get my bearing. Then I spied a building that held promise. The set of bells at the entrance were well lit, but no entry was listed for Ernesto Moos at the left. Let's try the right side, I whispered to myself. Again no entry for Moos, but lo and behold, a familiar name jumped at me. Letter for letter it matched Susanna's maiden name, by no means a common surname. It was too late to ring that bell. Besides I had to find my temporary home. Finally my wanderings led me to a luxurious hotel. I ordered a drink and a telephone (I don't have a cell phone). Ten minutes later Ernesto turned up in his Volvo. I quickly told him of my discovery.

The next day I telephoned Susanna to ask what we should do. After that conversation I rang their doorbell daily for the duration of my visit, but with no success. Finally, on the last evening, I wrote a letter to the unknown person or persons, explaining our surprise and interest in whoever they might be. After having dropped my note in the namesake's mailbox, we waited and waited for a response. The summer turned to winter—my discovery had not panned out. Then out of the blue, I received an email: "Sorry, we are answering so late. But we only use the Minusio apartment twice a year as a vacation home. We live in Germany! Let's get together!"

We did so in Renée's apartment, the following year. The first time Susanna laid eyes on Dieter, she almost fainted: He looked like an older version of her deceased father. It turned out that Dieter had been born in her parents'

Silesian hometown of Beuthen in Germany before the war. Susanna was born in the same town after the war, then Bytom, in Poland! Even though they were not able to figure out if or how they are related, Dieter suggested that didn't matter: Let's just decide we are family! Since Susanna is in regular touch with only one of her relatives, a cousin who lives in Nuremberg with her husband, friendship is very important to her and she invests a lot of time and effort maintaining it. I, too, grew very fond of Joanna and Christoph Konopinski, whom I see almost every year in Nuremberg and whose hospitality is incomparable.

Since 2009 we have spent a week each year in Stratford, Ontario. Susanna always has been a theater aficionado and the Stratford Festival (formerly called the Shakespeare Festival) offers plenty of opportunities to indulge in world-class plays. We are lucky—friends of ours from Detroit, Elin and Barry Becker, have retired to this wonderful little town and become ushers at the festival. We are very grateful for their hospitality. This annual trip is—as Susanna calls it—the highlight of the year for her.

How to describe the last love of my life? I liken her, the writer, to the masterful technique of her short stories. They appear to navigate on the even flow of her narrative, and you figure that you can see her toss the anchor at a predictable harbor. But woe to you if you adhere to that assumption! In her stories, in her life—I mean in our lives—there is a sudden resetting of the sails. And you know you have been had! Examples abound. One year we joined a Christmas party of my department at Wayne State University. Close to the building in which it takes place, we witnessed an elderly homeless man sitting in the snow. Susanna was devastated. When all the guests had arrived, she whistled loudly through her teeth and asked the crowd for a moment of attention. Within five minutes she had collected about seventy dollars and stuffed a bag full with food. This pittance she handed over to the old man, who was totally dumbfounded.

She is not just practically minded but also manually skilled. When she immigrated to the United States, she brought her huge toolbox along, fixing almost everything in the house except electrical stuff. She also shipped an immense number of books to her new home. This is her weak spot. Even though we virtually live in a library, she still buys books. Both of us believe in exercise. My lifetime sport has been swimming. Susanna's life sports are different. She is a walker, preferring nature walks. Yet while walking fast, she is fully attuned to her surroundings. There isn't a plant, an herb, a bush in bloom, or a caterpillar or a bird that escapes her attention or fails to evoke her astonishment. Hardly a day goes by that she comes home from a walk without having found at least one coin.

She takes a fifty-minute walk through our subdivision almost daily, while nervously spotting the overly aggressive Canadian geese that have spread out in the last years. One day they made a foray into our short road for the first time: a flock of about forty were on the lawn in front of our house. To my surprise Susanna opened the garage door, grabbed a huge umbrella, and rushed toward her enemies, vigorously opening and closing the umbrella with raucous noises that swallowed up the tooting of the frightened birds. At last sighting, the geese were taking flight in the direction of the Canadian border.

Since 2016 she's been playing Ping-Pong again and enjoys it immensely, after having paused for about forty years. She has two partners, and for her it's all about the fun of playing—no matter who wins—even though I have told her that if she loses, she needn't come home. And as I mentioned, she loves to dance, and boy, she's got rhythm—who could ask for anything more?

When Susanna wanted to get a divorce from her first husband, she waived her right to alimony, even though he was a well-paid physician. Before she and I married, she told me she didn't want to inherit anything from me, arguing that she had entered my life when I was already in my eighties and had a son. As I continued to find out over the years, Susanna is a giver rather than a taker. I quickly learned that Susanna does not want to receive any gifts from me. Even uttering a thought in this direction upsets her. Instead, she occasionally asks me to read a book she likes. My taking the time to do so, and being able to discuss it with her, she considers a wonderful gift. She doesn't mind—and actually is delighted—when I write her a poem. Also, when I sometimes dare to buy her a little something, for example a beautiful calendar with a squirrel on it (her favorite animal), she is deeply touched. Before joining me in my condominium in West Bloomfield, she uttered just one wish: to install a bidet. She got it.

Like me, Susanna is as punctual as a Prussian officer (that must be a German thing); she is very quick-witted, and we make each other laugh a lot. She hasn't changed from that first evening in Minden, when I noted how smart, funny, cute, and creative she was. What I did not know then is how loving, caring, and highly sensitive she is—the latter, I sometimes assume, a consequence of a troubled childhood and youth with a bitter and very sick father who became an invalid at age twenty-four, due to undetected hepatitis. This fact actually allowed the small family (Susanna is an only child) to leave Poland in 1965 and move to Germany, where he underwent lifesaving surgery. He was also told that his maximal life expectancy was no more than ten more years. This had a huge impact on the family. Since early childhood Susanna has been a constant worrier, and she suffers from extreme sleeplessness. My wife lets nobody down: since her mother's death she took over the financial support of a former colleague of hers in Poland, a woman Susanna had only known as a two-year-old prior to her emigration to Germany. But she didn't just send parcels and money. For many years, until the woman's death in 2017, she also wrote letters and called her.

Needless to say, we have a dishwasher. But from the beginning my wife told me she prefers to hand wash the dishes. That would warm up her constantly cold hands, she claimed, and at the same time she could indulge in audiobooks and NPR. That's the story about the fate of a dishwasher that hasn't been in use for many years. It serves as a repository for bakery goods, cookies, chocolate, and bread. Dark chocolate and Indian food, by the way, are things she scarcely can resist.

I have rarely been challenged so intensely by conversations such as ours; they are every evening's bill of fare and they vary from taking a stand on world politics to the sophistication of Bach's compositions. Some evenings we read our favorite poems to each other or sing together. When I met Susanna, I was very astonished and delighted to find out that she knows so many songs and lyrics of my time, especially songs from the Big Band Era. She has always loved this kind of music.

And what about our age difference? When we married I quipped, "My wife is half my age and has double my brains." Of course that equation no longer holds because of mathematical stringencies. But Susanna drew even with her own aphorism. Quoth she: "I fear when I turn fifty, he, with his unbounded energy, will trade me in for two twenty-five-year-olds." Well, her fiftieth has come and gone and that eventuality did not materialize.

Admittedly, the first years of our married life required some adjustments across different upbringings: my insistence on male prerogatives, reliance on diplomatic circumlocution, and indifference to outside appearances clashed with her distinct sense of justice and fairness (even if it is to her disadvantage), her insistence on straightforward honesty at all times, a meticulous adherence to nonclashing attire, and so forth, to mention just a few examples. But I guess we knew that give-and-take was the demand of the moment and minor differences had to be buried. We managed their entombment. Thank God we are aligned on the major issues that bedevil us today. We agree politically and economically; we see eye-to-eye on the need for women's rights, equity of income, liberal ethics, environmental protections, and many more. And yes, we have a fondness for punning in German, the language we speak at home and when we are by ourselves. Both of us having the same sense of humor and being pretty good at repartee helps cope with a world that at times seems to have lost its compass.

On June 9, 1944, as a soldier, I conquered Normandy. On June 9, 2004, as private citizen Stern, I conquered what turned out to be my soul mate. One of Rodgers and Hammerstein's songs ends with the line, "Once you have found her, never let her go."

I followed this advice.

Working Past Ninety

*A Salute to the Holocaust Memorial Center
Zekelman Family Campus*

TRANSITIONS CAN BE SPRUNG upon us as slowly as evolutionary changes or in the blink of a split second. My transitioning from professor to department head to provost to professor emeritus traveled a course of about fifty years. Yet when each rung up the ladder (or down, as the case may be) occurred, it came about with some combination of excitement, sadness, hope, and fear.

As early as 2002, I realized that there is a time to teach and a time to retire (or perhaps it wasn't early—I was eighty at the time). Yet I did not walk gently into that good night of retirement when I said goodbye to my university. I foresaw that I would miss my classes and my students—and I railed against that loss. Fortunately, my university career ended on a note of triumph: the College of Liberal Arts, on the initiative of its dean, had organized a retirement party that broke precedent. The triumph came first; in fact it had been preceded by a prelude of trumpet blasts. That same month a select committee of faculty and administration had named me an outstanding university citizen. Only four such awards were given out that year. My socially conscious efforts beyond the campus had been recognized.

Then came the retirement party at a filled-to-the-brim festive hall, where almost all of the colleagues closest to me, including the president of the university, were in attendance. Among the array of speeches was one by Donald Haase, senior associate dean and a student of mine as an undergraduate. He spoke of me as an adherent and guardian of academic integrity. But that led to an evening of self-examination, as I recalled an insightful German truism: "Lob verpflichtet." (Praise puts an obligation on us.) An adherent of professional ethics? I thought that fit me. But had I also been its guardian?

When I was asked to become part of the Holocaust Memorial Center Zekelman Family Campus Academic Advisory Committee in Greater Detroit, I took it as merely another application of my educational expertise, coupled with my personal experiences and my supposed leadership skills. Rabbi Charles Rosenzveig, as the founding member of the Holocaust Memorial Center, spelled it out for me. I was asked to help the Center become "a world-class facility educating the public on all matters regarding the Holocaust and genocide." I fully understood his stated goals and was, of course, familiar with the name Zekelman, the family that had not only most generously contributed financially to the institution but had also benefited it with its advice and wisdom. Yet I could not overlook my shortcomings when it came to tackling this new task. Though I was, beginning at age six, a lifelong museum visitor, what on earth did I know about the management of a museum? Fortunately, the designation "Advisory Committee" was somewhat of a misnomer. Neither Rabbi Rosenzveig nor Henry Dorfman, the chairman of the board, appeared to be in need of my advice as they were set in their convictions. But "my" committee became an aggregate of talent scouts for the Center, whose members throughout the years would lead colleagues and well-wishers within its orbit. We recruited Kenneth Waltzer from Michigan State University, head of the Jewish Studies Department and a well-known Holocaust historian with an encyclopedic knowledge about the Buchenwald Concentration Camp. We also gained the volunteer services of Melvin Small, who was teaching World History at Wayne State University. He caught even slight mistakes, including mine, before they could become the "gotcha" criticism of censorious visitors. These experts and others put their storehouse of knowledge at the Center's disposal. And without noticing it, I myself became tied to the Center beyond escape.

Our gifts as talent scouts extended beyond the fertile grounds of academics. At a party I heard a razor-sharp debate between my wife Judy's friends—Alex and his wife, also named Judy—about God's role during the Holocaust. Both

had miraculously survived. From that outcome, Alex had drawn his own conclusion. "I followed every one of God's commandments and I'm convinced
that my conduct led to my being saved."

"Nonsense," Alex's wife said, pointing to the loss of her family. "My parents
and my entire family were decent people who helped others wherever they
could. God should have saved them." She concluded that God was indifferent
to people's actions or had died in the course of the centuries.

"Stop right there!" I said. "You are both mighty debaters! How would you
like to appear before a general audience?"

They became spellbinders at an event before a large audience that, typical
for HMC, represented the whole spectrum of Jewish observance from agnos-
tics to undeviating traditionalists. Questions from the audience resembled
debates more than queries. But what lent further piquancy to the proceedings
was the well-advertised fact that Judy and Alex were (at that time) husband
and wife.

Many of HMC's loyal followers began showing up at neighboring campuses and contributing to their intellectual environment. One event lingers in
my mind, perhaps because it recalls a time when one could respect a speaker's
opinion at a forum even when it greatly deviated from one's own. After a
lecture tour through Germany, I convinced several German political leaders
to pay a countervisit to my campus. Otto Schily from the Social Democratic
Party of Germany came, then West Germany's Minister of the Interior, and
also Countess Marion Dönhoff, a German journalist who participated in the
resistance against Hitler's National Socialists. I persuaded Joe Stroud, the editor of the *Detroit Free Press*, to come in as moderator, since the topic was
"Fairness between Rich and Poor." I tried to bring in a point-of-view representative from the Center.

I also invaded a neighboring campus for an event that touched on the controversy reminiscent of the arguments of our friends Alex and Judy. I was
invited to a special event at Michigan State University to duel verbally with a
most formidable adversary on the subject of whether God survived the Holocaust. The Catholic spokesperson had no doubts; I verbalized my uncer-
tainty. There were no winners or losers.

Before my retirement from the university, it came about that several vacancies occurred on our board of directors. One afternoon Rabbi Rosenzveig tapped me on my shoulder and asked whether I would be interested in being appointed to the board. I didn't have to think long. It was a flattering offer and entirely doable despite my obligations at the university. I said yes, and a whole set of monthly meetings unfolded, frequently involving household decisions, with the weightier ones remaining within the capable hands of the rabbi and the president. But then a momentous decision arose. The museum, located in the basement of the Jewish Community Center, was running out of space. We couldn't accept all the high school and college visitors within our orbit. I suggested that we look at all the modern Holocaust memorials in the country and ask them for architectural suggestions. But the rabbi's ambitions went beyond those. He engaged British interior architect Richard Houghton to lead a delegation of his advisors, including me, on a trip to Berlin, justly regarded as one of the leading sites for modern museums. The building, now standing at a busy thoroughfare of suburban Detroit, ended up winning several architectural awards.

The new location was completed and opened in 2004. Concurrently the rabbi asked me to vacate my board membership and take charge of an institute he had long contemplated and had incorporated in his plans for the new museum. He named it the Institute of the Righteous, and it showcased righteous actions throughout history, as well as during the Holocaust itself. We displayed the historic friendship between David and Jonathan, as articulated in post-biblical writing, when Jonathan protected David even though he thereby lost his chance of becoming the king of the Israelites. We included images of Rodin's famous statue *Les Bourgeois de Calais*, which depicts an elder who was willing to sacrifice his life to save his fellow captives. As far as the Holocaust is concerned, we highlighted pictures of Raoul Wallenberg, and the Japanese Consul Chiune Sugihara, and eight other equally heroic persons from various nations and all walks of life. The visitors see these displays at the very end of their tour, and therefore are left with the only ennobling impression to be extracted from the Holocaust when altruistic persons took it upon themselves to help the potential victims of murderous Nazi actions.

I took on the rabbi's task and defined it, with his approval, as a twofold undertaking. We were going to explore the motivations for altruistic action, drawing on specialists beyond our own constituency, importing social scientists and psychologists from both the United States and abroad to lecture on their theories of the incentives behind people's unselfish actions. We would also give lectures to high schools and colleges, trying to instill this spirit of idealism in their students. With the help of a devoted committee we advanced these causes, and we also recruited a promising intern, Rebecca Swindler, to research and publish the first bibliography of studies on altruism.

Though he lived to see the opening of the new structure of the Holocaust Center, four years later, on December 11, 2008, Rabbi Rosenzveig succumbed to heart failure. The board asked me whether I wanted to be a candidate for the post of director. Being in my upper eighties, I thought I had done my fair share of carrying administrative responsibilities and politely declined to be considered. But I couldn't refuse an alternative solution. When I was asked to become interim director until a national search could be concluded, I accepted that responsibility "for a short period." It turned into a ten-month stint.

Having held different posts at the museum, I felt that I could do a reasonably effective job as interim director. After all, I had held administrative posts at two universities whose size dwarfed the facilities and the staff of the HMC. I wasn't altogether wrong in that assumption, but I hadn't calculated the personal effect the daily responsibility would exert on me. Even my service on the board and my delving into the exploration and dissemination of ideas about altruism had not prepared me for the daily encounter with the nightmarish details told to me about the Holocaust.

Numerous visitors, either survivors of the Holocaust or their descendants, came to me as acting director to share their own memories, or those they had heard secondhand. Many of these narratives contained harrowing details. They frequently did not convey new information, but what bestirred me was the daily exposure to these tales. I obviously was not inured, and I could not prevent my thoughts from being thrown back upon the loss of my own family whenever one of the victims or their relatives told me of theirs. As a result, those ten months were, emotionally, the most trying of all my tasks at the Holocaust Memorial Center.

One hopeful thing that occurred during my interim directorship was that we acquired a most valuable artifact, thanks to Feiga Weiss, our head librarian. She had spotted an announcement from the Anne Frank Foundation in Amsterdam. The chestnut tree on their property, which had stood for Anne as a symbol of the nature from which she was barred in her hiding place, was slowly dying. But several saplings could be salvaged and distributed, on a competitive basis, to various institutions in Europe and beyond. Feiga suggested that we compete for one of them. I thought it was a superb suggestion and drafted a proposal on behalf of our center—and we were awarded one of eleven saplings that went to US institutions. It did not diminish our joy that the US Department of Agriculture, to protect our native trees from diseases, stipulated that our sapling had to be sequestered for three years. We gave it our tender loving care, and so it survived its "hiding place," and now graces the immediate surroundings of our institute as a sturdy tree, a visible reminder of the talented young girl who has become one of the icons of the victimized European Jews during the Holocaust.

We found yet another way to celebrate the survival of that chestnut tree on our grounds, when Stephen Goldman became our director. I had kept up with cultural events in Germany beyond my retirement and learned that two prominent German artists, the composer Volker Blumenthaler and the librettist Alexander Gruber, had created a cantata in memory of Anne Frank, titled "My Name Is Anne Frank." Encouraged by Director Goldman and James Hartway of the WSU Music Department, we were able to premiere the work under the auspices of the Holocaust Memorial Center in collaboration with Wayne State University and Berkley High School, whose orchestra was invited to play at President Obama's inauguration. A capacity crowd of more than eight hundred people filled the school's auditorium as the Berkley orchestra and an a capella choir, reinforced by two cantors, Dan Gross of Congregation Adat Shalom and Penny Steyer of Temple Shir Shalom, celebrated the talent and spirit of Anne Frank. The two artists who had composed and written the cantata came to the opening and, together with the performers, got standing ovations. The librettist of the work, Alexander Gruber, sent us an email afterward: "I never shall forget the Holocaust Center. . . . And never the great and overwhelming experience the singers and instrumentalists of Berkley High created with their . . . loving rendition."

One of my disappointments was that I wasn't able to convince the board to have us initiate a publication outlining the achievements of our Center in a richly illustrated volume. As is so often the case, creativity may be thwarted by an empty pocket. All in all, though, I liked my interim stint, including Sunday morning rap sessions with the Executive Committee of the board and planning the Annual Dinner with the expert advice of one of the spouses of a board member, with tasty and generous samples of the menu offered by competing caterers. But I was equally happy when we all decided on a permanent director.

When an outstanding leader with multiple years of experience in the administration of Holocaust museums was inaugurated, I enthusiastically stepped back into my former position as director of the Harry and Wanda Zekelman Institute of the Righteous, and we resumed research on altruism and the spreading of that ideal among younger generations. We try to analyze what has impelled people from all walks of life to act nobly in defense of the persecuted, even if it meant personal disadvantage, losses, or a threat to themselves or their families. Some scholars argue that this noble impulse comes from an upbringing in a loving family or from a person's religious persuasion. Others trace it to an impulse stemming from the survival instinct during evolutionary times, when man had to compete with stronger mammals and could only persevere by altruistically banding together. Still others hypothesized that a sense of gratification produced by a noble deed is a further incentive. In a small way, we have explored the road that might someday lead us from that small candle to a beacon. Our hope rests in the new generation, which one of Germany's liberal poets, Ludwig Uhland, addressed as such:

Ihr seid das Saatkorn einer neuen Welt.	You are the kernel of a world renewed.
Das ist der Weihefrühling, den Gott will.	That is the consecrated spring that God demands.

As it turned out, Director Stephen Goldman found additional uses for me. During my stays in Germany, I was able to enter the negotiations for acquiring one of the Center's most spectacular and effective exhibits: a boxcar that in all likelihood was used for the nefarious deportations the Nazis had in store for their Jewish fellow citizens. While other museums had been able to secure boxcars from stock held by the Polish railroad authorities—Goldman had bought one for his museum in St. Petersburg, Florida—I tracked down the relevant German surplus agency. I located a boxcar of German origin with some bureaucratic inscriptions. On an administrative level, I was also able to reestablish a more positive atmosphere between the museum and the German Foreign Office. That improved relationship may have contributed to receiving a grant that helped in the restoration of the acquired boxcar.

Goldman encouraged me to make use of my contacts at Michigan universities and with particular ethnic groups for the sake of HMC. For instance, we worked to inaugurate meetings of interest to the Greek community and the Armenian consulate. Born out of a relationship of cordiality and friendship, we also gave radio and television interviews as a team, addressed civic groups such as the Rotary Club and the Shriners, and pursued an invitation from the Eisenhower Memorial Library for me to address a crowd during a commemoration of Victory in Europe Day. At times I felt like an ambassador of goodwill, as when the Michigan Veterans Administration invited me to speak on Memorial Day at the National Veterans' Cemetery in Holly, Michigan, and I found myself addressing an audience of four thousand people. Needless to say, I called attention to the Jewish War Veterans and to the Holocaust Memorial Center, but also gave examples of the heroism of Jewish soldiers throughout American history. I cited the courage of Tibor Rubin, who held off an entire North Korean battalion and became the recipient of the Congressional Medal of Honor, bestowed upon him by President George W. Bush. It will not surprise anyone that given my admiration for Tibor Rubin I went to extraordinary lengths to secure his presence as the keynote speaker at the Holocaust Memorial Center for Memorial Day, 2009. His appearance constituted a dramatic rebuttal of the age-old canard, denying the heroism of Jewish men and women.

One of the most satisfying excursions was a joint journey to Germany with Stephen Goldman when one of the exhibits developed by us opened at the University of Bamberg, and subsequently went to the Free University of

Berlin. The exhibit featured some of the exploits of the Ritchie Boys, with particular emphasis on their role in preparing the way for democratic media, free of the propagandistic content and jargon of the Nazi years. During our stay in Europe, we crisscrossed southern Germany and laid the foundation for future collaborative efforts with German museums. Both aims of our trip offered new challenges and gave me a sense of fulfillment.

As I conclude this tome, I am still gainfully employed at the Holocaust Memorial Center Zekelman Family Campus. The task left unfinished is a project very much within the purview of altruistic deeds. While the rescue or attempted rescue of persecuted Jews during the Holocaust by non-Jews has been extensively and most justly recorded and commemorated, the self-help of Jews for other Jews has not. The reasons for such an omission are manifold, prominently among them the claim that Scripture enjoins Jews to help their co-religionists, and thus such assistance isn't considered altruistic in the way it might be for non-Jews. To our minds, however, it has become imperative to recognize the extraordinary valor Jewish rescuers displayed, and I was charged with forming a committee to commemorate such superhuman efforts. Our mission statement reads:

> In honor of those who risked their lives to save others, the Holocaust Memorial Center Zekelman Family Campus is working to ensure that the heroism and altruism shown by Jews who helped their fellow Jews to survive through a time of unspeakable horror, will find its rightful place in the vast compendium of tragic events that took place during the Holocaust. As the surviving rescuers and survivors age and pass along, we owe it to them and to those who have passed to do them justice.

I was authorized to employ an assistant, Shirlee Wyman Harris, to share this new and difficult assignment. Harris engaged herself in researching information on the Nazi-occupied countries and coordinated her research with the committee members. The committee found a wealth of examples to prove the implicit assumptions of the mission statement—and the work continues. All of us feel gratified and honored that we can resurrect memories of altruistic heroism frequently not recorded elsewhere.

But then, into these rigorous and at the same time captivating largely scholarly activities a personal pursuit snuck in. It started with a telephone call. A
gentleman introduced himself as Bruce Henderson. He needed to talk to me
and asked for an appointment. "No trouble," I said. "I have an open door policy." We arranged for a meeting; he would fly in from California two weeks
later. His research topic was "The Ritchie Boys." After the phone call I rushed
to the computer. Who on earth was Bruce Henderson? I discovered he is a
bestselling nonfiction writer, who had chosen hitherto little known but totally gripping stories from the peripheries of various US wars as his subject.
With one of them, *Hero Found: The Greatest POW Escape of the Vietnam
War*, he had monopolized the number one spot on the nonfiction list of the
New York Times. Our West Bloomfield Library, rated one of the best in the
nation, carried the volume. The light in my bedroom burned past midnight.
That fellow could write! When we became closely acquainted, Henderson
told me one of his secrets of nonfiction writing, which he had shared with
several generations of Stanford University students: "Details, details, details!"
He had practiced what he preached.

Bruce arrived. With no time lost, Feiga Weiss and I took him to our archive
on the Ritchie Boys, started when we mounted our exhibits and sponsored
the first reunion of those stalwarts. He thanked Mrs. Weiss profusely as she
produced her treasures. "My job and my pleasure," she answered. And then
he started to interview me. The exchange, scheduled for two days, turned
into a week, even though he was a quick study. One evening during that week
he took my wife and me to dinner. I looked a bit closer at him; most of the
time before we had looked at papers and artifacts. Across from us sat a broad-
shouldered, wavy-haired, informally dressed gentleman in his late sixties. He
exuded a warm, winning smile and poignant wit. "What made you hit upon
the Ritchie Boys?" Susanna asked him. "Well, I was reading an obituary in
the *New York Times*," he answered. "I habitually read them. You discover the
craziest stories within those entries. And this one briefly mentioned the membership in your outfit of the deceased. I got curious and found out that there
was no book about the Ritchie Boys in English. So I resolved to write it."
"I'm glad," I said. "We are little known in the US. I think we deserve to be
'resurrected.'" "I will try to do just that," he promised. Actually he has more
than lived up to that promise: the hardback has sold well and the paperback

appeared on the *New York Times* Bestseller List for several weeks. He promoted the book in various cities in the United States. Here in Detroit the past chair of the Jewish Book Fair, Gail Fisher, scouted him during his appearance in New York. He spoke as well as he writes. Finally a miniseries based on his book is in preparation. In a fit of vanity I bargained out that I, appearing as a young man in his twenties, would be played by a handsome actor.

At this writing my daily work at the Holocaust Memorial Center continues. I consider myself an ambassador of goodwill for the institution that I have been connected to for such a long time. I am one of the very few people to hold an office under all the directors, temporary or permanent, who have headed this much respected Center. Our new leader since 2017 is a person who holds two different titles that rarely are attached to the same person: Eli Mayerfeld is a rabbi who also holds an engineering degree. He developed a new mission statement for the Center: to engage and to educate and empower by remembering the Holocaust. He established a new focus for our activities based on that mission, and with his leadership we set four initiatives: lead in statewide Holocaust education, integrate HMC visits into a broader Holocaust education, raise awareness for younger generations, and refresh our exhibits in order to keep them current. We will concentrate on the needs of our immediate constituency.

Eli has convinced me that I have not completely fallen victim to the vicissitudes of old age and can at least cheer on my colleagues in their exploration of new paths and new pursuits for an organization that I, in my heart of hearts, also see as a commemoration of my own murdered family. One of those new initiatives resulted from a most positive development. Michigan's State Legislature passed Public Act 170 of 2016, which made the study of the Holocaust mandatory for all eighth- through twelfth-grade public school students in Michigan. Our state is one of only ten states in the Union to mandate Holocaust education.

It was an occasion for jubilation. As Michigan's governor came to our campus to sign the bill into law, we held a large-scale celebration in which I enthusiastically participated. For me it marked the end of a long march. Many years before our founder, Rabbi Charles Rosenzveig, had argued for just such an action. He finally was given a hearing before a governmental committee in Lansing, the state capital. He asked me to accompany him—and to lend my arguments to his. We did our best; but our efforts languished until several years after Rabbi Rosenzveig's passing.

With passage of PA 170, HMC's board resolved to make the Holocaust Memorial Center the nexus for Holocaust education in Michigan. As a result, HMC launched an ambitious plan of action: to train one thousand Michigan teachers in Holocaust content and pedagogy by 2020. To meet that goal, part-time director of education and member of the Governor's Council on Genocide and Holocaust Education, Robin Axelrod, cultivated HMC's team of educators and requested the appointment of a full-time department head. She aided CEO Mayerfeld in the national search for her successor, Ruth Bergman.

With Bergman at the helm, supported by Axelrod as senior education specialist, the Education Department's leadership is solidly in place. Bergman's vision is to "blend the dissemination of accurate information with the instilling of ethical principles concerning the Holocaust and genocide. Pedagogically, never suppress the facts of the horror, but tailor them to the level of maturity of your students. Condemn actions of the perpetrators, but do not spare the indifference of 'mere bystanders.' And leave your audience with salutary role models: the heroic Christians and Jews who risked their lives and the safety of their families in extending their 'daring and doing' to help the persecuted." Although not involved in the fulfilling of Bergman's program, as the director of the Institute of the Righteous at HMC, I feel free to applaud her plan and the work of her team. I believe we are moving forward in the right direction at HMC!

The ambiance of the museum embodies a close-knit family. The various individual fates that the museum brings to life through its displays bear many similarities to my family's ethics—the unceasing hard work they engaged in to try to improve their situation, their belief in doing everything possible to secure the lives of their children, and sustaining their determination even to the end as Nazi cruelty dashed their hopes and extinguished their lives.

CHAPTER ELEVEN

Thoughts after Visiting France, 2016

A T THE BEGINNING OF this chronicle, I compared my life to a roller coaster. At its conclusion another analogy comes to mind: a carousel. So many situations from my childhood and my adulthood link to similar ones in the life of this old guy or old Guy.

During this last phase of my life, the three relatively short years of my experience as a Ritchie Boy have come to the forefront. I have been asked to give innumerable speeches and interviews about those momentous wartime years, including on television. Yet the most reverberating echo came in May 2016, when, for the first time in seventy-three years, I returned to the most dramatic episode in my life as a soldier, known to historians as the Invasion of Normandy. For reasons not entirely clear to me, for years I had declined invitations to come to Normandy, even those issued by well-meaning colleagues, such as Professor Helge-Ulrike Hyams, whom I had met at a scholarly conference in Laupheim, Germany. She owns a summer house in Sainte-Marie-du-Mont, close to Foucarville, where I had first slipped into my role as an interrogator of German prisoners of war. So many fellow Ritchie Boys, who came ashore with me before or after D+3, had died in the meanwhile, and some, of course, had not lived beyond that fateful day in June 1944. I thanked my colleague for the invitation and used an easy out when I declined it, simply saying that my schedule as a professor and administrator completely filled my calendar.

But I hadn't been candid with her. While I was working on this manuscript, an editor pressed me into self-examination, arguing that my readers were entitled to know the reasons for my reluctance. I followed her advice and forced myself to think back to the days after D-Day, when I had to steel myself against the horrors that I was exposed to on the beach. Against all my expectations, I was spared from being the squeamish person I had been all of my life. I have told in an earlier chapter that I was suddenly able to perform my duties on that day, no matter how horrific the experience was. Then, as a civilian, I returned to my hypersensitivity. I thought I wouldn't be able to deal with the memories evoked by returning to Normandy.

But now, in May 2015, came an additional invitation. It was one that I, cast in the role of one of a small number of surviving witnesses, could not ignore without doing a disservice to my comrades in arms. Monsieur Gérard Viel, the cultural coordinator of the tiny town of Foucarville, with 250 inhabitants, was in the process of mounting an exhibit about the first POW enclosure, located on a huge meadow on the outskirts of the town. It had served as the first holding cage of our prisoners and would grow to be the largest enclosure on the Western Front, at one time holding more than sixty thousand prisoners. The cultural coordinator had ferreted out my whereabouts, after speaking with the aforementioned Professor Hyams, and he sent me an email. He explained his plans for a day commemorating the Invasion and the significance of Foucarville. Our mutual friend, Professor Hyams, had suggested me as an eyewitness who could give an account of his participation. The email was signed:

Gérard Viel
Consultant Culturel
Conseiller artistique
Communication culturelle
Management d'artiste
Régie générale

When I didn't answer in good order, Monsieur Viel followed up with another, more urgent email.

Given that I was already toying with the idea of a European trip and was invited to a family affair in London, I tentatively agreed to accept Viel's offer. Yes, I would think about giving the opening address at his exhibition, dealing with the camp in Foucarville and our activities there. But then a question crossed my mind. I called my French correspondent, telling him that I had written accounts of my Foucarville adventures in both German and English. Which one would he prefer? His response came out in bullet-fashion. "En français, naturellement!" I didn't tell him that I hadn't given a speech in French in decades—and that was a very short one given at a conference at the Sorbonne Nouvelle.

But then I had all but committed myself to be present at Viel's opening. I felt obligated. The translation of my English manuscript took the full weekend's work of Maissa Saker, a French doctoral candidate at my university (with only occasional input by me). The results were greatly to the credit of my collaborator. Still, a month later, stage fright was my steady companion as I boarded the suboceanic railroad known as the "Eurostar," which took me from London to Paris.

Professor Hyams met me at the train station in Paris; we continued by train to her house in Sainte-Marie-du-Mont, passing locations that I suddenly perceived in dual perspective. Cities like Caen, Isigny-sur-Mer, and Sainte-Mère-Église flashed before my mind's eye as I had first glimpsed them during that June of 1944. Now, a new reality of carefully tilled fields, flower gardens, and baby carriages superimposed themselves in a paean to peace upon my remembrances of bomb craters, devastated houses, and people just emerging from the oppression and depression of years of tyranny.

My exploration of peacetime Normandy unfolded to be also an unexpected discovery. Shortly after we came ashore in 1944, we spotted a US paratrooper whose parachute was impaled on the spire of the village of Sainte-Mère-Église's most prominent church. Still alive, he was hanging there without a chance of rescue. A single shot by a murderous German would give him the coup de grâce. We were sure he wouldn't survive longer than a few hours. But against all odds, he made it. I was told during that reception, hosted by the village's mayor, "When you Americans had retaken our village, he was cut loose, and was hospitalized, and we were told that he wasn't seriously wounded. And we got living proof. He came to visit us after the war and we gave him a hero's welcome." The news cheered me for days.

This dual vision returned repeatedly during my three days on the Normandy coast. Nowhere else, with the possible exceptions of the British War

Museum and the Eisenhower Memorial site in Abilene, Kansas, has this moment of world history been more faithfully preserved than in Normandy. Museums have sprouted, even in small fishing villages. And none of the German bunkers has been torn down. I walked with local citizens through a mile-square bunker, which had housed the so-called Nazi defenders of the "impregnable" Fortress Europe. Powerful memories of my comrades in arms, especially my fellow Ritchie Boys, returned, as well as the memory of a couple of hours I spent with a private from the Ranger Battalion, an elite assault troop, who, just a few days before, had climbed up those steep, heavily defended cliffs, topped by German strongholds. He was four years younger than I and was able to tell of his climbing those cliffs as though it had been a cakewalk. We two had to see to it that waves of German prisoners were evacuated to a holding camp for transportation to England. He carried a rifle, but was in no way worried that one or more of the prisoners would make an attempt at escape. Completely in character he said to me, "Make them double-time, Sergeant!" He meant make them run. He didn't mind that he himself (and I) had to race alongside with our captives. I never saw him again, although I didn't have to conjure up an image of him seventy years later; he stood before me as he had on that day in June.

I stopped during one forenoon at the US Military Cemetery to place a wreath near a memorial monument. The wreath was handed to me by French Count Charles de Maupeou, whose family's nobility traces back to the thirteenth century. He owns a castle in nearby Colombières, shared with him by his father, who is alive and well and remembers not only the Invasion but also, with fondness, several teams of Ritchie Boys. They had been bivouacked in his castle for a short time during and after the Invasion. "These memories," said Charles de Maupeou Sr., "should never be forgotten, and new ones must be added! Hence, you, Professor Stern, should spend your last day and night at the castle." I did find myself there two days later, and rarely have I slept better.

My stay at Normandy became a movable feast. The mayor of Sainte-Mère-Église gave a champagne reception in my honor. Not to be outdone, her counterparts at five other coastal towns pooled their resources and hosted a five-course banquet. As one of them whispered to me, they were miraculously able to forget their political rivalries and territorial disputes for this occasion. A newly founded community, Utah Beach, named after the code word for one of our invasion spots, presented me with a medal designating me as an honorary citizen.

Exorbitant praise, particularly of my college French, followed my public presentations about my activities at Foucarville of seventy-three years ago. In a spirit of noblesse oblige, Monsieur de Maupeou rented the local movie house for my speech, charged no admission, and provided me with an interpreter in the person of a local high school teacher for the inevitable question and answer period. He also corralled his three offspring to assist me in my presentation. They went far beyond his terse instructions. His daughter Marie, a student at the famous Paris University Sciences Politiques, continued to help with the arrangements for my visit. She had mounted posters announcing my presentations and assisted her father in writing opening remarks. The older son, Nicolas, an engineer specializing in renewable energies, and his younger brother, Albéric, a student at a school of aeronautics, took charge of a copy of a recent film I had brought along, which gave a compact history of the Ritchie Boys, with me as the talking head. They inserted French translations into the documentary for the benefit of my French audience.

Why all the fuss for this one superannuated veteran and retired academician, I asked myself. I got the smattering of an answer toward the end of my stay. It seems my appearance among them reminded my well-wishers of a time when liberté, fraternité, egalité returned to them with the end of the Nazi occupation, and their traditional and revered order reemerged. In short, I was merely the catalyst of feelings remembered firsthand by some of my listeners, or passed on through the generations following them.

I returned from France glad that I had accepted the invitation of returning to the scene of the most eventful years of my life. I knew the added memories of those few days in Normandy with old and new admirable French friends would never leave me. And I felt a chapter of my life had now closed.

But it had not. A year passed. On a fall day, no different from all the others in Greater Detroit, I was following my daily routine. It always starts with swimming and exercises at 5:30 a.m. at the Jewish Community Center, consuming my wife's precooked breakfast in the Center's dressing room, and then rushing off to work. Upon coming home in the evening I usually glance at the day's mail. On this fall day I did more than glance because a fairly large letter immediately caught my eye. The envelope displayed the French tricolore and the return address bore the seal of the French Consulate General in Chicago. I opened the letter and nearly dropped it after reading the opening sentence. "The Government of the French Republic is most pleased to bestow upon you the Legion of Honor, the highest award within its giving" or words to that effect.

Details were worked out quickly. The consul himself would present the medal, the Holocaust Memorial Center would assume the sponsorship, and the Jewish War Veterans would furnish the Honor Guard and both the French and American national anthems would be played at the beginning of the ceremony.

On that day, January 27, 2017, the large auditorium was completely filled. I spotted many of the people close to me in the audience. The consul gave an inspired speech about the liberation of France in 1944. He spoke in English and mentioned the Ritchie Boys several times. My response, to return the courtesy, was partially spoken in French, this time thanks to the translation skills of my colleague Anne Duggan from Wayne State University. I had realized that the occasion could not have come more propitiously. I quoted a speech by the past French premier, who at the time of rising anti-Semitism had made a historic pronouncement: "France without Jews would not be France."

I also declared that I accepted this high honor in the name of all the Ritchie Boys. I pointed out the Jewish background of so many of them, their achievements and the recognition they had received by a high-ranking army historian, a specialist in intelligence work during World War II. I thought it was fitting that I concluded my thank-you speech by recalling a peaceful action in the midst of war: a kaddish, a Hebrew prayer for the dead, was held on French soil for the wife of one of us who had died in childbirth in faraway Brooklyn. It was equally fitting that the award ceremony was concluded by an ordained rabbi, our director, Eli Mayerfeld.

A reception followed the official aspects of the day's proceeding, minutely arranged by Sarah Saltzman, in charge of Events Planning at HMC. As women and men, old and young, Christians and Jews, people of all walks of life approached me and showered me with kind words, I was overwhelmed by contrasting emotions. I felt totally accepted and more, as if engulfed by a sea of affection. And then I said to myself: they are not really applauding you, because their approbation is going to a young man of twenty-two years who didn't really know what he was doing. In consequence I was laughing at myself. And that sense of ludicrousness intensified when I reflected on the fact that two and a half years of my much earlier life should reverberate into my nineties. In a milder form that sense of humor carried me through the rest of the day. I could quip to the next well-wisher: "Okay, okay already! Sure, the consul made me a chevalier, but where is the cheval, the horse that should come with the medal?"

And to a broadly smiling Susanna I cackled: "I am suspicious of the consul general's praise for my 'soldierliness.' You better widen my old uniform a bit. I think the French want to draft me for their next foreign conflict!"

But if I were to be asked, with all those emotions astir in me, which image from that day and from my stay in France arises most frequently before my mental eye, I can answer spontaneously: "The scene that followed my laying down that wreath handed me by Monsieur du Maupeou."

A person whom I had never met before intuited my feelings. Professor Hyams's daughter Judith, who had journeyed to her mother's house from Berlin together with her bright ten-year-old child, wrote a feature about me for one of her German outlets, "Die Allgemeine Jüdische Zeitung":

Descending from a car in Saint-Mère-Église, Guy Stern at first only has eyes for a baby in his stroller, being fed by his parents. "What a picture of peace and what a difference from the times of long ago," the man of ninety-four years comments with a smile. "Naturally the remembrance of this giant bloodbath of the war comes back to me and with it the despairing recognition that all this carnage could have been prevented, if the politics of that time had only been more intelligent. But I look forward and hope that the world has learned something. It feels great to be here [at the scene of war] and yet to be so far removed from warfare."

Hyams, the roving reporter, also called me a "Menschenfreund," a friend of humanity. But to be honest, when she saw me placing a wreath at the cemetery, could my face have mirrored anything else at that heart-wrenching moment? Only a very hard-hearted person would have been able to resist such an expression of empathy when suddenly, and seemingly out of nowhere, music began resonating from a loudspeaker across miles and miles of graves, intoning an anthem fought for long ago, followed by the familiar taps that will sound for us all.

CHAPTER TWELVE

In Pursuit of the Past

I N THE YEARS FOLLOWING my departure from my hometown, a building in Hildesheim visited my mind at regular intervals and became a living symbol. It is a tower without a function, unless you believe in the magic power of its name: Kehrwiederturm (Tower of Return). It serves as the antithesis to Thomas Wolfe's famous slogan, "You can't go home again." It worked its magic on me repeatedly and unexpectedly, and some of the most surprising turn-about pilgrimages resulted from letting my more mature judgment overrule my rash decisions during my youth.

Thomas Wolfe's admonition has fortunately been disregarded by innumerable writers. Add me to the list! As a scholar I could write an article, say, "Echoes of the Past," without much additional research. I would start with the German Romantic Age and go beyond, and quote such lines as "I dreamt my way back into my childhood" (Adelbert von Chamisso); "My soul spread its wings, homeward bound" (Joseph von Eichendorff); and "Sometimes the boy who bore my name comes visiting" (Oskar Loerke). The imaginations of these writers let all of them reconquer times and places once inhabited.

In my personal case such forays are incessant, even though many are far from being "romantic." But their insistence on being heard tells me once again that the well-meant advice of friends to "forget that horrible past" is futile. All of us are composites of our experiences. Mine are geographically fixed and are centered on my hometown, Hildesheim. That is easy to explain. As a child, up until the time I left for America when I was fifteen, I only sporadically visited other parts of Germany.

Right after the war, when I returned to Hildesheim still in uniform, the news I received from the parents of one of my schoolmates was crushing. The faint hope of finding any member of my family alive was shattered. Encounters with former acquaintances also reinforced my impression that I had no longer any ties to this society. One remark made me leave a party, as I recalled how the woman's brother had harassed my brother and me at the local swimming pool. The incident evoked nothing but revulsion. At the end of my first visit to Hildesheim, I would have scoffed at any prediction suggesting that there might be a rapprochement between me and my former home.

But was it a homecoming? Virtually every exile, then and now, who has returned to his/her former residence has asked him/herself that question. The answer hinges on the individual's perception of "Heimat," or home. *The Return of the Native* is the title of a nineteenth-century novel, *Childhood Country* the title of a more recent one. Other authors perceive "home" as something spiritual or religious or ideological. Or you can be cynical about the concept. The dramatist Bertolt Brecht claims that moving to a different town means that you no longer know to whom you must kowtow or whose face you can slap. One Berlin theater critic, Alfred Kerr, told his disconsolate young daughter, who had to flee her home during the Nazi period, "a person can have many homes." I am inclined to agree with him.

But that first visit, while it didn't in any way reestablish ties to my hometown, did return me to the day of my earlier departure. It forcibly impressed upon me the thin thread that had led that "invisible ink" fifteen-year-old boy from Hildesheim to St. Louis. I pondered how there must have been additional forces at work, still shrouded in mystery, that allowed me to escape my family's terrible fate. Concrete questions came to my mind, the answers to which were held at bay for an additional forty years or so.

I asked myself, wasn't my rescue an unlikely story? Here was an unemployed baker who had pulled the wool over the eyes of a seasoned consular official. And why did he, Malcolm C. Burke, pitch that ridiculous question to me, "How much is forty-eight plus fifty-two?" that someone half my age could have answered? And why, during my emigration, did I encounter so many members of a committee whom I'd never heard of before? Surely there were gaps in my understanding of my own story!

About eight years ago, Stephen Goldman, then director of the Holocaust Memorial Center at which I am employed, charged me with curating an exhibit dealing with the Ritchie Boys. Well, I needed help. So I solicited it from two friends, living in or near the District of Columbia. They were to do hands-on research at the Library of Congress and the National Archives. While they were digging up manuscripts and artifacts, one of them, Dan Gross, who had become a fan of the Ritchie Boys, found a curious entry at the Library of Congress. He, together with Steve Goodell, another helper and past department head at the US Holocaust Museum, called me one afternoon. "Guy," they said, "we have run across a document in which you are labeled as one of the Thousand Children. What on earth does that mean?" In an attempt at humor they added: "And we always thought of you as unique!"

"I haven't a ghost of an idea," I replied. But being a curious sort, I hastened to my favorite research person at the Holocaust Memorial Center, Head Librarian Feiga Weiss. I always say about her in German or Yiddish, punning on her name, "Feiga Weiss alles!" (Feiga knows everything!)

"Oh yes," she said, "you are talking about a group of Jewish women who banded together in 1933 under the label of German Jewish Children's Aid Project. They pledged themselves to rescue at least one thousand children from Germany and Austria. Therefore, people referred to them as the Thousand Children Group. You can compare them in a way to the British Kindertransport. Were they successful? Oh yes, by the end of the war they had rescued 1,400 youngsters from Germany, Austria, and a few other countries."

"Thank you, all-knowing Feiga," I said, "but why haven't I ever heard of that organization?"

"Oh, that is explained in one of the articles that we have in our archive and in a book about the organization. Knowing of the anti-Semitism in our State Department, they wanted to avoid any publicity and sail under the radar of the Foreign Office. Their fear was, of course, that those ideologues in Washington could stop their efforts."

"I see," I answered. "Apparently I was one of those thousand youngsters. Would there be a file about me?"

"Quite likely," she answered. "All the papers are at the YIVO (Institute for Jewish Research) archives in New York."

"Well, I would love to get a hold of a copy of my files."

"Sure. I will call Gunnar Berg, my opposite number at YIVO."

Within three weeks I had my complete file in hand, consisting of more than fifty documents. My father had petitioned the German-Jewish committee in Berlin on my behalf. They, in turn, had forwarded his request to this wonderful group of determined women, who immediately started working on my case. The New York office entrusted my application to the Sommers Children's Bureau, a collaborating Jewish children's organization in St. Louis, close to the home of Uncle Benno. It finally landed on the desk of one of their social workers, the amazing Mrs. Margaret Esrock.

The agency conducted a lengthy correspondence that weighed the pros and cons for extending help with my emigration. I read that correspondence with great excitement, as if the decision were still pending. Mrs. Esrock became my heroine. She highlighted all the points that spoke for me, including the recommendations I had received from my teachers, even those from my high school; she praised the goodwill and the experience of my aunt and uncle in raising children, and emphatically recommended favorable action by the St. Louis office. She downplayed any strikes against me. For example, I was close to the upper age limit of sixteen (should my journey be delayed, I would no longer be eligible for assistance).

Also she ignored the fact that the Sommers Children's Bureau had already overdrawn the budget allocated by the New York office, and the fact that the national office preferred helping youngsters with no relatives in the United States. As I pored over the reading of that correspondence, I noticed with growing excitement that it was all coming to a head at a meeting scheduled for July 1937, devoted completely to my case. Mrs. Esrock, however, was at that point already looking beyond the meeting. For the first and only time, she wrote directly to the New York office to get their endorsement, assuming the St. Louis meeting would turn out favorably. In short, she went over the head of her superior in St. Louis when she sent off a letter with her signature. The decision of that meeting in St. Louis is contained in the next letter within the file. It speaks for itself:

Sommers Children's Bureau
3636 Page Boulevard
St. Louis, Missouri

July 6, 1937
Re: July 8, 1937

Miss Lotte Marcuse
German_Jewish Children's Aid
221 West 57ᵗʰ Street
New York City

My dear Miss Marcuse:
   We recently called a meeting of our local committee in order to discuss Guenther Stern. Since the Silberberg's are so eager to do what they can for this child since the child himself is nearing the age of 16, the committee decided that St. Louis would attempt to be of service to the boy. It is hoped that the child will not become dependent upon the community and that the family can meet his needs. Although our quota is filled, I have been authorized to inform you that we should be glad to help Guenther. Therefore, you can start negotiations for having him leave Germany. This note will therefore serve to inform you that we will be glad to take responsibility for Guenther.

                         Sincerely yours,

                         Viola Oschrin, Director

And then, the committee in New York wasted no time; it sent eight copies of a perfect affidavit to the collaborating Jewish committee in Germany. Perhaps influenced by Mrs. Esrock's unauthorized enthusiastic endorsement, my name was on that list. But the committee's care and concern for me didn't end with my move to my relatives' home. After my arrival in St. Louis, I got to know her. She came to our house once a month and inquired about me, much to the chagrin of Aunt Ethel, who called her "Buttinsky" behind her back. At the time, I certainly didn't know whom she represented. Of course, in the final analysis, she represented me.

Mrs. Esrock completed periodic reports after each of her visits to our house. She even inquired about me at my high school and communicated with my university teachers. And then it was finally time to let go. She reported that her former protégé was now serving in the US Army in Europe.

Reporting this at a time when we hear so much about the selfishness of human behavior, I feel unending gratitude to a largely unrecognized group of American Jewish women who saw to it that Günther Stern took a boat to a harbor in New Jersey rather than a cattle car to Auschwitz. I'm currently hoping to prepare an exhibition of "Jews Rescuing Jews." Margaret Esrock rightfully belongs in it.

My several subsequent visits to Hildesheim in the 1980s, prompted by an invitation to speak at my former high school and at the local university, left me largely uninvolved because I was lecturing on being a former pupil there. I approached this task as an academician; my emotions were neutralized. Yet my step-by-step path of reconciliation with new and progressive generations in the country of my birth did finally include the streets of Hildesheim after all. The extraordinary attempts to ease my steps, undertaken by the kindest people possible, became the palliatives. I received an invitation to speak once again at the University of Hildesheim. A colleague, interested in my contributions to Exile Studies, asked me for a guest lecture in his seminar. As I observed elsewhere in Germany, the attending students represented a new breed—informed, inspired by the exile writers, and enthusiastic when posing questions. My sponsor, Professor Ernst Cloer, was in tune with me on a subject we both were diligently pursuing in our research.

In 1988 my home city once more remembered me. The spot where our synagogue had stood was to become a commemorative site. Four sculptors had collaborated in creating a stunning monument. I had been invited to the unveiling. I attempted to resurrect in spirit the glorious interior of the violated building. My presentation was well received, but more dramatic and lasting was the speech at the end of the ceremony, given by my former German youth leader, Fritz Schürmann (Fred Sherman). He closed his speech with a stentorian recitation of the Hebrew declaration of faith, a prayer that hadn't been heard in public since that disastrous November of 1938.

In 1988, I was on a specific assignment when I once more came to my hometown. The US Holocaust Memorial Center, then being built, asked me to do further research on one of the American rescuers during the Shoah—the Holocaust. The person the museum wanted to honor was Varian Fry, who, working out of his headquarters in Marseille, had been instrumental in the rescue of hundreds of German-speaking artists and writers. After finding a few less-than-sensational documents at the Library for Contemporary History in Munich, my task was made effortless. I had mentioned my mission to my friend and former colleague Dr. Oskar Holl. "Interesting," he commented. "You will have seen the Varian Fry documentary by my good friend, the filmmaker Jörg Bundschuh."

said, "You will be much more in tune with high school kids than I. Go teach them." She did admirably. The students kept her for an additional half hour.

In time my eightieth and her sixtieth birthdays were approaching. The decennial birthdays inspired her to a giant conspiracy, arranged with nano precision behind my back. Under the pretext that we were going to celebrate our coinciding birthdays at a hotel with exquisite cuisine, together with her brother and his companion, she chauffeured us to an upper-class suburb of Detroit. My first suspicions arose when she rushed us not into but across the general dining room to a chambre separé at the back of the faux-Baroque edifice. I opened the door and my knees buckled. My world of respected, admired, and beloved family and friends had assembled, arriving from two continents. My cousin Renée and her South American companion had come from Switzerland; my cousin Marianne from New York; my colleague Leo Fiedler was there from Germany, carrying a mammoth manuscript of a speech he was forced to cut; my colleagues from past and present affiliations were celebrating a reunion, mingling with the faculty of Judy's high school. Her principal was there, and my president, and at least two dozen relatives of my wife, the conspirator. The German Consul General attended. He was a man I admired for his occasional departure from diplomacy when outspokenness was called for. Judy and I had scarcely gotten through embracing one and all, when we heard most accomplished piano playing, emanating not from the usual hired hands that played at parties but from my admired colleague, Professor James Hartway, composer and master pianist. With each handshake and embrace, as we later told each other, a phase of our lives became resurrected, both happy and tragic moments. My cousin Marianne's presence stirred up Auschwitz, Renée's evoked the incredible beauty of the surroundings of the Lago Maggiore, where she lived. Recalling all of the associations here would double the space of this narrative.

Unfortunately, it turned out to be Judy's last "big" birthday. Four years prior to this joyous event she got a horrible diagnosis: inflammatory breast cancer. We fought against it as a team: I; her brother, a prominent physician; and most notably, Judy herself. We visited cancer centers here and abroad: our local Karmanos and Beaumont Clinics, Sloan-Kettering in New York, and on a hunch of Judy's, hospitals in Freiburg and Hinterzarten. During her daily life, Judy ignored her illness and—how to put it?—defied the possibility of death. She rushed from chemo treatment to her classes, and in the last months given her during her five-year battle, she planned a new course, "Modern American History through Feature Films." When she succumbed she had just put her faith and resolution in yet another treatment center, to no avail.

Judy died on June 29, 2003. Relatives, friends, faculty, and students from Kimball High School accompanied her to her rest. Rabbi Schwartz, who had married us, surpassed his own eloquence at the gravesite. A good part of what has been written here was contained in his eulogy.

I missed Judy, even her shortcomings. I think arriving on time was anathema to her. Once she even missed a plane. This clashed with my Prussian punctuality. And she was a collector. Our numerous closets were unable to accommodate her collection of dresses and our spacious basement was replete with her assembly of jewelry, most of it costume. That clashed with one of my many flaws. I was mostly indifferent to clothes, but I am to this day addicted to clinging to documents, papers, other articles yearning for the wastepaper basket.

Aside from those admitted impediments, we appeared to be and were an ad for married couples. At a time when other variations of living together were becoming the vogue, I looked back in sorrow to her and our conventional marriage. I was sure I would not marry again. Yet the roller coaster of life and love decreed otherwise.

During the summer of 2004, I was, as so often before, a houseguest of Ute and Dieter Blanke in Herford, Germany. I had met Ute, then a city councilwoman, and Dieter, the legal counsel of a utility company, about ten years earlier when Ute had been the prime mover in Herford's efforts to bring to the city the surviving former members of its once thriving Jewish community. I came along as the traveling companion of my cousin Marianne, who was no longer able to travel alone. She had gone to a Jewish school in Herford, when Jewish children were no longer permitted to attend public schools in and around Herford beginning in 1937.

During that reunion, with many events taking place at the home of the Blankes, we discovered a whole set of common interests. A chance encoun-

"What are you telling me?" I exclaimed. "You know of a recently produced film about Fry?"

He answered, completely matter-of-factly: "Exactly! It's playing right now at one of the movie houses in midtown."

I saw it, was enchanted by it, interviewed the director, Jörg Bundschuh—and was immediately told to invite the filmmaker for a showing and commentary at the Kennedy Center in Washington, DC. Rather undeservedly, I was lauded for my research skills.

I also went to the Kennedy Center for the showing, and afterward Jörg and I had an opportunity to talk in private. We talked about our past. "What did you do during the war?" he asked me. "I was in Military Intelligence," I answered.

"What!" he yelled. "Were you trained at Camp Ritchie?" I was flabbergasted. How could this German know about such a secret facility? Jörg explained, "My collaborator, Christian Bauer, is familiar with your former unit. He's planning a documentary about it. So I have an urgent plea. Please come to our studio the next time you're in Munich!"

About six months later, I was able to comply. Christian Bauer was sitting across from me in his studio on Pfisterstrasse, excited about his first meeting with "a genuine Ritchie Boy," and he came right to the point: "Tell me something extraordinary about your wartime duties."

"No problem," I said. "Imagine we are at that famous American breakthrough in France, at the Battle of the Falaise-Argentan Gap. I came upon a German prisoner of war and discovered that he, just ten years earlier, was in the same gym club as I had been, in fact in the same squad as me. I waited till nightfall before taking him into a darkened space, so he couldn't recognize me."

"What a coincidence," interrupted Christian. "And where was your common gym club?"

"In Hildesheim," I answered.

"Hildesheim?"

"Yes," I explained, my civic pride a bit wounded, "a midsize town in Lower Saxony."

"I know all about Hildesheim," he shouted, and asked a question that floored me. "Did you attend the Jewish elementary school there?"

I affirmed that I had. Very excitedly he tossed the next question at me. "Then you must have known my mother!"

"No," I said calmly. "There was no girl there named Bauer."

"Nonsense," he said, abandoning his role as a cool film director. "Before her marriage her name was von Rossen!"

"Eva von Rossen," I responded, almost whispering.

Christian jumped up and crossed the room. "What are you doing?" I asked him, now a bit shaken myself.

"I'm calling my mom. She must speak with you!"

"But what would I say to her? There have been almost 70 years between now and our last meeting!"

A minute later I heard myself say, "Eva, how are you?"

Two days later, we met in a Munich restaurant; Eva had come in from Upper Bavaria. She was still that lithe and graceful person fixed in my memory. Our conversation began with a question from Eva that tolerated no delay in answering, "I have worried so much about our schoolmates. Do you know what happened to them?"

I gave her multiple answers. The geographical cues were Australia, London, New York, Switzerland, and Auschwitz. We became rather emotional. Recognizing the intimacy of the reunion, her son Christian and my wife Judy excused themselves. We were alone together with our memories.

Later, much later, I asked her, "How did you, a Catholic girl, come to attend our Jewish school?"

"Oh, I can thank my father for that. He noticed that I was turning into a wallflower in that enormous Catholic school in which I was enrolled. As a good father and sensitive artist, he went from one school to the other within Hildesheim to find the right one for me. Finally, he came across your famous teacher 'Uncle Oskar' and they immediately got along. I arrived at my new school, was warmly received, and quickly became friends with everyone. Even you winked at me," she laughed, "and I blossomed." "I am glad I contributed," I grinned.

Then she became more serious. "My father's decision for me had a sad ending. As the Nazis came to power, they resented that he had sent his daughter to a 'Jew School.' He received no further artistic commissions from the city and was tormented. Almost overnight we moved to a secluded village in Upper Bavaria. I crawled back inside myself. But finally I followed in Daddy's footsteps and became a painter."

I visited Christian and Eva a few times in Landsberg. The last time she gave me one of her own creations, a copper etching of an illustration for the works of the German writer and composer, E.T.A. Hoffmann. It hangs today in my house in a suburb of Detroit, a memory of my schoolmate from Hildesheim.

This extraordinary chain of events was further validated when, a year later, I received in the mail Christian Bauer's and Rebekka Göpfert's book, *Die Ritchie Boys*. In it, he described our first meeting, beginning with my memories of the interrogation of my Eintracht partner from Hildesheim's athletic club, and extending to the memories Christian's mother and I shared. He recalled his mother's reports about her schoolmates, including me ("A most attractive boy with tar black curls, who would always turn around to her, when the teacher wasn't looking"). He also supplied his reaction to our chance encounter: "It was a lucky day. Unexpectedly I wiped away a bit of the sadness and guilt from my mother's life. I now knew why I became a filmmaker." Of course I understood what Christian meant; but why did that wonderful woman, Eva, have to feel saddled with sadness and guilt?

CLOSE TO MY NINETIETH birthday, the Kehrwiederturm (Tower of Return) bid me once again to retrace my steps. The Tower of Return had the assistance of my wife. Susanna took the initiative to glamorize the occasion in a most imaginative way—without a single word of warning to me. She contacted an acquaintance of ours, Herbert Reyer, the archivist of the city of Hildesheim. She wrote: "On the occasion of the ninetieth birthday of Guy Stern, my husband, which is on January 14th, 2012, wouldn't it be the crowning achievement of his life if he were to be named an honorary citizen of Hildesheim? He has not even an inkling about my inquiry, hence it will come as a surprise." Dr. Reyer, as the ensuing correspondence demonstrated, created a dossier showing my efforts on behalf of my city of birth. He relayed my wife's suggestion, and the relevant credentials found in his archive, to the office of the city's mayor, Dr. Kurt Machens, and asked for a date for the event, if the mayor and the city council would approve. He suggested that it should be coordinated with my next trip to Germany in the spring of 2012.

The two conspirators should be proud of their work. On the day in question, Susanna and I found the auditorium of Hildesheim's city hall to be completely jammed. Many of my friends and colleagues had traveled to Hildesheim, some of them from faraway cities in Europe. The mayor gave an eloquent speech, stressing my efforts to have the new generations understand, but by no means endorse, the crimes of a heinous past, and to restore the spontaneous feelings between the various religions in our common hometown. Across the width of the back wall hung a large display board recounting my life through articles and pictures. I came to the realization that my hometown had done all it could to extend its hand to me. I knew that the dark years that had robbed me of my citizenship had not as yet completely faded, but I also felt that a beam of light had broken through the darkness.

The formal ceremony had several repercussions. My wife and I were having breakfast in our hotel the next morning when visitors arrived, about ten of them in fact. A spokesperson emerged who introduced himself as Rolf Altmann, the president of the gym club Eintracht. "The entire board is here to apologize for your exclusion from our club in 1934," he said. "You are now a lifelong honorary member." During a later visit, I astounded members of the club and the press when I divested myself of my coat and dress shirt, thereby displaying the club's logo on my T-shirt. I then mounted one of the machines to prove anew that I was a qualified member of that venerable club. Whenever I am in Hildesheim, Rolf Altmann and his friend Hans-Jürgen Bertsche take me under their wings and arrange for unforgettable days.

Beyond this amazing coming together of circumstances, in which Hildesheim again figured in my experience, the town appeared often in my thoughts and dreams. And as this memoir draws to a close, I want to mention a few other times when the place of my birth and my childhood suddenly emerged in the life I was living decades later.

In 2004, Christian's film *The Ritchie Boys* opened the yearly Toronto documentary film festival. My friend and war buddy Fred Howard and I were there. Christian's introduction emphasized the impact of his mother's description of her Jewish classmates in Hildesheim on his resolve to film the story of the Ritchie Boys. After the screening a woman introduced herself as Debbie Filler, dramatist and actress. "My mother was a Rothschild; she also attended the Jewish school in Hildesheim." I knew her as Ruthie, who irritated us "older" students. I met her again as a grandmother in New York. She now lives in New Zealand. I asked myself, how many more links from this chain of astonishing chance encounters would emerge?

One year earlier, in 2003, I'd been sitting in my study in West Bloomfield, Michigan, with the latest publication about exile and exile literature in my hand. What began as a little-known specialty is now an expansive area of research. One has to work hard to stay current. I reached for a title, *Escape to Manila*, the first scholarly work about the Philippines as an asylum country, written by Frank Ephraim. Interesting topic! Soon I was on page 37 and suddenly thrown back once again to the Hildesheim of my youth.

For eleven years I'd met every Saturday with nearly all the youth of the Jewish community. We sang patriotic, folk, and Hebrew songs, listened to a round robin reading by the participants, read a verse in German from *Pirkei Avot* (*Ethics of the Fathers*) and discussed its meaning. This was all under the leadership of our cantor, Joseph Cysner, born in Bamberg, Germany. We had taken him into our hearts and nearly cried as the "diabolical" and much larger Jewish community in Hamburg hired him away from us in 1937. We surprised him with a gift upon his parting. Having gone through our "Heimnachmittage" (Saturday afternoon meetings) minutes and reports, we collected the typed and handwritten pages. They blossomed into a grand tome, bound by an excellent bookbinder. On the cover was the ambitious title *Our Work*. Seppl was moved to tears. After his departure, we listened for news from and about him—his success in Hamburg, for example—until we Hildesheimers were scattered to the winds or tragically to various concentration camps.

From the top of the aforementioned book and its page 37, I was back in the community room of our synagogue. Seppl Cysner had ended up in Manila, as Ephraim's book reported:

With his hard-won consent [to hire a Cantor] Rabbi Josef Schwarz turned to his old acquaintance Joseph Cysner, who served with him in Hildesheim and whose last-known post was in Hamburg. A telegram was sent to Hamburg, which in English read, "Do you want to come? Minimal salary. Supplemental work supplied. Send response today. Heartfelt regard. Schwarz."

The telegram reached him indirectly. Cysner was the son of Polish immigrants to Germany and was soon after the Night of Broken Glass deported to an improvised internment camp between Germany and Poland. He responded to the invitation immediately. His choice was no choice at all.

Heinrich Heine writes, "When words leave off, music begins." The story of the haven for Jewish refugees ends here, but the music and songs of beloved Cantor Joseph Cysner that sustained the Jewish community and particularly the children whom he loved, are everlasting. The young man who was twenty-six years old when he arrived in Manila in 1939 brought with him a golden voice, a personal warmth, and an infectious spirit. For more than seven years Cantor Cysner taught Jewish history and music to children and adults, and every festival centered around his immense artistic capabilities. The Torah sections each Bar Mitzvah boy in Manila learned to chant were taught him by Cantor Cysner, and the Temple choir that he had organized, trained and directed was his and the congregation's pride and joy. He taught secular courses when schools were closed or unavailable. For both young and old his home served as a center for Hebrew language, Jewish history—and, of course, his memorable skill for giving piano and singing lessons.

The book describes the happy turn of events in his life, and his untimely death. In the spring of 1945, Cantor Cysner and his mother left Manila for the United States after the Japanese occupation had ceased. There, in San Francisco, he was reunited with Sylvia Nagler, whom he had first met at the Bamberger Synagogue in 1934. She had escaped from Germany and spent the war years in England. They were married on August 22, 1948, at Temple Sherith Israel in San Francisco, where Joseph served as cantor. In 1950 he accepted a post in San Diego with Congregation Tifereth Israel, and the cantor's melodious voice resounded in the synagogue as he led liturgical passages of the service.

While leaving behind an enduring legacy, his life was cut short. Just past noon on March 3, 1961, Sylvia Cysner answered the phone at home to receive the tragic news of her husband's death. A massive heart attack had felled the man who, more than any other individual, had always given his heart to the Manila Jewish community. He was forty-nine years old.

I can still see him before me, even hear his singing. Just by changing a few minor details, my own tribute to my former teacher in Hildesheim would be as resounding. I have come to believe that Seppl was the most important influence on my life during my adolescence. With positive memories of those happy, beloved Saturday afternoons spent with Cantor Cysner and my friends, I would in time restore a guarded attachment to the city of my birth.

In Basel, Switzerland, in June 2011 Dr. Vincent Frank, the son of writer Rudolf Frank, born in Mainz, and Wilfred Weinke, a Germanist and curator from Hamburg, collaborated on an exhibit sponsored by the main library of the University of Basel. My connection to this event is quickly told. Rudolf Frank's emigration novel *Ahnen und Enkel* (*Forefathers and Grandchildren*) was my favorite book. It was the last Hanukah gift from my parents, one of the few books by a Jewish author that in 1936—obviously under the aegis of a Jewish publisher—was allowed to be sold in Nazi Germany, though to Jewish buyers only.

The exhibition opening was a rousing success that had to be celebrated. Spontaneously, Vincent Frank and his wife, Melinda, invited presenters, librarians, speakers, friends, and acquaintances to a party. "Incidentally," added the host, when asking me to come, "the daughter of a deceased lady from Hildesheim will be there. Aren't you also from Hildesheim?" At his home Vincent introduced us. I was stunned. Before me stood the reincarnation of my first love.

Gerda Schönenberg and I had known each other from grade school onward. The sister of my schoolmate Robert, she was one year older than I. After grade school she went on to the Goethe High School for Girls, joined the Sabbath youth group of Cantor Cysner, and like Robert and me was a member of the scout-like troop Bund deutsch-jüdischer Jugend (Association of German-Jewish Youth Group). In addition, she also belonged to a sports group under the aegis of the Hildesheim Center of National Jewish Veterans. She had made a strong impression on me. When our gym leader had taken umbrage at the fact that girls and boys were changing in the same room, Gerda admonished him, "Don't get hyper."

We fell in love at Lappenberg Place, right after an afternoon with the good Cysner. Before we separated I offered a suggestion. "Would you like to go for a walk?" It lasted almost two hours, beginning in front of our synagogue, passing Lake Kahlenberg, and ending at the aptly named Liebesgrund (Vale of Love).

Our walk became a weekly routine. We talked for hours. In between discussions we learned the pleasures of kissing. We participated in a three-week-long bike tour along the Rhine with our friends, Lieselotte Rosenberg and Fritz Palmbaum. We occasionally embraced, but "nothing happened" during that trip, which was the same year I would leave Germany. As that day drew nearer we stopped once in the Liebesgrund. We held each other and cried.

As I related this to Gerda's daughter, she in turn told me of her mother's many struggles during her exile years in Switzerland. All around us the excitement of the party in Basel continued. We had no part in it. Hildesheim, with all its memories, expunged what was probably a wonderful party in Switzerland.

In 2012, after I gave a lecture in a high school near Konstanz, Germany, the teacher huffed that her students had called me an "old fogey." As a ninety-year-old, one can laugh at the obviously inapplicable nickname. But the smile passed me by when, back at home, I found a balled-up advertisement for a chain of cremation services under a pile of birthday cards. In light of my advanced age, the ad said, I should take care that my burial fees wouldn't leave my progeny in ruins. "Compare!" I was admonished. They had kindly printed a table, which explained how inexpensively the heirs get off if the oldster—in this case me—prearranges for his cremation.

The tactlessness enraged the birthday geezer. I was ready to call the Better Business Bureau when a sudden reminiscence from Hildesheim displaced my displeasure. As a schoolboy I had walked across the marketplace at least once a week, leaving the city hall on my right and the cremation service on the left. I still can remember every step of that walk, including the more elegant and homey advertising for making the right choice in selecting our post-mortem disposal. In the show window was a dignified sign displaying a poem, which, translated, reads:

No revolting worms my corpse shall feed,
The cleansing flames are what I need!
I've loved the warmth and daylight bright,
Therefore, friend, burn me—let there be light!

The poem is by Peter Rosegger; peace to his ashes. Jamie Woodring, a Michigan high school teacher, former student, and friend of mine, translated it.

I once recited this poem to my fellow Hildesheimer Dieter Sevin—and he also recalled that deathless poem. In fact, whenever I met with my friend and colleague, we reminisced about Hildesheim. We could still swim with the same correct strokes we'd learned from our swim instructor, the somewhat corpulent Mr. Bode. Either he or I cracked a pun regarding this common experience. "We were both baptized with the same bath and Bode water." Once Dieter and his wife offered their beautifully located Hildesheim home to Susanna and me for a few days. Hinting at my always tight schedule, my wife expressed her joy and gratitude that we had spent a whole week in Hildesheim: "I really fell in love with this town. The town has grown on me." Immodestly, I was moved to make this declaration of dual love myself.

To round off this chapter—and this book—I need to relate one more moving encounter with the city of Hildesheim and its inhabitants. A year after being awarded the title of honorary citizen, I received another invitation. At the house 36 Hoher Weg, where I spent a large part of my boyhood, a memorial plaque was being placed to honor my family. I stood by as Mayor Machens said some fitting words, followed by a small band playing Klezmer music. Around us stood a whole group of Hildesheimers, once more my fellow citizens. I gave a short thank-you speech and more light broke through the darkness of the past. As I am writing this, my good feeling toward my hometown continues. When Mayor Machens left office, he was replaced on the strength of a bipartisan vote by Dr. Ingo Meyer, who has been equally eager to make me feel that I truly belong to my place of birth. He asked me to join a committee meant to showcase Hildesheim as the "Cultural Capital of Europe." I felt honored.

Having established such new stable bonds with people from Hildesheim, I had to cope with the most sustaining part of my life, the human relationships that have vanished from it. As I have learned from close associations with fellow victims of the Holocaust, each person so afflicted has found a highly individual answer. A frequent one is a fictional resurrection of the departed, often by immersion in genealogy. By intense research the information is unearthed to devise an elaborate family tree. A network of offspring of the victims demonstrates that they have not lived in vain.

My own version took recourse in a more concrete pursuit. A Hebrew saying had promised that "some shall survive." I went in search of the relatvies of the few survivors who had somehow escaped the mass extirpation. On this search born of desperation, I sometimes located relatives who before lived solely on the periphery of our family circle. I wanted them for their consanguinity, simply put, to regain the feeling that there was a place where I belonged. The vestiges of my murdered family, however remote, were the solution.

And I found them. On my mother's side there was my cousin Marianne, daughter of my mother's brother, Willy, the wounded veteran of World War I. She had miraculously survived Auschwitz and contacted me a few months after she had arrived in New York. I was able to help her in minor ways.

My mother also had a cousin in Cologne, Rudi Minden. A bundle of energy, he had smuggled his way across the Belgian border, together with his wife and small child. He had skirted capture by constantly changing hiding places in the capital city of Brussels and by entrusting little Renée to a Catholic family in Brussels. But where was Rudi now? I found a recent book, *Juden in Köln (Jews in Cologne)*, in a specialty library. Lo and behold, on the very last page was a list of the postwar Jewish community leaders. Rudi was one of them. I was in Munich at the time with my wife and son. I made one telephone call. The next morning our VW Beetle was taking us to Cologne. Rudi and his wife, Loni, and later their daughter Renée and Renée's children became additional members of my inner circle. Five years ago I was present to help Renée, her son Alan, and Alan's wife celebrate the Bat Mitzvah of their daughter.

On my father's side I also found a survivor. My father's brother David, greatly respected as a teacher at Germany's only ecumenical high school, had managed to escape to Argentina with his wife, Thekla, and his son Heinz. After the war he located me in Cincinnati and wrote a letter similar to mine, in short meant as a search for surviving Sterns.

We started to correspond. And then he came up with another suggestion. "Wouldn't it be a great idea if our older son, now at high school age, would spend half a year with your family and 'widen his horizon'?" "We would greatly welcome that," we wrote back. We enrolled Mario in Walnut High School, the highest-ranked secondary school in Cincinnati, and he thrived there. After his return we paid a countervisit at his parents' lovely home in La Lucilla. Today we visit Mario and his brother Claudio every time we are in Munich.

Even though I moved to New York after returning from the European battlefields, I maintained close ties to my Aunt and Uncle Silberberg, my rescuers from Nazi rule. They attended my wedding to Margith. With Uncle Benno restored to his former job, they looked more elegant than I had ever seen them at 1116A Maple Place on St. Louis's West Side. And then there is my cousin, Bobby, now more formally known as retired Missouri State Representative Robert Feigenbaum. He is the grandson of my aunt and uncle and the son of their daughter Bernice and her husband, Victor Feigenbaum. He holds a record: elected to office at age twenty-three, he is one of the youngest persons to be elected to the Missouri State Legislature and one of the first ones to sponsor bills for environmental protection in Missouri. He retained his seat for twenty years and became my conveyor into an in-and-out dive into Missouri politics.

As I have told elsewhere, Bobby invited me to his inauguration in Jefferson City and thereby enabled me to identify, in the person of Missouri Senator John Danforth, an erstwhile high school student who had performed brilliantly in a session of Columbia University's "Forum on Democracy," led by me. Bobby also became the catalyst for a second, equally unlikely chance encounter. In 1988 he decided to run for the US Congress and asked me to be one of his campaign speakers. (I hasten to add that he didn't win despite or because of my oratorical arts.) One of those was in a manor house on St. Louis's elegant Lindell Boulevard before a predominantly Jewish audience. The host was Ronald Reich, a prominent community leader. Talking about my continued Jewish upbringing since coming to St. Louis, I mentioned that for economic reasons, we prayed in a humble prayer room, where the service was conducted by a gifted volunteer, Mr. Ansky. Hearing this name, a cry of surprise emanated from the back of the spacious room: "Why, that is my uncle!" exclaimed our host. Candidate Feigenbaum was greatly pleased that my memories of my St. Louis past had brought Mr. Reich even more closely into his fold!

There was yet another tributary to be explored. My wife Margith left me a legacy. She maintained a close friendship with one of her cousins. Jo was a frequent visitor to our apartment in Queens and that continued when she moved to Tampa, Florida, and married Robert Franzblau, co-owner of a cigar factory. When Margith and I got divorced, the Franzblaus decided to retain me in their family. There has been scarcely a family celebration, including two huge family reunions, one in Tuscany and another in a luxury hotel also in Italy, to which we were not invited.

And one other addition stepped into my reassembled family circle. Susanna is very attached to her cousin Joanna and her husband, Christoph. When they introduce me to their friends, it is invariably as their cousin. I feel honored and pleased that I have gathered these remnants and new additions around me.

CHAPTER 13

A Broken Promise

THIS BOOK STARTED WITH the promise that this "confession" would be irrevocably the final word on the subject of the life and times of Guy Stern. But as has happened so often before, a chance encounter would decree otherwise and in a most extraordinary way. A new acquaintance, Chuck Bernard, fellow member of the Association of Former Intelligence Officers, asked me whether he could nominate me as "Veteran of the Game" at the football homecoming game at the University of Michigan on October 6, 2018. I simply and obligingly told Chuck: "Why not?" I was absolutely convinced that the selection process wouldn't settle on a member of an obscure army unit nicknamed "The Ritchie Boys."

Also, my acquaintance with that quaint game called "football" was infinitesimally small and sporadic. My first distant encounter came during my freshman year at Soldan High School. Our principal announced at short notice that all 11:00 a.m. classes were canceled in favor of a "pep rally" in the high school auditorium. What happened there was both noisy and, at least for me, mysterious. We were to encourage our football team, prior to the decisive game for the league championship, by shouting dubious poetry during their efforts. So we rehearsed under the guidance of our cheerleaders (all males) such memorable verses as the following:

"Izzagasiss, izzagasane,
Knock 'em down, yeah man!
Hit 'em high, hit 'em low,
Come on Soldan, let's go!"

I joined in the shouting match but saw no reason to go to the game, nor to any other one at my high school or my first year at Saint Louis University. But in my sophomore year, Mary Jane, a fellow student in Professor Mihailovich's sociology class, approached me: "Hey Guy, my dad is driving me to Saturday's football game. Want to tag along?" I was surprised and pleased. She and I had locked horns all through the semester. Mary Jane supported our professor throughout the spreading of his conservative views, for example, that divine punishment after death would have something to do with fire, because so many societal myths around the globe supported such a hypothesis. Like one of the iconoclasts I had, not too politely, opposed the assumption of both the professor and her. My dissent carried the day. After all, I had sat at the feet of that master logician, Father Reeve. During the game she was appalled at my abysmal lack of even the subbasics about the rules of football and never invited me again.

The years went by, as told in these pages, and I, the warrior, student, and professor, had ascended to the post of vice president of Wayne State University. On a fall day of 1993 our president, Tom Bonner, called me to his office. "Guy, next Saturday is the opening game of our football season. As vice president, you must go!" That was a command. I went to our library and immersed myself in a book on the rules and maneuvers of football. Mary Jane's contempt had taught me a lesson. I memorized terms such as lateral, double reverse, penalty because of unnecessary roughness, and quarterback sneak. I liberally threw these terms around and thus avoided being tagged a nerd.

Well, as you might surmise by now, the ladies and gentlemen of the University of Michigan's Selection Committee for the Veteran of the Game chose me. The contest was to take place between the stalwarts of the Michigan Wolverines and their opponents, the Maryland Terrapins. And I was briefed: "Your wife and you should arrive two and a half hours before the game and participate in a tailgate party. You'll be assisted throughout by a group of the U of M–Dearborn Student Veterans, led by Tom Pitock." (I made a valiant effort to remember all the names that would lead me through that unknown territory of a huge football field.) I got further briefings. My fans, old and new, coming from near and far, would gather under a tent for food and drink and greet one another across the years. Idyllic weather was predicted.

The latter factor prevailed upon Susanna to come along. She hadn't felt well the days prior to the event, but she didn't want to miss that stellar moment when I was to earn applause from the capacity crowd of 115,000 spectators. But that was not to be. A rainstorm threatened to lift the sheltering tent from its moorings; a particularly violent squall opened the tent's top and poured streams of water down on us, specifically down Susanna's back. I convinced my freezing, thoroughly miserable better half that this tent and stadium was no place for her. She went home with our friend Diane Bouis, our host during our overnight stay in Ann Arbor.

Michigan has a traditional saying: "Don't curse the weather; within ten minutes it will reverse itself." Although it was far longer than ten minutes and the game was delayed for over an hour, we had mild sunshine when the opening whistle blew. In the meanwhile one imaginative volunteer, Ken Magee, asked for silence in the tent and introduced us to an annual custom he had started many years earlier. Ken had obtained, in advance, a picture of the veteran to be honored and made it the centerpiece of an ID card with its back side retelling the daring deeds of the honoree. He made numerous copies of his creation and liberally distributed them to the invited guests of the tailgate party. Ken Magee followed his speech with a sharp command: "Outside everyone!" The largest band I had ever seen was preparing to pass and salute the tent housing the honored veteran. The size of the band dwarfed the seventy-six trombones blasting away in the musical *The Music Man*. Oldsters and freshmen, representatives of dozens of different nationalities, but all with the same serious mien, blasted, drummed, and whistled their way past us, with nods to me. And with that, Act I of my part seemed finished. But no, I was told to stay put. The majorette of the band was rushing back, embraced me, and planted a chaste kiss on both my cheeks. She was truly attractive, the picture of an athlete, and the thought bestirred me that she could easily be my great-granddaughter.

We were rushed to our protected booth; the game was about to begin. My friends wildly cheered the home team. I joined in. No longer any sing-song like "Izzagasiss." Instead there appeared flashing announcements on the scoreboards: "Make noise!" The game itself was hard fought and the lead shifted. But to my delight the University of Michigan, "Champions of the West," "creamed" the invaders from Maryland. I hadn't forgotten my sorrowful days on the campus of that institution.

I was completely absorbed in the game and had all but forgotten that I had a role to play. Bryan Assenmacher, a student army veteran, interrupted my removal from reality: "Time to go downstairs! The wheelchairs are waiting!" For that I was unprepared. In a fit of annoyance I protested that anyone else was welcome to take my designated seat. But I was quickly quieted. A person in charge of that whole enterprise told us it was a precautionary rule that obliged us to take advantage of the wheelchairs. Also my escort was a USAF veteran by the name of Joe Melcher, who seemed in need of such a contrivance. He was being accompanied by his daughter Kate, a retired air force captain and now spearheading the drive for the establishment of the nonprofit Fisher House (for veterans' families) in Ann Arbor. So in tandem we went down dark corridors, steep inclines, and past dressing rooms, which, rumor had it, were never meant to be seen by the general public. (I was reminded of a murder mystery by Scott Turow, taking place in a similar setting, populated by a basketball team.)

But nothing untoward happened to us. We were deposited behind the goalposts of the Michigan team during the third quarter and trotted out during the first break. We walked in military steps to the thirty-yard line, as though we wanted to demonstrate to the crowd that we were years removed from requiring those mandated wheelchairs. All of a sudden an abbreviated biography of me appeared on the scoreboard, describing my "exploits" in World War II and highlighting, as I had requested, the tragedy of my family.

While we were standing there, the thousands of spectators broke forth in shattering applause. For me that was the experience of a lifetime. As we retreated, strangers rushed up to me, thanking me for my service and erasing so many self-doubts going back to my years living under a dictatorship and being the victim of discrimination and harassment. I felt enveloped by the total approval and acceptance of my fellow Americans and I gloried in that approbation.

In Pursuit of the Future

L
OOKING BACK ON THIS account of my life written as truthfully as
my memory could evoke it, I feel an additional need of self-reflection.
What is my attitude toward my country of asylum? Under normal circumstances and throughout all the years of my US citizenship that answer
need not have been written. The United States, to put it simply, saved my life.
Without allowing me to arrive at its shores, I would have been on the train
taking me to perdition as was the fate of my immediate and extended family.
As my life took root here, there were so many additional benefits bestowed
upon me. Without those benefits my saved life would not have unfolded as
fully. I was able to complete my twice-interrupted education, first through a
free public school and then at college and university because of the liberal gift
of the so-called GI Bill of Rights.

My country financed my schooling through two years of undergraduate
work and through five years of graduate study and left even enough of a fund
to pay for the typing of my dissertation. During my first years in the United
States the Jewish community of St. Louis paid for my health and dental insur-
ance and for occasional short stays at a hospital. If I think of the heavy debt
that many students incur these days, I become doubly conscious of that generosity. There were other grants and benefits, too. Many came to me through
the Veterans Administration, where I received exemplary treatment, including a cataract surgery. The fact that I can still adequately hear and see I owe to
the care of the dedicated and highly skilled medical staff. I shun long-distance
driving at my age. Fortunately, a VA volunteer came to my aid. I had met

Mark Lindke earlier when he donated World War II artifacts to the HMC. We liked each other and stayed in touch. Every time I had a doctor's appointment at the clinic in Ann Arbor, Mark came through. Countless times he drove me back and forth—no matter the time or season. The seventy-mile round-trip drive encouraged many deep and humorous conversations, from war memories to baseball to politics. We often concluded our get-togethers with a nice lunch or dinner at the Red Lobster in Ann Arbor. In short, the VA founded a friendship.

Finally, another kindness came to me as a veteran. An extraordinary group of American women reward veterans for their service in a most original way. They put their craft of knitting to work toward creating unique and artistic quilts. Once a month, they present them to several veterans in a heartwarming ceremony. It is a national organization called Stitching Sisters Quilts of Valor. My benefactresses perform their work in Clawson, Michigan. To me, they represent America at its best. Bless their hearts!

I was very grateful when after some years the opportunity arose to "pay back" a little. The aforementioned Kate Melcher, "Captain Kate," was spearheading a drive to found a Fisher House near the Ann Arbor VA hospital, where relatives of wounded veterans could stay while their loved ones receive medical care. Enthusiastically, I offered to volunteer on her committee. Kate said she would have to interview me first. "Quiz me, Kate," I replied. I passed and served.

To put my thankfulness in one sentence: I became an American patriot, I hope, in the best and most positive sense of the word. In looking back on this enthusiasm for the country of my asylum, I conclude that this attitude wasn't free of criticism of my country, the United States, as not having fulfilled some of its promises and potentials.

Can I sustain this attitude for the rest of my life? In posing that question I look back on moments in my army career when we pledged a vow of allegiance to this country with the unambiguous phrase, "One nation, indivisible." So I ask: can this avowal be maintained at the time of this writing? Have not events occurred that split our nation—beyond the necessary debates of the ways and means of reaching that goal? Or is it not true that this oath, taken by all servicemen and women and many other citizens, has to be reattained? Should we not rededicate ourselves to unite our country again, to paraphrase Henry Clay? We found that strength after the Civil War. My affection for this country endures, but I would like to be reassured that the country that harbored me for more than eighty years has reaffirmed the idealism of all patriots who lived before me throughout our history.

ACKNOWLEDGMENTS

I needed help. When relatives, friends, and colleagues greeted my narratives about my checkered life with the exclamation that I absolutely must write my autobiography, I was rather skeptical. Sure, I had written scholarly books and articles and still do, even some short reports about my life as a soldier during World War II, but these suggestions loomed as something formidable. Also, I was now somewhat older.

But help was at hand. The first offer came from my wife, Susanna. She would keep other scholarly demands from my doorsteps, discuss my work with me, and do proofreading. Many of her thoughts turned out to be useful and inspirational. And so it is no surprise that this book is dedicated to her and the acknowledgments section starts with a thank-you to Susanna.

There are many others to whom I owe thanks. The first chapters show the fingerprints of my then assistant at the Holocaust Memorial Center Zekelman Family Campus, Rebecca Swindler, who had come to us as an intern under the auspices of the University of Michigan–Dearborn. There were other invaluable helpers. From "Day One," the department secretary of us all in the Ancient and Modern Language Department at Wayne State, Amanda Rayha Donigian, applied her unsurpassable organizational skills to my project. Parallel to the beginning was a rescuer at the very end. I had scouted for a bilingual office assistant for some time. What I got was not only a German speaker but a most sensitive observer and practitioner of English, nicknamed at one time "the grammar police"—Liesa Hess Helfer turned out to be a multitalented editor.

But then I needed more than fingerprints. I needed space and calm. My new bosses at the Holocaust Memorial Center, Stephen Goldman and his successor, Rabbi Eli Mayerfeld, encouraged me to work at the "new book," when otherwise unoccupied, and the spiritual leaders at my synagogue, Temple Shir Shalom, Rabbis Dannel Schwartz, Michael Moskovitz, and Daniel Schwartz, gave me a quiet space in an annex to the house of worship.

Then, in collaboration with the museum, I found an able and meticulous assistant who accompanied my labors for the two and a half years to its conclusion. Shirlee Wyman Harris typed my quirky handwriting—even when she had to intuit its German content—looked up data for me, and told me when I had lapsed into academes. Best of all, she convinced me that the title of the book, *Invisible Ink*, was more fitting than all alternatives.

There were two teams that encouraged me when I was showing signs of tiring. They were my colleagues at Wayne State University, Don Haase, Al Cobbs, and Walter Hinderer of Princeton University. The second team that selected itself as my research assistants was made up of Dan Gross, a retired engineer; Stephen Goodell, a former department head at the United States Holocaust Memorial Museum; and Feiga Weiss, the HMC's head librarian and chief archivist.

Last, but way beyond least, I want to express my gratitude to Mr. Joel E. Jacob. We had met at the Athletic Club's dressing room of the Jewish Community Center. During a subsequent encounter, he told me he had heard that I was writing my autobiography for Wayne State University Press: "You know, I really admire Wayne State and its press. I would like to support the press—and your book." The support turned out to be generous, indeed. And that inspired me to conquer writer's block whenever it lurked.